Being Góral

SUNY series in National Identities

Thomas M. Wilson, editor

Being Góral

Identity Politics and Globalization in Postsocialist Poland

Deborah Cahalen Schneider

STATE UNIVERSITY OF NEW YORK PRESS

Published by
State University of New York Press, Albany

Printed in the United States of America

For information, address State University of New York Press,
194 Washington Avenue, Suite 305, Albany, NY 12210-2384

Production by Kelli Williams
Marketing by Michael Campochiaro

Library of Congress Cataloging-in-Publication Data

Cahalen Schneider, Deborah, 1969–
Being goral ; identity politics and globalization in post-socialist Poland / Deborah Cahalen
    Schneider.
        p. cm. — (SUNY series in national identities)
    Includes bibliographical references and index.
    ISBN 0-7914-6655-8 (hardcover : alk. paper)
    1. Group identity—Poland—Żwiec Region. 2. Social classes—Poland—Żwiec Region.
3. Żwiec Region (Poland)—Social conditions. 4. Żywiec Region (Poland)—Politics and
government. I. Title. II. Series.

HN539.Z94C34 2006
305.5'09438—dc22   2005007997

ISBN-13: 978-0-7914-6655-1 (hardcover : alk. paper)
ISBN-13 978-0-7914-6656-8 (pbk. : alk. paper)
ISBN-10: 0-7914-6656-6 (pbk. : alk. paper)

10 9 8 7 6 5 4 3 2 1

Ziemia Żywiecka
Wanda Miodonska

Jak kolia z pereł i złota
Otoczona tęczą wielobarwną
Jesteś piękna moja ziemio żywiecka
Bliska sercu—jak matka
Wśród zieleni groni i gór
Które nieba sięgają błękitu
Pnę się stokiem by ujrzec cię
I powiedzieć—to ziemia rodzinna
I tak patrząc z zielonego wzgórza
Na błękitne rozlewisko wody
Przystrojone w łodeczki żaglowe
Widzę piękno mej ziemi rodzinnej
W twoich ramionach ziemo matko
Chcę czerpać siłę i natchnienie
Ty bądź tą kromką żytniego chleba
I dobrą matką

Żywiec Lands
By Wanda Miodonska

Like a necklace of pearls and gold,
A colorful rainbow setting,
You are beautiful, my Żywiec lands,
Close to the heart—like a mother.
Among the green foothills and mountains
Which reach for the azure heavens
From the lovely slopes, I would glimpse you
And say—there is my native land.
And so, gazing from the green landscapes
Onto the azure flood of water
Adorned by sailing craft,
I see you, my beautiful native land.
Within your arms, earth mother,
I draw strength and inspiration.
You are that crumb of rye bread,
And a good mother.

Contents

◀◉▶

Chapter 1

◄o►

The Day the Pope
Came to Town

On May 21, 1995, Pope John Paul II came to town. I had been living and conducting research in Żywiec for almost nine months. Excitement had been building for weeks, ever since the pontiff announced that he would have a "private" visit to Żywiec, meaning that only town residents would be allowed on the main square while he was speaking. Everyone had an explanation for why the pope had picked Żywiec: it was close to his birthplace (the town of Wadowice), and he was very ill, so most of the explanations had to do with his coming home one last time before his death. But why Żywiec rather than Wadowice? The two towns are not that much different in size (about twenty-four thousand people), and more or less the same distance from the county seat (Bielsko-Biała), where he was celebrating mass that morning. For that matter, he could have gone to Oświęcim (otherwise known as Auschwitz), another nearby town of similar size, and made a different kind of symbolic statement.

The deciding factor in many townspeople's minds was that the town of Żywiec lies at the heart of the Żywiec region, a place with its own claims to a particular regional identity, that of the Żywiec Górals.[1] By some estimates, the Żywiec region makes up about half of the county of Bielsko, all lying in the Żywiec Hills foothills of the Tatras Mountains. There are several different groups of Górals, all living in

1

the mountains bordering Poland, the Czech Republic, and Slovakia, and the Góral identity as a whole is accepted by other Poles as a distinct regional-ethnic identity. Because Pope John Paul II was born in Wadowice, which is within the Żywiec region, and also grew up within the Góral area, he is seen by these primarily Catholic Górals as a native son who attained the highest honor possible by becoming pope.[2] Also, because Żywiec is the center of the Żywiec Góral region, many townspeople felt that the pope was showing that he was a real Góral by coming to Żywiec, symbol of his homeland, possibly for the last time before he died.

In the weeks before John Paul II came to town, extensive renovations were done to prepare for his arrival. Buildings facing the route he would take were repainted. A huge stage was constructed on the main square, and several kiosks were moved to make room for it. Half-bombed-out buildings, left to decay after World War II, were bricked and boarded and painted. All the Catholic churches in town handed out tickets for the event, and every resident living on the main square was interviewed by special security forces and given a list of security requirements. (A more cynical resident told me that this was "just like when the First Secretary came through.") These security measures, along with other aspects of the pope's visit, were hot topics of gossip in the town for months before the visit. Town residents told me about the security requirements they had been hearing about: there would be a policeman at every window looking out onto the square, families would not be able to look out of their own windows, people would not be allowed to move in and out of their houses during the pope's visit, and no guests would be allowed to stay with families who lived on the square during the visit.

A newly built traffic roundabout was interpreted by many residents as being created especially for the occasion. "The smallest rondo in the world," as it was called, became the town joke. In a town in which until recently there was only one traffic light (there were now three), the idea of a traffic roundabout seemed a ridiculous pretension. (The mayor, as we will see later, had a very different justification for the building of the rondo.) Pictures of the pope and flags flying the colors of the pope (yellow and white), the Polish nation (red and white), and the Virgin Mary (blue and white) crowded every window, fence, and signpost in town.[3]

When the big day finally came, I went out with all of my neighbors to see the Holy Father drive through the neighborhood. We waited for an hour and were finally rewarded by the sight of the popemobile cruising by. We waved and snapped pictures, and the town's mountain horn players, dressed in full Góral costume, played a special Góral horn salute on our very corner as the pope passed. None of us had been so lucky as to obtain tickets for entrance to the cordoned-off main square (which were free to town residents, but limited in number and distributed through the Catholic churches in town to their members) or to the apartment block where he would supposedly be stopping for a papal visit. (I heard various stories that they were free, and also that some people were selling them at high prices to both town residents and out-of-towners). So, we retired to our houses to try to tune in the festivities on television. The TV showed us a packed, cheering throng on the main square, waving papal flags and pennants with the word "Żywiec" printed on them, with many Żywiec residents wearing "traditional" Góral costumes.

After the pope had finished his speech, I left my neighbors and, with camera in hand, went out to see if I could get some pictures of the crowds leaving the main square. As three helicopters buzzed overhead, carrying the pope, his car, and other dignitaries back to the Czech Republic, I photographed some of the street vendors as the jubilant waves streamed past. One elderly woman, whom I knew slightly, was decked out in beautiful old-fashioned clothing and posing for some photographers. Her costume was what is touted as the "traditional" Góral dress for townswomen in the late nineteenth and early twentieth centuries: a white blouse with laced bodice, long petticoats and skirt with an intricate lace apron, and thick, knitted woolen socks with leather slippers tied on with leather thongs. It is likely that her mother wore such clothing for holidays when this woman was young, and she herself probably had worn a child's version of this outfit for special occasions. Although I do not normally take photos of people, I decided that I would ask her for permission because she was already posing. She nodded pleasantly and posed for me to take a snapshot, then sighed sadly and said to me, "Everyone wants to take a picture." Shocked that I had done something inappropriate, I tried to apologize, but she brushed it off and then commented, "People should know what Górals look like." The crowd from the main square and the vendors selling papal paraphernalia were dispersing, so after this encounter I headed home to rehash the day's events with my landlady, puzzling over the woman's remarks.

THEMES: CLASS, IDENTITY, AND GLOBALIZATION IN ŻYWIEC

The community of Żywiec had something that made it special in Poland—the Góral identity. This identity, which was the subject of

contention in the postsocialist era, was intimately linked to responses
to political and economic change. For some people, the Góral regional-
ethnic identity provides a sense of local autonomy from outside forces,
and a sense of identity that gives weight to arguments to avoid global
capital and focus instead on regional economic ties. Others disagree,
believing that the community needs global capital for development,
and they express this belief in part through arguments that the Góral
identity is part of tradition but not relevant to contemporary political
and economic issues. An important finding of this study is that class
position was a major determinant of one's views on the relevance of
Góral identity. Exploring this relationship between class and identity
allows one to understand the point of view of the frustrated woman
in Góral dress, and the story of the pope's visit provides a context
within which to introduce important actors who attempt to construct
differing Góral identities in this community.

Poland was facing escalating economic difficulties and social
tension. The problems Poland's government had experienced in implementing policies for a shift to an entirely market economy were, in
part, a result of the conflict between the assumptions underpinning
government policy and patterns of lived experience familiar and available to the vast majority of the Polish people. This disjuncture led to
a steep decline in popular support for politics in general and the national government in particular. In Żywiec, it also led people to feel
more distant from the national government, and more in need of local
solutions to their problems. One local resource on which they could
draw was the regional-ethnic identity, Góral. This process of declining
nationalism and increased importance of other identities is a much
debated aspect of globalization, on which this project sheds some light.

An examination of Żywiecers' responses to political and economic
change in previous eras suggests that it is not unique to the postsocialist
era that Góral identity had been used as a resource for mediating the
community's relationship with states and economic systems. In both
the pre–World War I period, when Żywiec was part of the Austro-
Hungarian Habsburg Empire, and the socialist period, from the end of
World War II up to 1989, Góral identity seems to have been linked to
ways of negotiating the preferred relationship among the community,
the state, and community economic strategies. By falling back on the
meaning of their past during times of change, Żywiecers have been
able to create new strategies for dealing with transition, while at the
same time reinterpreting the meaning of their past to better serve their
present needs. This is in no way an uncontested process, however. The
class politics of recreating this identity, and the implications for

Żywiecers' visions of postsocialist politics and economics, is the major focus of this book.

The primary process explained in this book is how class conflicts shape claims to group identity. This is not to say that class is the only determinant of identity process, but that it is an important one in this case. Class dynamics in the postsocialist era split the elites in Żywiec roughly into two groups—one favoring "globalization," attempting to involve foreign investors in town businesses, and the other favoring "regionalism," a more insular economic strategy involving increasing ties with neighboring towns across the nearby Czech and Slovak borders. The second group justified regionalism by invoking the Góral identity as a meaningful contemporary category, which tied the region together regardless of national borders. In contrast, the first group claimed that the Góral identity was a thing of the past, and that modern residents should look outward, especially outside the nation, for economic help. Ironically, both results of class politics involve a pulling away from nationalist politics, bolstering other claims on identity— regionalist or pan-European. What happened in Żywiec is a concrete example of a general trend: the contemporary spread of transnational capital and a growing, global cultural system of symbols and meanings pull in two directions, toward global (suprastate) systems of meaning, politics, and economics, and toward particularist (intrastate) backlashes. Whether called postnationalism (Matustík 1993), neonationalism (Wicker 1997), or simply a change in how nationalism functions (Llobera 1994), these processes "do not reinforce the ideological constructions called nation and state, but actually undermine them by pulling ahead of them on a trajectory of their own" (Wicker 1997, 32). Contrary to the strawman argument that postnationalism would mean that the nation-state is no longer meaningful in any sense, from an instrumentalist viewpoint it seems likely that the strength of nationalism will fade as the state plays a smaller role in the fate of the community, and other kinds of identities will gain salience. And in fact, the Żywiec case is one in which nationalism simply is not an ideological card that is played. No one there is trying to create a separate state (the idea of a separate Góral political homeland would be humorous to them), but no faction invokes the Polish state as useful or meaningful in their attempts to create a viable economic future for the community. National economic policy is designed to force communities, businesses, and individuals to be self-sufficient—with radical effect.

I began this research by doing semistructured interviews with individuals about how they were adjusting to these economic changes, primarily in terms of their personal economic strategies, and how their political outlook might be changing. I asked them about the kinds of adjustments they were making at various levels—nuclear family, kin group, local organization, business, or community—because most individuals do not have the resources, inclination, or opportunity to make purely individual decisions about economic strategies. The interviews were designed to shed light on a set of related questions: How do people in Żywiec respond to the effects of political, economic, and cultural changes at the level of class? How have class categories been maintained or reworked through the changes that led to socialism and the changes away from socialism? And how are class, identity, and globalization currently being articulated in contexts of local, national, and global power? The results formed a picture of how important class reproduction, fractioning, and formation were in the current debates over the community's future and over conceptions of the current identity of the community. The answers to these questions also challenge our views of the political economy of postsocialism in the former Eastern Bloc.

I suspected that the reality of the "transition to capitalism" in provincial communities was out of sync with national reports and Western expectations of a rapid and easy change toward individualism, the main building block of liberal capitalist modernity. This was indeed what I found. As the current transition to decentralized economic and political structures in Poland proceeds, it is increasingly evident that the benefits of this transition are distributed unevenly. Provincial communities suffer at the expense of urban centers for a number of reasons. Foreign investors and in-country capital sources are more likely to invest in large cities that have well-developed infrastructures, so expansion of existing businesses and creation of large new enterprises and joint ventures happens more in cities. Existing enterprises in smaller cities and towns have a lower profit margin, due in part to a lack of infrastructure, and so are more likely to be liquidated during the privatization process. This last means that unemployment will rise most in the very places where new businesses are least likely to open. It also plays into a circular process in which the national government attempts to make the economy more cost-effective by cutting infrastructural support, such as railroad service, in places that "don't need it" because industry is shutting down there. As the socialist landscape is reworked into capitalist geography, areas outside the major cities increasingly and disproportionately suffer.

Many Poles in provincial communities thus feel abandoned or betrayed by the national government and new economy that had given them such high hopes in 1989. They are left on their own to puzzle out ways to support themselves and their families, and to overcome these new obstacles of high unemployment, high inflation, decreasing infrastructural connections, and little or no support from outside sources. In the process, most people draw on their own past experiences and the traditions of their communities to come up with survival strategies. They do not have the resources that would allow them to open their own businesses or move to cities, the new way of doing things promoted by government and international development policies. Responses such as migrating to big cities to find jobs, which might be expected in the First or Third Worlds, are not viable strategies for most people in Eastern Europe, as I will explain.

An important factor in the responses of some people in this community to these problems is a defensive regionalism connected to the Góral regional-ethnic identity. As I discuss in chapter 2, the region around Żywiec historically has been passed back and forth among various nations in Central Europe, and thus has been the object of many different policies of nationalist politics and economics. Even after the region returned to Poland in the post–World War I era, it has been subject to the Nazi occupation, a socialist regime tied to the Soviet Union, and current attempts to integrate into the capitalist system. Each successive wave of changes has brought attempts by governing states to blur or eliminate this regional identity. Some Górals have resisted these attempts and entrenched their identity at each stage, because that very identity has helped them to process and mediate the community's relationship with each successive incursion. This identity affected strategies (economic, cultural, and political) at the family, local organization, and community level.

Before I ever came to Żywiec, I had heard from Poles living in other regions that Żywiec residents were Górals—that they spoke the Góral dialect and embodied a number of stereotypes, such as being less educated, rowdier and more ready to fight, fiercely independent, and generally ornery. I was told that I wouldn't be able to understand these people because the Góral dialect was so different from standard Polish.[4] On my initial visits to Żywiec, however, I discovered that I had no trouble understanding the few people with whom I spoke. I saw some few pieces of artwork and furniture in the Góral style, but I chalked it up to romanticization of the traditional. Only after several months of living there, I realized that I had difficulty understanding some people because they used certain idioms and grammatical aspects that were different from standard Polish, code switching between the Góral dialect and Polish. (This was certainly a relief to figure out!) At the same time, I was attempting to make sense of various statements that people made to me about who "real" Żywiecers were, and who I should be interviewing for my project. When people asked me who I was interviewing in Żywiec, I usually asked them who they thought I ought to be interviewing—a serendipitous question, as it turned out. Some people inquired whether I was interviewing only "town residents," because in their opinion the "real traditional Żywiec folk" lived on the outskirts of town. Others informed me that the real Żywiecers were those who lived in the main town, who had a family history there and relatives who been merchants or artisans prior to World War II (Żywiec residents call it simply "the War"). Still others thought that I should go beyond the bounds of the town to interview people from various parts of the Żywiec region, but I was not sure exactly where that region ended (neither were they) or what it meant to them. It was only several months into my project that someone actually used the term "Żywiec Góral" to me, and I began to pay more attention to whether people were implying the Góral identity when they said Żywiecers.[5] I started to put the pieces together and developed an idea of how and why this identity is important to various groups of people in the community.

The Góral identity is not important to every Żywiec resident: its strength of appeal is based in large part on how useful people find it, and class position is important in understanding its potential usefulness (or uselessness, or even disadvantages). I found that some people in Żywiec were repositioning and entrenching the Góral identity in attempts to improve their own situations by exerting influence over the economic choices of local businesses, the community, and one another. I call this group of people the "prewar elite"; they are currently in conflict with an emerging class I call the "neocapitalists." Identification with this regional identity is also a response to their own political feelings about national leadership. Some self-folklorized[6] markers of this identity, such as ostensibly traditional dress and crafts, or the dialect being used by people who normally speak standard Polish, are intentionally adopted by members of the prewar elite to reinforce their meaning of Góralism and their social claims to authority in the community. Other markers, such as speaking the Góral dialect mixed with standard Polish, or cultural rootedness in the geographical place where Góralism is a way of life, are implicit markers that are reworked as other aspects of people's lives change. For example, some Górals who moved to Kraków and Warsaw founded chapters there of the Friends of the Żywiec Region (FZR [*Towarzystwo Miłośników Ziemii Żywiecki*], an organization whose importance will become clear later), and Górals who moved to some foreign countries can purchase the *Żywiec Gazette*, the local monthly newspaper, through Polish-owned businesses abroad.

To understand the social crosscurrents of this complex factor in townspeople's responses to the post-1989 political and economic changes, I had to explore what "being Góral" meant to different parts of the community, in both the past and the present. The "town" version of being Góral in Żywiec is certainly a more objectified identity than it is among those who live in outlying rural districts, which were formerly separate villages and have recently been incorporated into the town. Both Góral speech characteristics, varying from differences in pronunciation to distinctly different vocabulary and grammatical structures, and artistic traditions, such as knowledge about the production of traditional Góral instruments and possession of Góral-style furniture, are more likely to be found in the rural areas. Yet the emphasis on community identification with "Góralness" is being promoted by a group of local cultural and political elites (the prewar elite) centered in the town proper. Likewise, the push to consider the identity part of the traditional past is championed by individuals with links to global capital (the neocapitalists). Thus, the identity as conceptualized by any member of the population is in dialogue with different external forces, depending on who that person is and how they are connected to groups outside Żywiec.

The anecdote about the pope's visit to Żywiec provides a framework within which I can illustrate the interaction of the major actors of this community and show how class drives claims to identity. Central to understanding several aspects of this anecdote, and the major theme of this book, is the conflict between the prewar elite and the neocapitalists over which group should have the authority to shape a Żywiec community strategy in the postsocialist era. This conflict links the fate of the Góral identity to the role of local and global business in the community. Ultimately, these conflicts involve questions about the relationships among the local community, the Polish state, and the global economy, which result in the growth of postnational identity processes. Understanding the ways in which the Góral identity is used by the two opposing elite groups in town helps in understanding the subtexts of globalization, ethnic revitalization, and class formation that are present in everyday life and are given concrete public shape in major community events. In the next section, I reexamine Pope John Paul II's visit from the point of view of three group actors who play key roles in town: the prewar elite, the Żywiec Brewery, and the neocapitalists. This closer reading illuminates the "behind the scenes" significance of class formation, ethnic resurgence, and postnationalism during the event.

The Prewar Elite

My conversation with the woman I photographed on the day of the pope's visit still stands out in my mind. Some important pieces of information that helped me make sense of it include the facts that she was not speaking in Góral dialect, that she lives in town rather than in a rural area, and that she is involved with the FZR in town, an arts and folklore group whose membership is predominantly made of up of prewar elite. People who have lived in the main town speak standard Polish and have largely lost the Góral dialect over the last one hundred years. This is particularly true of the prewar elite, because they were small business owners or managers of Habsburg businesses in the prewar period—the town elite who had business relations with outsiders who spoke standard Polish or German. A few older people who live in the large apartment complexes known as "settlements" retain the dialect, but their children quickly learned a more standard version of Polish. People in the outlying areas of town, however, tend to have been farmers much more recently in their families' histories, and they have retained Góral speech characteristics, even if they do not speak completely in dialect. The members of the FZR, the Żywiec Culture Club, and other artistic, cultural, and folkloric groups in town come primarily from the prewar elite, the more cosmopolitan main town residents. These groups are very active in trying to promote Góral arts and crafts among the residents and in organizing folk festivals and exhibitions. Together, the groups constitute a solid power block of upper-class town residents who retained much of their social status through the socialist era, a process I explain in detail in chapter 3.

Prewar elites' construction and use of who and what is Góral conforms to Polish ethnographers' vision of traditional Góral culture— a self-folklorizing, romantic view frozen in the early twentieth-century costume, rural lifestyle, and defining dialect. At summer folklore festivals, for example, ethnologists from universities are brought in to advise Góral dance and acting troupes and to judge the festivals. This folkloric view permeates the community to such an extent that individuals who in fact do incorporate characteristics of the Góral dialect into their speech and maintain small farms on the outskirts of the town sometimes don't consider themselves to be "real" Górals if they do not know Góral dancing or crafts.

These members of the prewar elite embody and privilege certain markers of Góral history that could be easily discarded—dialect for writing purposes, dress on occasion, and folklore—over other Góral characteristics such as farm life and actual incorporation of the dialect into everyday speech. This vocal and influential group of townspeople maintains that Góralism is rooted in community solidarity against the outside, for example, in regional autonomy from the national government or resistance to Western popular culture and Americanization. In promoting this ethic of solidarity, they also attempt to use it to discipline and control individuals (local and national politicians) and businesses that they believe are not doing enough to help the community.

My interpretation of the actions of the woman who was dressed in Góral finery hinges on her involvement in the various cultural groups in town that were interested in entrenching this identity and my understanding of her as one of the prewar elite. In my interviews with members of these groups, they suggested that by focusing on being Góral, and remembering the community's history, the community will be better able to weather the homogenizing cultural and economic effects of capitalist transformation. It soon became clear to me that a similar strategy had been used during times of political and economic transformation in the community: during the socialist period to distance the community from communism, during the World War II Nazi occupation to maintain community morale in the face of devastating attacks, and, before that (up to 1919), during the feudal period and Austrian partition. Thus, I argue that this recent response to policies of capitalist transformation is part of a historical pattern of relying on the local identity in instrumental ways to mediate colonizing forces, and in the same process, redefine the identity.

I would suggest that this particular woman was exasperated with the other residents' emphasis on the anomaly of her wearing of Góral costume, because her intent was to make a statement that the Góral identity is a given for everyone in the community. Wearing a beautiful traditional costume reflected her class status as well, because she was certainly part of the prewar upper class in Żywiec. More important, it was clear from the particular style of costume she wore that she was an upper-class resident, because there is not a standard traditional dress; dress differs by class and occupation as well as by gender, age, and, for women, marital status. The prewar elite are in key positions to construct, manipulate, and monopolize the cultural capital invested in Góral identity in an attempt to control the changes wrought by national programs on their community and in their families.

Globalization, International Capital, and the Żywiec Brewery

The global political economic system within which Żywiec is situated has prompted many changes in the town since the 1989 decisions to move away from the previously existing socialist system. One major player in this process is the Żywiec Brewery, which produces the best-selling beer in Poland, Żywiec Beer. Discussing the actions of the brewery and the reactions of town residents to the evolution of the brewery sheds light on the process of globalization in this community and the place of both class and identity in reactions to globalization.

The Żywiec Brewery has been around in one form or another for several centuries. In the late nineteenth century, when Żywiec was under Austrian rule, a branch of the Habsburg family made Żywiec a summer home. They built two small castles, and purchased and expanded the brewery and several other enterprises. They stayed even after the reconstitution of Poland after World War I, finally leaving Żywiec for good when the Nazi front came through during World War II. According to older members of the community, many of whom remember the Habsburg period as a golden age for Żywiec, the family always took care of the community and used brewery proceeds to support the workers. This fit in well with the historical construction of a community sense of morality attached to industry in Żywiec.

The Żywiec Brewery was one of the first enterprises in Poland to be privatized after 1989 as part of the Polish Privatization Plan, and it is widely touted as a success story—an example of the triumphal ideology that capitalism will inevitability "win" in Eastern Europe. Its profits are good, the stock is steady, and with the changing of national law on foreign ownership in 1994, the Heineken Brewery Company was allowed to purchase 25 percent of the stock.

Local residents see a different side of the story: the Żywiec Brewery is currently a primary target of anger in Żywiec. Before 1989, the brewery employed around two thousand people, but as a result of intensive capital investment in mechanization, it employed fewer than eight hundred in 1994–95, and over one hundred more were laid off in 1997. Since its privatization in 1991, benefits such as health care, child care, a kindergarten, sports activities, vacation arrangements, and help obtaining winter potatoes and coal have been slashed or eliminated. Brewery donations to the town library and cultural activities have dropped, except for large-scale activities that will bring international exposure or result in profit from beer sales, such as the Polish Góral and International Folklore Festival. There is widespread resentment—expressed through rumor, jokes, angry stories about unemployment, constant requests from community groups for brewery funds, and statements of currently employed workers—that the brewery seems to have turned its back on the community. The brewery has set up a special requests fund in an attempt to distance itself from the process of handing out funds for sponsorship of various community activities. The idea was that town groups would all apply to this fund for money, and thus the bureaucratization of funding would show people that money was given out on the basis of merit, and there was a limited amount to be given out. Community groups, including the town council, see this fund as far too small in proportion to the perceived resources of the brewery, and also inappropriate because it does not recognize the moral economy of the town—the personal relationship between the town and brewery, and the necessity of dispensing help through affectual ties.

Currently, many people in town see Heineken as the moving force behind the changes in the relationship between the brewery and the town. The new marketing department (the Poles borrow the English word but pronounce it with the accent on the second syllable) is often spoken of with derision, as the puppets through which Heineken's will is done (as in "those marketing guys don't care about this community, they only care about profits"). These results of privatization and globalization are clearly something most Żywiec residents with whom I spoke would like to do without.

The brewery is also tied to the idea of Góral identity. For more than a hundred years, the Żywiec Brewery has used Góral images and the Żywiec name in its advertising and marketing strategies, from the dancing Góral couple on the label to hiring costumed Góral bands to play in grocery stores during promotions. The town council and cultural organizations have begun to use this identification with Żywiec and Górals against the brewery, threatening to give sponsorship of major events such as the huge summer Polish Góral and International Folklore Festival to another brewery. The objective is to pry more money out of the brewery for various town projects, including sponsorship of the festivals. A different but related control issue is that the brewery wants sole rights to the name "Żywiec" for its products and is negotiating with the town council for this. This was spurred by the use of the name by a new and very successful mineral water producer (Żywiec Zdrój mineral water) in a nearby town, which irritates the Żywiec Brewery now that it too is marketing its own brand of flavored mineral waters (Żywiec mineral water). (The town council's response was to propose a tax on the brand name "Żywiec" for all products that are sold other than locally, which the brewery would be able to absorb because of sheer size. Needless to say, this is not an acceptable compromise to the brewery.) The brewery is using this Góral imagery and name, which has cultural meaning in Poland, and thus has to fight with the town over what that meaning is and how it can be used.

The reverse side of this issue is that the brewery still has substantial economic power in town. Most of the time, it is the first choice for sponsorship of community events, and it holds a commanding position in negotiations for excellent product placement when the town of Żywiec gets publicity. By pouring on enough money, it can try to leverage issues such as the trademark of the Żywiec name. Thus, flags that bore the name Żywiec in the trademark style of the brewery appeared on the town square during the pope's visit. However, the town was able to stall the brewery on the issue of trademarking, while at the same time acquiring money from the brewery, so this strategy of passive resistance was standing the town in good stead in the mid-1990s.

Just as the Góral images attract buyers to the beer, the beer attracts people to the Górals. At least a part of the fun in going to a folk festival in Żywiec is buying the beer made there. So, although alternate sponsorships lose product placements for the brewery for publicity purposes, and there might be some shame attached (though I could detect little sign of it among the brewery workers or management), the brewery will certainly continue to profit from its use of the Żywiec name and Góral imagery.

International Exposure, Economic Links, and the Neocapitalists

If the prewar elite class and the Żywiec Brewery are the first two actors, the third is the emerging elite class of neocapitalists, a group that included the mayor, the town council, and local managers of international businesses. The neocapitalists were a group in formation in the mid-1990s—some came from prewar elite families, others emerged onto the local political scene after 1989. This class was attempting to convince itself and others, via a discourse of development that includes various promotional pamphlets, videotapes, and newspaper advertisements, that Żywiec is "modern" and thus able to support foreign capital investments and tourism. The mayor of Żywiec, for example, told me that the extensive repainting and renovations in Żywiec were not just for the purpose of honoring the pope, but also to look good for the international exposure the Holy Father would bring. Several national and international news organizations were covering the papal visit—in the mayor's own words, "the whole world will be watching us on that day"—so people all over the world would know that it was a great place to be a tourist, to relocate one's business, and to invest. The rondo, he said, was actually to ease the traffic flow through Żywiec and to help all the tourists. Any claims that the rondo was constructed solely for the pope were pure fantasy, according to the mayor. Żywiec is, in fact, on a main road to newly opened border-crossing points with Slovakia and the Czech Republic, and there has been an increase in traffic, which led to the repaving of several roads, installation of traffic lights, and construction of a new road that bypassed the downtown area so that traffic would not be tied up.

The number of tourists who actually stop in Żywiec to enjoy its scenic castles, museums, and hiking and boating venues is small, but the town council and most residents believe that tourism could become a real economic force in Żywiec. For tourists to be attracted to Żywiec, however, they feel that there must be a blend of "old world" charm and folklore with modern tourism facilities. The town council ordered that the roadwork and rondo construction be sped up to complete it in time for the papal visit, so that people around the world would see that Żywiec is pleasant enough for vacationers and developed enough to handle modern needs. I later discovered that the town had also hired a film company to film and edit the papal visit in videotape form, to be available both to residents, through the town hall and local churches, and to tourists at festivals and in town museums. This partnered another promotional videotape about Żywiec made the year before, which was designed to increase tourism and business investment.

Where did the resources come from to do all of this work? Partly from the town budget, but a large donation was made by the brewery. In return, the brewery stipulated, the town was to look more favorably on its request for the trademark rights to the town name (which it still had not received in 1997), and was also to allow product placement—the display of the Żywiec Brewery logo during the papal visit where it would be sure to be broadcast by television crews. The Żywiec pennants given out for people to wave on the main square displayed only the name of the town, but this is also the name of the beer, and the pennants were printed in the stylized manner associated with the brewery's logo. This savvy technique allowed international television exposure for the brewery and looked appropriately patriotic, without causing worries about seeming impious during the papal visit. It also provided television cameras with an "appropriate" blend of folklore (people in Góral outfits, a Góral chorus to entertain the pontiff) and the modern (freshly painted buildings, a newly erected scaffolding for the pope's mass, the Żywiec logo recalling the town's modern industry) to symbolize the town's links to the past, present development, and vision of the future.

The neocapitalists had the advantage of holding major political positions in town, allowing them to set the stage to show off their version of Żywiec: the modern town with strong international investment. The prewar elite had their own version of what should happen: the papal visit should be a time to show off the unique cultural history of the Żywiec region, which gave them claims to authority in the community. It is interesting that nonelites in town seemed unmoved by the political stagings of either group. After a wave of initial excitement when the visit was announced, people became disenchanted by the demands on time and patience that all the reconstruction, repainting, and rehearsals required. Soon they became bored or antagonized and began to talk to me about the event not in terms of anticipation, but of anger. One woman, who had a daughter celebrating her First Communion that year, was annoyed that she was required to take time off from work to bring her daughter to the festivities, where First Communion celebrants needed to appear in special costumes. The kiosk where another woman worked was moved to a less desirable location, because it was placed exactly where a huge outdoor altar was to be built. Because the kiosk was now out of the hustle and bustle of the main square, she was afraid that it would be shut down after the pope's visit. At a pig-slaughtering I attended shortly before the pope's visit, the construction, road paving, and new rondo for the visit were hot topics of conversation among the adults. As one man exclaimed, with money being spent that the town could not afford, security precautions annoying everyone, and the whole thing being blown out of proportion, "it's just like when the First Secretary [an important communist politician] came to town." Though when I questioned nonelites about why the pope would choose to come to Żywiec, they almost without exception replied that it was probably because he had grown up in Wadowice and was from the Żywiec region, few of the nonelites followed this up with spontaneous remarks about importance of the Góral identity, as the prewar elite did.

THE SPECTER OF THE COLD WAR
AND THE TRANSITION FROM SOCIALISM

The reactions of these townspeople need to be understood as rooted in their hopes and fears about their own futures and the futures of their families and the Żywiec community in the particularly unsettled era referred to as "the transition." But trying to understand reactions to the papal visit solely in terms of a transition from socialism to capitalism leads to a number of problems. By making socialism our baseline era, we miss out on important social links to the more distant past. Ideologies of transition championed by consultants and policymakers stress the importance of supporting particular kinds of social actors (for example, entrepreneurs) over others (reactionaries or traditionalists), because these actors will help move the transition forward (toward capitalism). This is a rather flat portrayal of social actors, lacking a contextualized understanding of their histories and goals. It also requires a particularly shallow notion of political, economic, and social change to suppose that we know what the endpoint of a transition from socialism will look like, as if a radical break from the past would be either possible or predictable. The privileging of this kind of conception of the transition from socialism is rooted in an outdated paradigm in which the Cold War dominates analysis of Eastern Europe, and it is linked to modernization theories in Western social science.

Anthropologists frequently refer to gatekeeping concepts in discussing the significance of place in constructing theoretical paradigms. Following Arjun Appadurai (1986), a gatekeeping concept is one associated with a given region of the world, which is taken to stand for that region and becomes the only legitimate lens through which to view it. Appadurai outlined the implications for anthropological theory:

> From the start, the ethos of anthropology has been driven by the appeal of the small, the simple, the elementary, the face-to-face. In a general way, this drive has had two implications for anthropological theory. The first is that certain forms of sociality (such as kinship), certain forms of exchange (such as gift), certain forms of polity (such as the segmentary state) have been privileged objects of anthropological attention and have constituted the prestige zones of anthropological theory. The second result has been that the anthropology of complex non-Western societies has, till recently, been a second-class citizen in anthropological discourse. This second effect involves a kind of reverse Orientalism, whereby complexity, literacy, historical depth, and structural messiness operate as disqualifications in the struggle of places for a voice in metropolitan theory.

> Yet this characterization of the role of complex traditional civilizations in anthropological theory is too simple and conspiratorial. The fact is that the anthropology of complex

civilizations does exist, but in a peculiar form. In this form, a few simple theoretical handles become metonyms and surrogates for the civilization or society as a whole: hierarchy in India, honor-and-shame in the circum-Mediterranean, filial piety in China are all examples of what one might call gatekeeping concepts in anthropological theory, concepts, that is, that seem to limit anthropological theorizing about the place in questions, and that define the quintessential and dominant questions of interest in the region. (1986, 357)

I argue that for Eastern Europe and the former Soviet Union, the primary gatekeeping concept in American social science since World War II has been the Cold War. Some results of this have been an emphasis on politics as the defining object of Eastern European studies and the privileging of political science for the setting of research agendas. The Cold War became the idée fixe of thinking on the Eastern Bloc, thereby setting up the notion of the transition as the natural, or essential, object of current social science investigation once the Cold War was perceived to be ending.

This Cold War paradigm led Western social scientists to privilege state-level politics as the main frame through which the Eastern Bloc was viewed, so that the primary subject with which anthropology is concerned, culture, was believed by many to have been wiped clean by that monolith, communism. Thus, class, ethnicity, religion, and other hierarchies of power that would interest anthropological political economists were officially pronounced dead by the Communist Party. However, information about the Eastern Bloc had clear strategic importance, and thus was the bailiwick of many political scientists. One impact of this set of circumstances was that many Eastern Europeanists in anthropology and sociology virtually abrogated responsibility for setting their own research agendas, turning instead to political science and economics (Verdery 1996, 7). Getting past the Cold War paradigm will allow us to more fruitfully explore the realities of present experiences in the Eastern Bloc and will force us to rethink Cold War constructions of history and the relationships between the First, Second, and Third Worlds.

Certainly it is important to think about state politics and economics, which have an enormous impact on everyday life, and many valuable studies concerned with these concepts have shed a great deal of light on what life was like under socialism. Nevertheless, the current prevalence of "transitionology," the study of privatization, national elites, and civil society, eclipses other kinds of subjects in the Eastern Bloc. In the postsocialist era, the current gatekeeping concept for Eastern Europe and the former Soviet Union is that of the transition. Other concepts, such as civil society and nationalism, tend to fall easily under the umbrella of the transition paradigm. As Abraham Brumberg states,

> "Transition" is one name of the game. Another is the question, "Will Russia make it"? Both invite trouble, because both are based on dubious propositions: that the current period in post-Soviet history is by definition transient, with a clearly distinguishable point of departure and a discernible time of completion, and that the end of this process is either 'normality'—that blessed state of prosperous capitalism, democracy and enlightened relations with the outside world—or a backslide into a barbarism even more chilling that that of the past. (1996, 29)

I do not mean to suggest that the former Eastern Bloc is not experiencing change, but rather that the popular and scholarly construction of the transition as a particular type of change with a predetermined outcome has teleological elements that are intricately linked to the construction of the Cold War paradigm. The transition paradigm assumes that the Eastern Bloc will be transformed through the adoption of the free market in exactly the same ways that the Third World was, so that the former centralized economies will soon fit neatly into the capitalist world system, and fifty or more years of socialist history will be a historical fluke with no residual effects. Just as the Cold War was thought to wipe out presocialist history and social structures, so the transition will erase all vestiges of Soviet-era imposition. We need to get away from these gatekeeping concepts, reconsidering not just the current conceptualization of Eastern Europeanist anthropology, but challenging the entire paradigm of the Cold War and how it affected our conceptualization of issues affecting the Eastern Bloc. I would also challenge anthropologists to look at the privileging of the First World–Third World split, because I see this as flowing directly from the Cold War paradigm. Cold War rhetoric drove elimination of the Second World from discussions of the global economy and culture in the First and Third Worlds.

Thus, this project is not concerned with the Transition—the idea that there is a single process occurring in the Eastern Bloc that will move the countries there away from socialist government and economics and toward democracy and capitalism. The Transition, with a capital *T*, does not exist. There is no one process in Eastern Europe, or even in Poland: there are many different processes, many different kinds of changes. There is no inevitability to the process. The reforms that national politicians and Western advisors have put in place may result in some form of democracy and capitalism, or then again, they may not. As with so many things, it depends on the definitions of the terms, and it depends on where the definer stands in relation to these processes.

Of course, there are many transitions occurring presently in the Eastern Bloc, and 1989 was a watershed year for those transitions. However, this does not mean that every research project needs to be structured by the notion of the Transition, a unidirectional, evolutionary concept in which the beginning point is socialism and the endpoint is a capitalist industrial democracy. It does not mean that every research agenda situated in present-day Eastern Europe or the former Soviet Union needs to flow from the standpoint of the political, economic, and cultural changes taking place there, without linking these to other global matters as well.

This project is concerned with class processes and an ethnic identity that predate socialism, were maintained during the socialist era, and continue to be relevant in the postsocialist era. I seek to answer the questions of how class processes are related to the maintenance of the identity, in the past and under current conditions of globalization. I also seek to understand how the various classes, and the community as whole, have been constituted in relation to the nation-state in several historical eras: the feudal era, in which Żywiec belonged to the Austro-Hungarian Empire; the socialist era, during which Żywiec, like the rest of the Eastern Bloc, was subject to Soviet socialism; and the postsocialist era, in which the Polish state is attempting to integrate into supranational entities such as the European Union and North Atlantic Treaty Organization (NATO).

CHAPTER OVERVIEWS

The structure of this text is designed to introduce the town of Żywiec and its residents in a way that builds, chapter by chapter, to answer the questions of how people in Żywiec have been responding to political-economic transitions, past and present, socialist and capitalist, and what these responses tell us about the relations of class, identity, community, and nation-state in several different historical periods. I first set the stage with a discussion of the political-economic history of the community vis-à-vis the nation-state and then follow with a history of class structures in general and the elite classes in particular. Next, I explore nonelite, family-level economics and politics and how these are related to the elite classes and community strategies. This leads to a description of community-level politics and economics in the socialist and postsocialist eras. Each of these pieces contains a theoretical thread that contributes to the whole argument. Finally, I weave these threads together in a discussion and reconceptualization of the intersection of local, national, and global political economy, traditionalism and modernity, and local identity.

In chapter 2, then, I take up the specific history of Żywiec. Drawing on original historical manuscripts from the town, I show the development of Żywiec and its town industries until the end of World War II. I describe the effects of the German occupation during World War II on the town's industry and some of the socialist era changes in the town's geographical size, population, and trades. I consider the questions of how the community has been affected by its relations with the several nation-states that have engulfed it, and where the postsocialist transition is taking the town and townspeople in the contemporary era. Understanding how the Góral regional identity maps onto the Polish national identity requires an understanding of how Góralism has been shaped by the particular political and economic history of this region of Poland, and how Góralism has shaped the response of Górals to colonizing forces and other national identities in the past. Chapter 2 thus explores the interaction of Góralism with feudal colonial powers, and the continuing moral economy of Góralism in socialist Poland. I show how town businesses grew up amidst a Góral community ethos, and changed from feudal to small-scale capitalist to socialist within that ethos. The introduction of large-scale international capitalism in Żywiec is breaking larger enterprises away from the community and interfering with small, community-based businesses, a point I take up again in chapter 4.

Chapter 3 covers the history of the changing social structure of power in Żywiec, describing its class structure in the present era and previous eras. It shows how members and descendants of members of prewar power networks have been using the regional-ethnic identity of Góralism as a currency of authority under socialism and are attempting to continue this strategy of traditionalism in the postsocialist era. They are attempting to recreate the prewar authoritarian social power structure and, further, parlay their positions within this affectual authority structure into "modern," bureaucratic positions. Historically, I also explore the influences of the former Communist Party and the Solidarity movement in Żywiec, showing how members of these organizations have been absorbed into the new power structure. In the postsocialist era, I analyze the emergence of a new elite class, the neocapitalists, who are primarily the go-betweens and beneficiaries of international capitalist investments in Żywiec. This new elite class is in direct competition with the prewar elite, in the sense of both moral authority in the community and access to economic resources. I consider the concepts of traditionalism and modernity as cultural idioms through which these two elite classes, prewar elites and neocapitalists, maneuver and manipulate to characterize themselves, through various arguments, as the "true" inheritors of authority in Żywiec. This chapter focuses on the power structure of the upper class in Żywiec and is a counterpart to chapter 4, which discusses nonelite individual and family strategies without consideration of community-level power relations.

Chapter 4 explores the way in which economic strategizing for nonelite individuals, of peasant and worker classes, depends on family strategies and networks and is influenced by a felt sense of Góralism that is distinct from the folklorized Góral ideology used by both of the elite classes in Żywiec. This is a continuation of processes that were at work during the feudal and socialist eras in Poland generally, and Żywiec specifically, and continue today. I look at the differential effects of age, gender, class, and cultural and material rootedness in the region on possible economic strategies and outcomes. Different skills and differential access to bases of power result in differences for individuals and families within Żywiec. However, the culture of place that connects nonelite Góral inhabitants in a regional identity differentiates them broadly from urban residents and the elite classes in the community, who have greater economic capital and greater social and cultural capital, which can be used in political and economic ways. In this chapter, I also consider the instrumental use of Góral identity within family networks in justifying adaptive strategies, as well as arguments over maintaining or breaking the links of family traditions.

In chapter 5, I look at Żywiec's community-level strategies of economic and political responses to the national-level economic and political policies of transformation, primarily in the postsocialist era, but in part in contrast to those of the socialist era. Within the community, these transformations include changes in town management, struggles between the town and various businesses, and the budding tourist industry. In nearly all of these situations, the players (of all classes) invoke various ideas of Góral ethnic regionalism to bolster their positions. The ideological and financial conflicts between the town and the brewery, and the brewery and the metal factory, are explored in depth to show the ramifications of transnational capital on regional identity and resulting strategies of resistance. Between the community and the nation-state, the transformations involve control over the flows of labor and resources, and in the postsocialist era, they also include globalizing strategies that involve sidestepping national linkages and forming ties with other communities internationally.

In chapter 6, I return to the day of the pope's visit to reconsider the event in terms of the larger questions of class and identity, community and nation that have been raised in this project. The articulations of traditionalism and modernity in Żywiec, and in the former Eastern Bloc in general, are shown to be similar in their logics to those occurring in Western Europe, and indeed to some extent in the rest of the "globalized" world. I discuss the supranational, national, and regional processes that problematize the nation-state as an analytical category in Europe, and deeply affected the relation between subnational and transnational identities and the nation-state in the 1990s. I look at regionalism, nationalism, and transnationalism as responses to economic, political, and cultural change. In doing so, I bring together various levels of discussion about families, business enterprises, and communities to discuss strategic adaptations to the changing economic, political, and social environment. Returning to the main thesis of the book, I discuss how globalization and local identity interact to form a primary battleground for claims to authority, from which come political and economic responses to the many changes in Poland today.

"BAD TIME FOR DEMOKRACY": WRITING ABOUT A "TRANSITION" IN PROGRESS

Writing and conducting research about responses to broad political and economic change turned out in some ways to be as muddled a process as the "Transition" itself—in terms of both lived experience and theoretical modeling. Every day in Żywiec, I received new information, some of which contradicted information I had previously heard or approaches I had tried. Everyday I attempted to fit this in with my changing views—of Góral life, of the consequences of national policy, of something seemingly as simple as buying bread or what kind of train ticket to buy to get to Prague for vacation. Sometimes, I got so frustrated with the onslaught of change that I attempted to go back to old behavioral patterns or theories, only to be forcefully reminded that they didn't work anymore. At other times, I made confident plans based on the new order, only to find that it hadn't penetrated nearly as deeply as I thought. In the end, I managed to come through somehow, for better or worse. This basic pattern, of course, is more or less the same for everyone in every society today. The difference in Eastern Europe post-1989 is that the changes are so widespread; so thoroughgoing, so loved, hated, craved, and feared—brought on by themselves and now out of control. Historian and sociologist Jadwiga Staniszkis told us in 1984 that the Solidarity movement was proposing a "self-limiting revolution," which would result in changes only to bring a "socialism with a human face." In 1995, it felt to me, and to many others with whom I spoke, as though this self-limiting revolution had fed on itself and now appeared to be a limitless revolution, an uncontrollable monster rampaging through the countryside with endless demands.

The heading of this section, "Bad Time for Demokracy," is taken from graffiti scrawled across a wall on a building in the heart of Żywiec when I was living there in 1994–95. It caught my eye among the other graffiti because "bad time for demokracy" was painted in English (and misspelled). Underneath it, in a different color of paint, someone had declared in Polish, "I don't understand." As if to clarify, yet another respondent demanded, "Write in Polish!" This exchange was a daily sight for me from autumn 1994 until late spring 1995, when it was painted over to prepare the town for tourist season and the pope's visit in particular. This tragicomic interchange of social analysis, pleas for understanding, and whitewashing for outsiders could hardly escape me as an allegory of daily life during the transition. I interpreted this to mean that the writer, like many Poles with whom I spoke, took a dim view of the economic changes in Poland, and believed that the political changes did not and would not result in democracy.

The initial euphoria of 1989, felt by many people in Central and Eastern Europe as well as observers in the West, soon faded as the realities of life in transition sank in. Those who thought that they had supported the "add free market and stir" approach to decentralizing economic and political power found that this was not as simple as it seemed. A splintering into dozens of political groups occurred, where previously there had seemed to be such a clear division between the Communists and the opposition (Solidarity) umbrella organization. Workers, peasants, national and local politicians, and intellectuals discovered that they had very different expectations about how the dismantling of communism and the putting in place of market and democratic institutions should proceed. This has resulted in conflict and disappointments on most sides, and affluence and hope for a very few.

In this study, I try to portray the situations as they were explained to me by people in Żywiec and as I experienced them myself from the perspective of someone living in Żywiec. I sought to interview Żywiec residents from a variety of perspectives—members of different classes, women, men, local politicians, young, old, workers, and managers. I interviewed some people who had left Żywiec to live in other places, those who were unemployed or partially employed, and those who owned businesses. Some people identified very strongly with the Góral label, some did not. I do not claim to represent in any comprehensive way the points of view of national-level politicians or advisors, urban residents, Górals in other regions (such as Zakopane, a neighboring region, or Slovakian Górals), or foreign investors.

Nevertheless, this study is written to be read primarily by academics—in Poland, in the United States, and elsewhere. I hope that I can do justice to the many interviews with which I was gifted, and I hope that Żywiec residents who read this can recognize themselves and their descriptions of their lives, despite the academic analysis. In discussions of anthropological methods, the question often arises whether the anthropologist, as outsider, can see certain aspects of a phenomenon more clearly than those who are inside the culture, or whether we merely distort our findings to fit our analyses. A well-off, highly educated, widely traveled Żywiec resident might read my study and think, "But I'm not a Góral! That's a part of the past." No culture is entirely the same for all participants. However, the frequent and wide-ranging appeals to Góral ideology and imagery that I witnessed during my year in Żywiec seemed to me to be based in some solid notion of cultural meaning, was understood by members of the community, and frequently accomplished the task at hand. The fact that things got done when Góralism was invoked is a strong argument for me that Góralism is alive and well in Żywiec, whether in ties to folklorized images or in felt understandings.

There is a difference, of course, between community ideals of Góralism, which grow and change with the times, and the frozen, folkloristic idea of the "real" Góral, which some people have in mind if asked the question, "Are you a Góral?" I attempt to explain both aspects of the problem in this study and to show how they are both relevant to the lives of current Żywiec residents. Likewise, I would like to stress that there is certainly an expressive, affective, noninstrumental aspect to this identity—people do not appeal to Góralism merely to get things done, but also because it is personally and historically meaningful to them.

The community of Żywiec has survived many upheavals over the centuries. The much vaunted fall of communism is no different from any of the others, in that people pick up the pieces and move on. This project is about moving on. In the same sense that Chekhov's play *The Three Sisters* is not about wanting to go to Moscow, but about living while not going to Moscow, this project is not about the postsocialist transition, but about living while dealing with the many transitions that Żywiecers have experienced.

Chapter 2

◄○►

A Political and Economic History of the Żwiec Region

My very first visit to Żywiec occurred while I was a student at Jagiellonian University in Kraków, when a group of friends and I drove down to see the town. The group included myself, three other English and American women of Polish descent, and Jan, the young Polish boyfriend of one of the women. For the rest of the group, the point of the trip was to take a Saturday break from studies and see the famous Żywiec Brewery; for me, it would be a chance to see the community in which I was planning to live for at least a year.

We pulled into the town square, hungry for lunch, and decided to try the first restaurant we found. Entering the dimly lit space, we discovered that it was furnished entirely in Góral-style carved wooden furniture. Because we had previously visited the town of Zakopane to the east, another Góral community, we expected that the waitstaff would be Góral-speakers. The women who worked there, however, did not seem to speak in the Góral dialect. After lunch, we investigated the national park and castles, which were part of the former Habsburg estate. Eventually we asked for directions to the brewery and drove out to see it.

As we got closer to the brewery, the distinctive aroma of fermenting beer grew stronger and stronger until it filled the air. We approached the gatehouse and asked if they gave tours, and the guards laughed and joked with us about tourists who always wanted to see the inside of the brewery. We walked over to the brewpub, which was attached to the brewery property and open to the public, to see if Żywiec beer tasted different at the source. There were a number of people socializing in the brewpub, all men, who grew silent as four women walked in, accompanied only by one young man. We walked up to the bar and ordered beers, asking the barmaid about the souvenir Żywiec glasses, mugs, posters, and other items for sale, all eyes in the bar trained on us. When we finally settled at a table, conversation picked up again. Gazing around at the decor, I saw that all of the tables and chairs were carved in the same patterns as those in the restaurant where we had eaten lunch. Among the carved wooden plaques hanging on the walls was one that depicted a scene of three men: one of them was drinking beer, and another had what appeared to be horns on his head and was fighting with the third. These last two had blood on their faces and bodies. Puzzled, I asked Jan if the scene represented some sort of myth about the Devil. He laughed and told me that it was a Góral party—that there was a Góral saying that if there was no blood at a party, there was no party. Just how important was the Góral identity in Żywiec, I wondered? And why would the brewery, newly privatized and looking for a modern image, continue to hang such traditional plaques on the walls of its brewpub?

This chapter explores the unique history of the town of Żywiec and the Żywiec region, attending to the problem of how shifting relations to nation-states have affected local identity and how the Góral identity has mediated the community's relation to various polities. Historical investigation shows that the Żywiec community has belonged to the Czech monarchy, Silesian nobility, various Polish noble families (including the royal family at one point), the Habsburgs, the Nazis under the World War II occupation, and the modern Polish nation-state. Because this is an area of Europe that has passed back and forth between several states in the course of its long history, the political and economic impacts of various nationalist projects have been met with resistance from the community. I contend that because the relationship between the community and these various nation-states has been shifting, and the relationship between local identity and national identity is unclear, the community has developed an insular political and economic view that is distinct from national identity both historically and contemporarily. Thus, in the present era, as the Polish nation-state withdraws funding and infrastructural support from Żywiec as part of the "shock therapy" changes, the nation-state is becoming even less important to the local economy and identity. I first provide a brief political history of the town of Żywiec and show where this parallels the Polish nation-state and where it diverges from it. Second, I discuss Żywiec's economic development. The town of Żywiec has been relatively prosperous in comparison with the rest of the region. Despite ties to foreign capital up through the early twentieth century, and the nationalization of town industry under communism, a community-oriented moral economy developed, which I argue lasted throughout the socialist period and is only now beginning to be disrupted by the impact of global capitalism. I discuss the articulation of the local identity of Góralism within these histories with nationalist factors such as religion, language, and educational systems.

The history of political and economic resistance to national programs in the Żywiec region are often glossed over or entirely ignored in conventional histories of Poland. This makes it necessary to comb official histories of Poland and the Austro-Hungarian Empire for references to this specific province and town. Local archives containing regional newspapers, journals, and manuscripts were valuable resources for writing a richer local history of Żywiec. For descriptions of events occurring in this century, I also rely on oral histories as related to me by older community members.

ORIENTATION

The town of Żywiec lies in a valley at the crossing of the Soła and Koszarowa Rivers. The valley is approximately 355 meters (590 feet) above sea level, and the surrounding peaks are some of the highest in the Beskid Mountains, ranging up to 1,725 meters (2,875 feet) above sea level. The Slovak border is only 30 kilometers away.

Żywiec is widely touted by the inhabitants as a tourist attraction, and there are in fact many types of recreation available nearby. Locals go to the Żywiec Lake for fishing and swimming, hike on the mountain trails, and ski on the slopes in the winter. The Żywiec amphitheater, built during the socialist period, seats several thousand, and many events are held there during the summer, from rock concerts to folk festivals.

There are a number of sights to see within the town itself. A few wooden churches have been preserved and are some of the oldest types of this architecture in Poland. The Holy Cross Church was built in the fourteenth century, and the Church of Our Lady in the fifteenth. The Church of the Transfiguration was first built in 1701, and in the late nineteenth century, the wood structure was replaced by brickwork. The

Old Castle, some parts of which date back to the fifteenth century, stands in the center of town on the twenty-five-acre garden park that was the estate. The Habsburgs left their stamp as well, when they built the New Castle next to the Old, rearranged the park from an eighteenth-century Italian style to an English garden landscape, and built a Chinese-style summer house on an island in the park.

The Communist Party planners also added distinctive features to the Żywiec community. Large apartment projects in the downtown area, built during the 1970s, allowed the influx of several thousand villagers from the countryside surrounding Żywiec. This flow toward the town was engineered to ensure that there would be enough work-ers to staff the expansion of industrial production in Żywiec. The town as it is currently constituted also includes a number of districts that were previously outlying villages and that were incorporated into Żywiec over the course of the socialist period.

Markers of Góralism are dotted across the scene. In smaller vil-lages farther outside the town there are some "traditional" Góral wooden houses still in use by poor families. Góral-style furniture and decorations can be found in many homes in Żywiec and in restaurants and other businesses as well. Graffiti scrawled across whitewashed walls make frequent use of the word "Góral." Sports stadiums have Góral names. In the hum of conversation that drifts across the bustling outdoor town market, Góral phrases and jokes are interwoven with standard Polish.

POLITICAL DEVELOPMENT OF ŻYWIEC

The political boundaries of countries within Central and Eastern Eu-rope have changed many times over the past five hundred years as the rising empires of Russia, Prussia, Austria, and the Ottoman Turks vied for power. Poland's position in the center of three of these empires has meant a great deal of squabbling about the political authority over various lands claimed both by Poland and Russia, Prussia and Aus-tria. The region immediately to the west of Żywiec, Silesia, with its manufacturing and rich mining deposits, was the source of much of Austria's wealth during the Habsburg Empress Maria Theresa's reign in the early 1740s, and dispute over its ownership was a cause of the War of Austrian Succession between Prussia and Austria. Żywiec changed hands from country to country and from duchy to duchy within and among these empires many times.

The historical records on Żywiec go back more than seven hun-dred years, and archeological digs demonstrate evidence of Celtic settlement in the area beginning in the sixth century BC. The first mention of Żywiec in the historical records is a tax record from the Duchy of Oświęcim (Auschwitz) in 1308. At this point, the duchy was a part of the Czech kingdom under King Jan de Luxembourg. The foundation of the town apparently occurred somewhat earlier, in the thirteenth century. The region passed from one Polish noble family to another through the next few centuries, passing to the Piasts in 1433 and then later to the Skrzynski family, a branch of the Labedz nobility. Several manuscripts in the town archives, including seventeenth-century historian and mayor Andrzej Komoniecki's *Chronicles of Żywiec* (published in 1992 by a community group), note that this was a difficult period for the town, allegedly because several members of the Skrzynski family were themselves robbers who stole from townspeople.

In 1460, Żywiec became the property of Kazimierz Jagiellończyk, the king of Poland. In 1474, Kazimierz gave Żywiec to the Komorowski family, lords of Orawa and Liptow. Over the next several centuries, Żywiec remained in royal or noble hands until 1678, when then King Jan Kazimierz sold it to Jan Wielopolski, one of his chancellors and also the duke of Pieskowa Skala. The Wielopolskis kept the region for 140 years, selling it to Duke Albert von Sachsen Teschen, an Austrian nobleman who also owned the Teschen part of Silesia, in 1808. When he died in 1822, the region passed to direct ownership by the Habsburg family, rulers of the Austro-Hungarian Empire, where it remained until the end of World War I.[1]

Partitions

In 1822, when Żywiec landed in Habsburg hands, Poland as an independent state did not officially exist. This was due to the partitioning of Poland in the late eighteenth century, when Poland was dissolved over a twenty-three-year period, a situation that lasted until the end of World War I. Poland in 1772 was a self-governing nation, whose king was Stanisław August of the Poniatowski family. In the 1760s, however, Russia, Prussia, and Austria began planning the first partitioning of Poland, claiming that certain lands under the Polish crown belonged to these three nations. In 1772, 1793, and 1795, the three partitioning powers further subdivided Poland until the final partition in 1795, when Poland ceased to exist.

During the late 1760s and the 1770s, a Polish resistance movement (the Confederation of Bar) was fighting the troops of Catherine II of Russia and also Stanisław August's troops. The resistance was furious with Stanisław's weak stance toward the partitions, and the Polish Diet, or Sejm, eventually declared him deposed. The last stand of the Polish rebels took place at Częstochowa (at the shrine of the Black Madonna), their headquarters (Wolff 1988, 56). (During the battle at this shrine, the picture of the Black Madonna is reported to have wept—one reason why Poles refer to the Virgin Mary as the Queen of Poland, and why Żywiecers waved blue and white flags, the colors of the Virgin Mary, during the visit of the Holy Father.) Poland was divided up entirely among Russia, Prussia, and Austria by the end of the eighteenth century.

Thus, from 1795 until 1918, most of southern Poland, including the Żywiec region, belonged to the Austro-Hungarian Empire. This Austro-Hungarian partition area, known as Galicia, extended from Żywiec in the far west through what is now Ukraine in the far east. It was ethnically quite diverse, including large populations of Górals, Ruthenians and Lemkians (now known as Ukrainians), and Jews. Norman Davies (1982, 144) estimates that the population in the late nineteenth century consisted of approximately 3 percent Germans, 45 percent Poles, 41 percent Ruthenians, and 11 percent Jews, and each ethnic group maintained that they were oppressed by the others.

Polish nationalism in the Austrian partition of Polish territory did not run as hot as in the other two partitions, leading to a greater acceptance of the Habsburg dynasty's presence, particularly in the Żywiec region. Reasons for this include the Austro-Hungarian policies on language, schooling, religion, and serfdom, which differed significantly from those of the other partition powers. Davies (1982) states that Galicians were

> free from the social and political pressures which domi-
> nated Polish life in the other Partitions. They were free from
> the cultural imperialism of Russia and Germany; they were
> free from the atmosphere of deprivation and harassment
> induced by Tsardom; and they were free from the rapid
> social changes, and the mania for self-improvement, which
> beset the Poles in Prussia. For this, they were truly grateful
> to the Habsburgs. (161)

This relative acceptance of Habsburg rule did not mean that Galicians came to identify as Austrians—to the contrary, it was the perfect atmosphere for regional identities such as Góral to flourish. In contrast, Polish nationalism seems to have had a stronger grip on the imagination of people in the Prussian and Russian partitions. We can gain some understanding of this by examining the role of Catholicism, an important aspect of Polish nationalism both today and in the past. The Roman Catholic Church came to stand as a symbol uniting the

Polish people while Poland was split into three parts. Two of the partitions had to deal with conflicting religions, because the Russian state religion was Russian Orthodox and the Prussian was Protestantism. However Galicia did not have this divisive issue to deal with, because the Austrian state religion was Catholic. Schooling emerged as a primary site for resistance and nationalist sentiment in the other partitions. This relates in several ways to the link between the nationalists and the Catholics. First, prior to the partitions, the Catholic Church ran nearly all of the schools in Poland, in terms of both money and staff. Second, the Catholic religion was a required subject. Third, the curriculum was taught in Polish (and Latin in the universities). It is notable that during the partition period, the governments in Prussia and Russia used the schools in an attempt to fundamentally change the ideology and loyalty of their Polish subjects, by requiring education to be conducted in the language of the imperial power, and also by requiring religious education in the conflicting state religions. Polish religious instruction was banned in both of these provinces, and church property, including and especially schools, was seized and turned over to the state. School strikes over the issues of language and religion broke out periodically in these provinces during the partitions. In contrast, in the Austrian partition, especially after 1867, neither the schooling system nor other Catholic religious institutions were persecuted. Thus, nationalist sentiment did not run as high in this region of former Polish territory.

Another aspect of resistance during the partition period was language, and the connections between the Polish language, religion, and nationalism are clear: each of the three partition powers was at times trying to assimilate the population, and linguistic and religious nationalism posed serious problems. Because large differences existed in language, the answer for the partition powers clearly was to impose national language training, which would diminish differences between the Polish population and those of the partition powers. Depriving the Polish people of their most visible (or audible) signifying aspects would make assimilation easier. The school strikes of 1901–07 in Prussian Poland illustrate the importance of language training to the partition governments. As early as 1815, Prussia had made attempts to have German as well as Polish spoken in schools in Prussian Poland. There was some opposition, and the somewhat dispersed national government backed off. It was not until the unification of Germany in the late nineteenth century that the Prussian government insisted that German language training be given in all Polish schools. Though again there was opposition, the fact that religion continued to be taught in Polish seemed to play a role in Polish concessions toward bilingualism (Kulczycki 1981, xv). However, in 1901, the Prussian government instituted a policy of gradually replacing Polish with German in the teaching of religion, precipitating waves of school strikes that gradually picked up strength, supported by the growing nationalist movement. The strongest manifestation of the period was the general school strike lasting through 1906–07, in which more than ninety-three thousand children participated (Kulczycki 1981, ix). Antagonism over the issue fanned Polish resentment of Prussian rule, and the Prussian government tried to force Polish parents to send their children to school by instituting a heavy fine system. The situation escalated until the strikes were finally put down in late 1907 because of the heavy fines, but as Kulczycki states, the strikes "proved a hothouse for the growth of Polish nationalism" in Prussian Poland (1981, xvi). The connection between the Polish language and the Roman Catholic religion was one link in the further connection of religion and language to Polish nationalism. Embedded in the Polish-language religion classes was the sense that Poland, which had not been a nation for more than a hundred years, was still in some sense alive.

However, the position of the Austrian partition in general and that of the Żywiec region in particular differed substantially from the situation in the other two partitions. The Austro-Hungarian Empire was composed of many culturally and linguistically distinct fragments, and the state made little effort to impose homogeneity on the Polish population under its authority.

Norman Davies (1982, 141–42) states that during the first century of the partition period, Austrian policies in Galicia led to a quality of life far worse than that of peasants in the Russian and Prussian partitions:

> The state intervened in every sphere of social and political life. The labour services of the serfs were fixed by official *Robotpatente* or "work certificates", just as the duties of the clergy were controlled by the Governor's *placetum* or "statement of approval". The jurisdiction of the nobles was replaced by that of the mandatariusz or "state mandatory", who was paid by the landowner but was answerable to the state authorities. Taxation rose steeply above former Polish levels, bringing hardship to those least able to support it, especially to the peasants. . . . Surveillance and harassment of unreliable elements was accompanied by close liaison with the police forces of Russia and Prussia.

The poverty-stricken state of the Galician population, widely known as "Galician misery," led eventually to massive emigration. Davies (1982, 145–47) cites an 1887 analysis that claimed that Galicians were in a worse situation than the Irish during the potato famine, and fifty thousand people a year were dying from near-starvation conditions; he estimates that more than two million Galicians emigrated during the quarter century before World War I. Given this immiseration, why then did Galician peasants not turn to Polish nationalism and revolt against the Austro-Hungarian Empire?

Ironically, the out-migration of many Górals during this period served both to offset the widespread poverty and reinforce the Góral identity. Christopher Hann (1995) notes:

> Regional identities focused on cities, and even on small market towns, are sometimes very strong. . . .The Highlanders (Górale) of the Tatra zone of the Polish Carpathians are another interesting example. Physically quite isolated and long associated with a pastoral economy quite different from that of the lowlands, they speak a dialect that was problematic for most Poles. For a time in the nineteenth century it seemed as if their cultural distinctiveness might be eroded, as population growth induced changes in the economy and a high level of migration. However, attracted by the ethnographic color, the intellectuals who contributed to Poland's national awakening established the notion that the Highlanders were uniquely separate, and that their distinctiveness should be preserved. High out-migration proved to be perfectly compatible with a strong sense of group identity, and the funds earned in North America were used to subsidize the old economic base in the Tatra foothills. As incorporation into the modern Polish state proceeded and Highlanders spread to other towns as well as overseas, they maintained their regional loyalty. (89–90)

How did Żywiecers fare during this period? Because of Żywiec's special circumstances, such as being a center for trade and industry (detailed in the next section), in addition to having no local Polish nobility (the Habsburgs were themselves the local lords in the Żywiec region), Żywiec was in this respect in a position considerably superior to the rest of Galicia. In the second half of the nineteenth century, however, Austrian policies concerning all of Galicia changed considerably, easing the position of serfs and allowing freedom of religion, language, and schooling.

The Habsburg presence in Żywiec, for example, is well known locally for its feudal beneficence toward the town, donating money to churches and schools and investing in the town brewery. I heard many stories about the Habsburgs in Żywiec, not only during interviews on the subject, but in casual conversation with older people who remembered the prewar era. The Habsburg era in Żywiec is seen by many older people in particular as a sort of golden age for the town, and the last Archduke as a feudal patriarch, in the best sense of the term, who cared for the people of the town. In fact, there was quite a groundswell of support to return the brewery to its former owners, the Habsburgs, rather than selling it to the public, during the 1990–01 debate over the reprivatization of the brewery—a story I tell in detail in chapter 5.

Another reason why the language issue did not affect the Żywiec region as much as the other partitions of Poland is the presence of the regional *gwarą*, or dialect, of Góralism. The Góral dialects in Poland and just over the Slovak border on "the other side of the Beskid Mountains" are so close, and in pure form different enough from Polish and Slovakian, as to raise the question of whether the Góral dialect is in fact a dialect or a separate language. The dialect also shares similarities with the Silesian language spoken in the region west of Żywiec.[2] Thus, the problem of linguistic assimilation with their southern neighbors in the Austro-Hungarian partition was hardly an issue in Żywiec, where many residents who spoke the Góral dialect had as much linguistically in common with their Slovakian (Austrian) Góral neighbors as with Poles in the other partitions. The lack of imperial practices of linguistic domination, combined with linguistic differentiation from other Poles and similarities with other Austro-Hungarians, served to palliate the politicization of language in the Żywiec region during the partitions.

The Galician uprising in 1846 serves as a stark reminder of the consequences for the Polish nobles of the liberal Habsburg policies, intended to defuse nationalist sentiment among their conquered territories. In 1846, spurred both by nationalist uprisings in the other Polish partitions and by an increasingly Machiavellian Habsburg policy toward serfdom that threatened their livelihoods, a number of Polish nobles in Galicia attempted to forge an alliance with peasants and throw off the Austrian political claims. An Austrian district officer also tried to enlist the support of Galician peasants in putting down this uprising, promising them that they would be freed of their feudal obligations if they would help (Davies 1982, 147). Davies says that

> In the ensuing melee, the estates of the noble conspirators
> were invaded. Noblemen, landlords, bailiffs, and protesting

> officials were butchered in cold blood. The innocent suffered
> with the guilty. Before long, the peasant bands were offering
> the severed heads of their noble victims to the authorities as
> proof of their zeal. . . . For the [noble] Poles, it was a rude
> awakening to the fact that Polish-speaking peasants could
> not be relied on to support Polish noblemen in patriotic
> enterprises. But for the peasants, it was a liberating experi-
> ence of the first importance. Having once shaken off their
> feudal dues, they could not easily resubmit. (148)

The nobles were "cut down by their own peasants, more interested in
social emancipation than in national freedom" (Okey 1986, 86). The
nationalist ties of the Galician peasants to Poland were weaker than
their instrumental sense of the benefits of Habsburg rule.

For Żywiec and the rest of Galicia, however, limited freedom
from the Habsburg empire was just twenty years down the road. As
part of the internationally engineered Compromise of 1867, Galicia
gained limited autonomy within the Austro-Hungarian Empire. The
Habsburgs gave control of Galician lands back to the local Polish
nobility (Simons 1993, 13). The result was tightened serfdom, but liberal policies on the Polish language, religion, and education. This did
not mean either that Poland was born again or that the Habsburgs left
Żywiec—by the accounts of locals, the Habsburgs continued to play
an important role in the town, and they were, after all, the local nobility in that region.

What this limited autonomy did mean, though, was that Galicia
was later romanticized as the one place where Polishness had survived during the partitions. According to Davies (1982),

> Polish commentators tended to look back on Galicia with
> indulgence and even affection. For them Galicia was the
> one place where Polish culture and ideals had been kept
> alive, whilst the other partitions languished under the ham-
> mers of Germanization and Russification. . . . Despite the
> fact that relatively few Galicians were actively interested in
> the cause of Polish independence, it is undeniable that the
> Galician experience played an important role in fitting the
> Poles for the independent status which was thrust upon
> them at the end of the War [World War I]. (159–60)

In an odd contradiction, then, even though Górals themselves in this
area may not have had a strong sense of Polishness, after the
reunification of Poland, Poles in other areas looked to Górals to re-
mind them of what "traditional Poland" was like.

Reunification: World War I and the Interwar Period (1918–38)

World War I washed over Europe from 1914 to 1918 and changed the fate of Poland. Germany, the Austro-Hungarian Empire, and the Ottoman Empire lost the war. The final defeat of Austria actually occurred in Galicia, at the hands of the Russian army. One of the results of the end of the war was that Poland as a country was reconstituted from its partitions, with Żywiec landing on the Polish side of the border. When Poland appeared again on the political terrain, it extended nearly from Minsk in the east to past Poznań in the west, up past Vilna in the north, and down to Kraków.

However, all of these borders remained contested, and the years between the wars saw no settling of political disputes. Ethnic regionalism was quite a challenge for governors of the new nation-state. The problems of incorporating millions of people who identified themselves as Germans, Silesians, Belorussians, Lemkians, Ruthenians, Latvians, Lithuanians, Jews, Slovakians, Czechs, and, of course, Poles plagued the new government. Military action continued in Poland until 1920, and the newly free government sought to hold off Russian, German, and Czech attempts to seize its territory.

In Żywiec, the Habsburgs still remained in residence because they still owned their estate and much of the town industry. Their official status was that of private citizens, however, the Polish government eventually asked the family to take over some of the administrative tasks for the region because they had such political and economic influence. Though Żywiec was officially part of the Polish state, it was surrounded by wars contesting the southern border of Poland and thus was in the midst of constant political turmoil.

To the west, the Silesian uprisings raged intermittently from 1919 to 1922. The Czechoslovak war started with the invasion of Cieszyn (slightly to the west of Żywiec) in 1919 and was settled through arbitration by the Allied winners of World War I. In the mountains to the east of Żywiec, the districts of Spisz and Orawa were under attack sporadically until 1925.

In the mid to late 1920s, foreign attacks on Poland died down, and the Polish state could focus on attempting to construct a stable political and economic order. Polish state leaders were faced with broad ethnic diversity, political contention, and an economy in which almost 75 percent of the population were peasants or agricultural workers. Davies (1982) sums up the problems of integration of the three partitions:

> The population, institutions, and traditions of the three
> Partitions had to be welded into one new entity. At first, six

currencies were in circulation; five regions—Posnania, Silesia, Cieszyn, East Galicia, and Central Lithuania (Wilno)—maintained separate administration; there were four languages of command in the army; three legal codes; two different railway gauges; and eighteen registered political parties competed for power. (402)

Górals in this period retained many characteristics that set them off from other Poles. A young American woman, Dorothy Hosmer, bicycled through southern Poland in the late 1930s and produced a travelogue published in *National Geographic* in June 1939. This remarkable look at the Góral region, published on the eve of World War II, provides a view of Góral life in the interwar period. Hosmer's photographs of Górals—in traditional clothes such as embroidered, white wool trousers, herding sheep, shopping in the open-air market, and living in log cabins—give some support to claims of present-day Żywiecers that Góral life in the prewar era retained many elements of what they view as traditional culture.

Hosmer (1939) also mentions the ties between Górals in southern Poland and emigrés to the United States:

> When I stopped to adjust my rucksack on its carrier for the tenth time that day, I let out aloud "Oh, darn!" A laugh and the words in English, "Better leave it here," startled me. From his cottage door a farmer grinned good-naturedly. This was not the only incident of its kind; I came across many Górale [Górals] who had worked in the United States before the World War. They looked up from shearing a sheep or came to the door of a grain mill to question me, and then to chat. During a storm I took shelter in the cottage of one of them. We talked over the "good old days," and he expressed regret that his Polish-born son wasn't home to meet an American girl; only the day before he had taken their three cows and half-dozen sheep up into the high mountain meadows where, following the Góral custom, he would remain for months, tending the animals and making cheese in the company of other mountain shepherds, until the beginning of winter drove them down. (754)

World War II: The German Occupation

Hitler's armies invaded Poland in September 1939 and seized much of Polish territory, establishing the German occupation of Poland. Żywiec, lying so close to the border, saw much of the fighting, and the town industries were taken over by the Nazi army and put to producing war materials. The remaining members of the Habsburg family had fled in the face of the advancing Nazis. The Polish resistance movement was very active in the Żywiec region, with Home Army units hiding in the forested regions and attacking Nazi troops. Town records show a number of resistance leaders who were captured and confined to die at Auschwitz, the nearby death camp outside the Polish town of Oświęcim. The small Jewish village of Zabłocie, which abutted Żywiec and was later incorporated into it (and in which I lived during my time there), was decimated, the cemetery desecrated, and the inhabitants killed or moved to Auschwitz to be killed. When liberation finally came, in 1945, the town of Żywiec was left in tatters for the survivors to rebuild. Remains of buildings that were never rebuilt still stand in parts of the town today as a reminder of the war. Overall, Poland had lost approximately six million citizens in the war, half of them Jews, and more than half of all livestock had been destroyed (Okey 1986, 191).

After World War II, the borders of Poland were moved once again as part of the concessions of Germany and gains of the Soviet Union. A great deal of territory that was formerly eastern Poland became part of the Belorussian Republic of the Soviet Union (today known as Belarus), Ukraine, Latvia, or Lithuania. For Galicia, this meant that most of East Galicia (where much of the population identified themselves as Ruthenians and Lemkians) became Ukrainian. Poland's western border was extended two hundred kilometers to the west into formerly eastern Germany, to the border of the Oder River, and a great deal of the Baltic coast that had formerly been in German hands came to Poland as well. Most of the Jewish population in Poland, about 10 percent of the total population before the war, had been killed. About eight million Germans were expelled from new Polish territories in western Poland, and Poles expelled from the territories ceded to Belorussia and Ukraine were moved to these new western territories. Poland thus became nearly ethnically homogenous for the first time (Okey 1986, 191). The massive resettlement that these changes touched off in many parts of Poland did not have much effect on the Żywiec area, because the German population in the region was very small and no new populations were relocated there.

Conflicts along the border in the Żywiec region continued in the postwar era. Hans Roos (1966) states that

> Compared with the great problem of Poland's westward
> shift, smaller frontier conflicts with Czechoslovakia dating

from the pre-war period possessed, as it were, only epi-
sodic importance. The long-standing dispute about Teschen
. . . was checked by Soviet intervention. The restoration of
the frontiers of 1920–1938 did not rob the conflict of its
sharpness, as was shown by the repeated failure of negotiations on the subject. Not until the signature of the Polish-
Czech assistance pact on 10 March 1947 was tension relaxed
in accordance with Soviet wishes, both sides tacitly renounc-
ing any further attempts at frontier revision. (219)

It did result in yet another political change for Żywiec, however—
namely, that the area no longer had even the Habsurg family there to
tie it to the Austro-Hungarian Empire, but rather belonged outright to
Poland. The years immediately following World War II led to the establishment of communist rule in Poland, which had some unforeseen
effects on nationalist feeling and on the strength of the Góral identity.

The Communist Period

In 1947, the Polish Communist Party (PZPR) won the parliamentary
elections in a move that was hotly contested by the United States and
other Allied powers. There had been several competing communist
movements in Poland during World War II. The first postwar government in Poland (the Polish Committee of National Liberation, PKWN)
was formed in Lublin by the victorious Soviet Union. Davies (1982)
states that it

assisted its Soviet masters in administering the lands liberated from German Occupation, and in course formed the
core both of the Provisional Government of the Polish Republic (RTRP) from January to June 1945, and of the Provisional Government of National Unity (TRJN) from June 1945
onwards. In this way, its activities spanned the transitional
period which separated the collapse of the German Occupation from the full emergence of the communist-led regime in 1947. (556–57)

The takeover of the Polish state by the Communist Party was
thus contested within the nation as well as abroad. Antigovernment
violence in 1944 and 1945 resulted in killings of government officials
and their supporters. John Coutouvidis and Jaime Reynolds (1986)
describe the armed resistance as slight in western Poland, widespread
in central Poland, and "in the remoter parts of the east and south of
the country government forces were confined to the towns, under

virtual siege" (217). Underground networks consisted of former members of the Home Army and the National Military Union (both nationally organized groups of underground fighters during World War II) and guerrilla regional groups in eastern and southern Poland. A Ukrainian nationalist movement was also active on the southeastern border.

One of these guerrilla regional resistance groups existed among the Górals in the Tatras Mountains south and slightly west of Żywiec, where fighting with Russian troops continued in some parts of the Góral region into the 1950s. This made it extremely difficult for the PZPR to gain popular support. Coutouvidis and Reynolds (1986) state that

> this was particularly so in the remoter country areas where armed attacks made it difficult for the Communists to establish even the rudiments of an effective organization. But even in the towns it was not easy for the party to break the remnants of wartime solidarity, the prestige of the AK [the Home Army] and the widespread popular view that party membership was tantamount to collaboration with an occupying power. (220)

Many underground fighters from Żywiec during World War II were members of the Home Army, fighting against the German occupation. The regional Góral guerrilla organization run by Józef Kuras (Kapitan Ogień—"Captain Fire," also a former Home Army member) after the war, was, in contrast, purely anti-Soviet in sentiment (Coutouvidis and Reynolds 1986, 343). Former U.S. Ambassador to Poland Thomas Simons Jr. (1993) describes the effects of the ideology around these skirmishes in the Góral region more than a decade later:

> In the Tatras there was one commander nicknamed "Fire," Ogień, who had fought the Germans and continued fighting the Communists long after the war had ended, into the 1950s. He was supplied by the people in the valley villages, whence young men came to join him. A week after I went to Poland in 1968 five Warsaw Pact countries, including Poland, invaded Czechoslovakia. [N.B.: The army camped on the Polish border within sight of Żywiec.] I heard that in those mountains they were digging up and oiling the weapons they had buried after Ogień was taken, to be ready for the great day when the war of good and evil would begin again. When my wife and I went to the Tatras the next year, "Long live Ogień"—*Niech zyje Ogień*—was still written on the huts where the shepherds spend the summer with their flocks. (43)

Many Poles viewed the Polish nation and the Polish state as quite separate entities during the socialist period. That is, they felt that the governing body of Poland, which was socialist, was not truly Polish or representative of the Polish nation. This antagonistic relationship between socialism and nationalism did not hold in every socialist nation during the Cold War: in many republics of the Soviet Union, and in parts of Eastern Europe, socialist rule actually worked to increase nationalism (Livezeanu 1995; Schöpflin 1993; Verdery 1991a, 1996). In contrast, in Yugoslavia, socialism seemed to dampen nationalisms at least for some time. Polish nationalism was strong but was defined in large part by being anti-Soviet socialism. Many other, smaller regional or ethnic identities, such as the Lemkian identity, were assimilated into Polishness. In contrast, ethnic Ukrainians in Poland retained a strong sense of identity, but of course they could identify with an actual Ukrainian nation-state (Hann 1985). The Góral identity has never been nationalist, and has had a historically problematic and shifting relationship to the Polish identity, because the Góral region has belonged to several different polities over the past several centuries. The political struggles played out in this community during the Habsburg period were also far from the Polish national elites and their agenda. This border region contained numerous people who had relatives across the newly laid Slovak and Czech borders and thus were even less likely to be solidly Polish nationalists. All this makes it rather ironic that during the socialist period, Polish nationalist intellectuals would seize on and romanticize the Góral identity as the bastion of "true" Polishness. Yet some members of the Żywiec community, the prewar elite, were able to capitalize on these romantic notions of the unique qualities of political resistance of the Żywiec region to maintain a sort of power in the community. These individuals played a key role in the Solidarity movement in Żywiec in the 1980s.

The Rise of Solidarity

During the socialist period, there was always a certain amount of infighting within the Communist Party between those members who were supporters of Soviet policies and those who wished to limit Soviet involvement in Polish politics. In the early years, the question of agricultural collectivization versus privatization was a major source of contention between these two factions. Stanisław Mikołajczyk, an anti-Soviet Peasant Party leader, was instrumental in splitting up large noble estates and ceding land deeds to Polish peasants during the immediate postwar period, and he fought the notion of collectivization in the early 1950s. Though some small farms were collectivized at that time, the end of the Stalinist era in the 1950s portended a reverse movement toward decollectivization.[3] Żywiec thus retained much of its prewar character of tiny family landholdings.

The issue of trade unions was also a point of contention immediately following World War II, a point that resurfaced during mass protests against the Polish state in 1956 and 1970 (Laba 1991). In the late 1970s, several Founding Committees of Free Trade Unions (*Komitety Zalozycielskie Wolnych Zwiazków Zawodowych*, KZ WZZ) were formed by industrial workers; the KZ WZZ in Gdansk helped organize strikes during the summer of 1980 at the Gdansk Lenin Shipyard, which sparked the formation of the protest organization Solidarity (Persky and Flam 1982). Polish intellectuals as well as workers were invested in resistance against state policies: in 1976, a group of intellectuals formed the Committee for the Defense of the Workers (*Komitet Obrony Robotników*, KOR) to aid workers who were being persecuted in the wake of protests against rising prices (Lipski 1985). These two organizations, the KZ WZZ and the KOR, formed the backbone of the Solidarity movement, which emerged in 1980. They were soon joined by protest groups from across the entire political spectrum, as well as more than a million PZPR members—about a third of the total party membership (Kubik 1995). Robin Okey (1986) notes:

> National and religious traditions were especially strong in Poland and received a fillip from the tour of a Polish Pope that year. . . . A symbolic issue was to hand in government attempts to reduce the subsidies on meat which had already led to the riots of 1970 and 1976. . . . Thus disturbances beginning in central Poland spread to the dock workers of the coast and culminated in government ministers signing the Gdansk agreement of August 1980 permitting the formation of a free trade union, which within a year claimed 10 million members. The Solidarity era was to last sixteen months, punctuated by almost permanent confrontation with the regime, over the leading role of the communist party, the trade union rights of private peasants, the removal of corrupt officials and issues of censorship and police repression. On 13 December 1981, Solidarity was suspended by the declaration of martial law. (235)

The imposition of martial law as a method of squelching Solidarity proved ultimately ineffective. Jan Kubik (1995) argues that the anti-Soviet wing of the Communist Party was gaining the upper hand, the Soviets were not willing to intervene, and Solidarity, which went underground in the middle 1980s, resurfaced in 1988 as an organized aboveground political force. It is arguable whether there was truly an anti-Soviet branch of the party in Poland; however, in 1989, relatively peaceful roundtable talks between Solidarity and the PZPR resulted in the Communist Party giving up sole control over the government of Poland.

For the people of Żywiec, the imposition of martial law is vividly remembered as one of the harshest periods in Żywiec history. Shortages of food, energy, and clothing; armed guards at the factories and train stations; and suspicion and fear were the memories relayed to me in 1994 and 1995. A main organizer of Solidarity in Żywiec during the 1980s described his trip to Gdansk in 1980, where he was sent by a group of Żywiec prewar elite to hear Lech Wałęsa speak and bring back information about the Solidarity movement.[4] Żywiecers who were involved in the Solidarity movement told me of attending underground meetings, arranged to look like vacations at mountain spas, and discreetly passing back information at work. Many of the "movers and shakers" of Solidarity in Żywiec were not simply workers, but members of the prewar elite, who were disenfranchised of their property during the socialist era. Thus, the resistance movement in Żywiec was rooted in prewar social structures of authority, a point I elaborate on in chapter 3.

The fact that Solidarity leaders in Żywiec came from the prewar elite differed from the way resistance was structured elsewhere in Poland. Before the rise of Solidarity, with the exception of attempts at outright revolt, most resistance to the socialist government in Poland involved everyday acts of resistance, which were difficult to trace to individuals. Resistance was also at times orchestrated by the Catholic Church, an organization strongly tied to the Solidarity movement. Perhaps the most famous example of this last in Poland was Father Jerzy Popiełuszka, a labor organizer and Warsaw priest who was censored and prosecuted by the Polish communist government for his fiery sermons in the Solidarity cause. So zealous was Popiełuszka that he was officially censured by Polish Cardinal Glemp in 1984 for concentrating too much on union politics, when the unions had been declared illegal with the imposition of martial law in 1981. Popieł uszka was one of a number of priests under investigation by the government, on charges of abusing religious freedom and making antigovernment remarks (S. Ramet 1987, 133). At the time, many priests were jailed, housing was ransacked, lay volunteers were beaten, and one priest was killed by a car bomb (S. Ramet 1987, 133). Popiełuszka especially was singled out because he had been holding masses dedicated to "the people of Poland," which was a political statement about martial law (by distinguishing between the Polish people as a nation

and the communist government as a state), and was extremely vocal
in regard to the right of Solidarity to exist and the wrongdoings of the
state. His apartment was bombed in December 1982. In October 1984,
Popiełuszka was beaten, kidnapped, and murdered by the regime's
secret police (S. Ramet 1987, 168). Popiełuszka immediately became
known as a martyr for the "nationalist"—or Solidarity—cause. He was
buried behind his church, the Church of Saint Stanisław Kostka in
Warsaw. People were known to journey to visit the church and hang
political banners there, a common pronationalist practice, the significance of which was not lost on the government. The following
year, a government newspaper printed the complaint that

> the churches are becoming fronts for political opposition
> and priests continue to use the pulpits for attacks against
> the socialist system. . . . The churches continue to be used
> as places for clearly antigovernment hunger strikes. Some
> churches have already become symbols of opposition and
> have been plastered by banners, badges, and slogans whose
> eloquence is obvious to anyone who is able to think a little.[5]
> (quoted in S. Ramet 1987, 170)

Such everyday resistance in the political realm was linked to similar
kinds of resistance in the economic realm under communism. To understand the form this took in Żywiec, I need to outline the structure
of the town's economy under socialism, which in turn requires a discussion of the historical path of local economic development.

DEVELOPMENT OF INDUSTRY AND TRADE IN ŻYWIEC

As a study of a small community's resistance to and strategies of
dealing with capitalist incorporation, Żywiec provides a unique perspective on the effects of global capitalism. In contrast to studies that
have focused on the impact of capitalist transformation in the Third
World in which capitalism did not previously exist, Żywiec had experienced small, community-oriented capitalism followed by socialist
industrialization, and was now experiencing globalization. Further,
most other studies of privatization of industry have been carried out
in large cities in the former Eastern Bloc.[6] I chose Żywiec because I
thought that it would be an ideal place to study privatization and its
effects on community life, as well as the kinds of resistance engen-
dered by the results of transition policies. The Żywiec Brewery was
one of the first and largest state enterprises to be privatized in Poland,

and because it was located in a provincial town, I thought that the changes and responses to this privatization would be more clearly evident than in either large cities with many resources or smaller villages with little industry.

As described above, Żywiec's political history took a path quite different from towns located firmly within the boundaries of Poland as envisioned by nationalists. The nature of a border town is often that of a place where identity may be conflicted (O'Dowd and Wilson 1996). Żywiec in the nineteenth century was in a unique position within Galicia because the "local" nobility were Austrian rather than Polish. However, the special trade rights that gave Żywiec its strong position in the regional economy date back much further, to the fourteenth century. It is from then, with the development of influential town guilds and the absence of continuous feudal control, that we can trace the development of a community-oriented moral economy linked to the Góral identity. I use the term "moral economy" to mean community notions of how trade or industry and the community ought to interrelate, and how these notions were imbued with a sense of patron-client relations concerning the class structure in Żywiec.[7] Because this was a community-centered ethic of economics, it became associated with notions of Góral community insularity. This ethic persisted through the feudal and socialist periods, in part because these economic systems were both in many senses regionally based. It is only now, with the influx of global capital and nonlocal management, that this moral economy has begun to be significantly disrupted.

The Żywiec Guilds

The development of the town guilds led to the increase in prominence of Żywiec in the region. This history is described in various original guild-privilege documents from the fourteenth century kept in museums in Żywiec, in the seventeenth-century historian and mayor Andrzej Komoniecki's *Chronicles of Żywiec*, and in local historian Grażyna Rapacz's 1986 manuscript describing the development of trade and industry in the town. This wealth of historical documentation clearly shows the path of development of the local economy, and I draw from these documents to present a brief history of the town's trades.

Because of Żywiec's location, lying near the confluence of two major rivers and at a strategic pass through the mountains bordering Silesia, Slovakia, Bohemia, and Galicia, it was on a major thoroughfare for trade between Kraków and Vienna. However, it was the town charter and royally bestowed trade rights dating from the fourteenth century that led to the town becoming an economic and administrative center for guild regulation of handicrafts and industry. It is impossible to establish the exact date of the charter and rights because the original documents were stolen in the late fourteenth century. However, in 1448 the original rights were reaffirmed by the duke of the Przemysław family.

By the fifteenth century, the town of Żywiec held trade rights granted in the town charter by the noble family that held title to the region. The development of trade and industry in Żywiec was based primarily on these trade rights, which guaranteed advantages to the town at the expense of residents of other villages. Town residents (those living in the town itself or within a one-mile border around the town) held rights to use the local open fields and forest for grazing their animals and fishing rights to the local river. Żywiec residents could also collect and sell salt, produce lead and copper products, and collect tolls from travelers, and the district court was located in Żywiec. A one-mile border around the town was also used to limit Żywiec's population, eliminating competition in yet another way: the Żywiec guilds interpreted the royally granted trade rights to decree that no tradesman who did not have membership in one of the Żywiec guilds could settle in the town or produce within a mile of the town line. By using the trade rights in this way, the town guilds gained in stature, making themselves central to the local economy. After the Komorowski family purchased the region, Żywiec gained further trade privileges, among the most important of which were the rights to brew beer and distill liquor. As a result of this privilege, all of the surrounding villages had to purchase beer from Żywiec. The town maintained a manorial brewery, the beginnings of what would later expand to become a major brewing industry in Żywiec.

All of these privileges strengthened the economic development of the town, which quickly became the center of economic life of the whole region. The sixteenth-century beginnings of guild prominence in Żywiec coincided with the growing impoverishment of peasants elsewhere in Eastern Europe. This so-called second serfdom, in which nobles, pressured by the rising colonial powers in Western Europe, reasserted their power over their serfs, was described by Okey (1986):

> For one thing, the urban bourgeoisie, still weaker in Eastern Europe than the West, suffered from the dynamic development elsewhere which tended to reduce Eastern Europe to the level of provider of raw materials, chiefly grain, to an expanding West. Taking advantage of the grain trade's rural origins to wrest control of it from the urban

merchants, the East European nobility decisively asserted its dominance over the towns and pressed ahead to consolidate the weakened demesne economy so as to maximize the profits of grain export. But this required the revival of forced serf labour to man the demesnes. Secure in their feudal diets [demesnes], the nobles in province after province in the late fifteenth century began to pour out edicts restricting free peasant movement and tightening up half-forgotten labour regulations. . . . The peasants, in the language of feudalism, became "bound to the soil", their tenure no longer secure. Cut off from the market by heavy dues in kind . . . toiling for up to six days a week on noble demesnes . . . the peasants had been reduced by the seventeenth century to what historians have called the "second serfdom". (18–19)

The decrease in peasant power in the surrounding countryside no doubt also contributed to the growth in power of the Żywiec guilds, as the economic balance tipped away from the producers of raw materials and toward the processors. Thus, the beginning of the semi-peripheralization of Central and Eastern Europe by the core of Western Europe was mirrored on a local scale by the rise of Żywiec over the rest of the local region.

According to local manuscripts, the cobblers' guild was formed in 1544, and was probably one of the first guilds in Żywiec.[8] Several guilds followed afterward, such as the blacksmiths' and tailors' guilds. In 1546, Polish bishops gave to the guilds the rights to handle funeral services for their members, an important symbolic and economic service. The strength of the guilds grew in the seventeenth and eighteenth centuries, with guilds established for potters, weavers, linen workers, furriers, and tanners. Guild formation was capped off by the establishment of the unified assembly guild for trades that were not represented elsewhere.

Like guilds in Western Europe, guild statutes regulated details of trade and production as well as the relations between the workshops of masters and the relationship between apprentices and masters. Guild leaders held positions of great political importance in the community. The guilds shaped notions of town rights in the region and notions of moral economy within the town. Most important in terms of the local economy, the trade guilds had a monopoly on the production and sale of goods. At the head of each guild was the guild master, who was chosen annually by the elders of the guild. The guild master's responsibilities included representing the guild externally, sitting on the council of guilds, and calling the tradesmen to assemblies. The guild master also kept the guild chest, which contained the guild privileges and records of the guild as well as stamps and money. Several original guild chests, seals, and other paraphernalia are on display in the Żywiec Museum.

Guild assemblies, the annual election of the guild masters, became important in the political and social life not only of guild members, but of the entire town of Żywiec. In the seventeenth and eighteenth centuries, the guild assemblies were occasions marked by high ceremony, processions, feasts, and a variety of other festive traditions. The importance of guild traditions and customs lasted well into the nineteenth century, because Żywiec residents maintained a great many of the traditions even after the end of the guilds. The height of guild membership in Żywiec was at the end of the eighteenth century and beginning of the nineteenth century. There was a sharp decrease in guild membership in the nineteenth century, particularly in the guilds concerned with textile production such as weavers, dressmakers, dyers, and tanners, due to the effects of the industrial revolution in Western Europe.

Nascent Capitalism Comes to Żywiec

The end of the nineteenth century and beginning of the twentieth century saw the establishment of a number of industrial firms in Żywiec, some of which survive to the present. This was the beginning of small-scale capitalism in Żywiec. The community ethic or moral economy within which these firms operated was based on local leaders, a circumstance made possible by the fact that there were no local Polish elites who had rights to the profits from these firms. The oldest of these town firms include the Żywiec Metal Factory, which dates from 1832; the Żywiec Paper Company, founded 1833; and the Żywiec Brewery, 1856.[9] This brewery was independent of the manorial brewery established previously, although it took advantage of the same guild privilege of town monopoly over the production and sale of alcohol. A sulfur match factory founded in 1870 has passed through several hands and been reworked into an iron bed factory, a chrome furniture factory, and finally a hospital furnishings factory named Famed. The early twentieth century saw the addition of the Machine Factory (currently known as the Ponar Machine Factory), 1902; the Żywiec Fur Firm, 1919; and the Chelmik Southern Leather and Tannery Company, 1921.

The three largest of these enterprises were the brewery, metal factory, and paper factory. Drawing on the products of the Silesian mines, in 1870 the Żywiec Iron Mill (later the Metal Factory) produced 693 tons of forged iron and 381 tons of iron sheet metal and employed 115 workers (Rapacz 1986). The mill passed through the hands of all the noble families who owned the region until the Habsburgs, who sold it in 1900 to the Austrian Mining-Metallurgy Company. Shortly afterward, the firm came into the hands of the Galician Rivet and Nut Firm in Oświęcim, and next to the Brewiller Austrian Cooperative, headquartered in Vienna. In 1912, the firm began production of a new product, screws. By 1936, the Żywiec Metal Factory was producing 250 to 300 tons of various items and employed 350 workers.

Karol Schrotter and Franciszek Menchardt founded the Zabłocie Cardboard-Paper Firm (now the Żywiec Paper Firm) in 1833. At first, the firm did not specialize in paper, because the founders also produced cardboard in a neighboring property, ran a cloth factory, and had a farming business. In 1836 and 1837, the owners bought riverfront property and began installing milling equipment that would vastly increase their production capacity. By the turn of the century, the plant employed about three hundred workers. The plant attracted more investment and was reorganized in 1930, to be renamed the Żywiec Paper Factory Solali, Inc. At this point the factory was producing paper to wrap cigarette filters and high-quality writing paper and was exporting to Greece, Turkey, France, and England.[10]

Though there was a small brewery in Żywiec prior to the nineteenth century, the large Żywiec Brewery was officially founded in 1856 by the Habsburg family. At the end of the nineteenth century and beginning of the twentieth century, many of the brewery's processes were mechanized, electrical wiring was installed, and water pipes were built to connect the nearby stream with the brewery. From 1927 to 1930, the brewery was entirely revamped. Grain silos, fermenting halls, and storage warehouses were built; an administration building was constructed together with a social building for the workers; and an apartment building for workers was partly completed. Production of beer topped two hundred thousand hectoliters.

Smaller enterprises, such as the Ponar Machine Factory, the Żywiec Fur Firm, the Chelmik Southern Leather and Tannery Company, and the Famed Hospital Furnishings Factory, also had prewar origins, and went through various changes as the Żywiec economy was reorganized during the German occupation, the communist era, and the postcommunist transition. The Ponar-Żywiec Factory began as a workshop for wooden machines, which was owned by the Wrobel family in Żywiec. Their products were exported as far as Romania, Russia, and Hungary. By 1910, the Wrobel Brothers' Machine Factory in Żywiec and Galicia employed eighty-six people. Despite their growth, the factory went bankrupt just before World War I, and it was sold to a mining company in Kraków, for which the company produced mining equipment, and then later sold to an iron casting firm loosely held by a Lublin consortium. The Żywiec firm, as a division of the company, produced machines for flour mills and lumber mills, iron castings, and farm machinery. The Southern Leather and Tannery Chelmik in Żywiec was founded in 1920, and the Żywiec Fur Factory, founded in 1919, employed seventy-three people by World War II. The Famed Żywiec Hospital Furnishings Factory began life as a bed factory in 1870, and by the time of the German occupation, it was producing metal furniture and employing three hundred people.

The small-scale capitalist enterprises in Żywiec were not much disturbed by the events of World War I or the following shift in political allegiance from the Austro-Hungarian Empire to the newly reformed Polish state. The Habsburg family continued to be a presence in the region, in part because of their investments in local industry, but also because, in the post-World War I years, the new Polish government asked for Habsburg help in quelling local unrest and establishing peace in the region. It wasn't until the beginning of World War II that the political economy of the Żywiec town and region underwent substantial change.

World War II

In 1939, the German occupation began. The Żywiec Paper Factory was seized in the first days of September 1939 by the Nazi regime because the owners were Jewish. The brewery was occupied and intensively exploited by the German army; in fact, German citizens were relocated to Żywiec to manage the brewery, even though Żywiec workers were kept on to work. The Żywiec division of Lechia (Ponar) became a small German factory, producing among other things farm machines and parts for war equipment. The Żywiec Metal Factory was also taken over by Germans—an obviously valuable asset during wartime because of the metal-working capabilities.

During the six-week period in which the war front lingered in Żywiec (February 14–April 4, 1945), the Nazis destroyed many of the area's homes, warehouses, and factories to keep them from falling into the hands of enemy armies. On their retreat, they crippled the region by burning homes and businesses and looting equipment, which left much of the industrial capacity in ruins. The Nazis also took a large archeological collection from the museum and a number of valuable old pieces of art from the churches. On April 5 1945, the Soviet and Polish armies liberated Żywiec from the German occupation.

It took the surviving residents several years to clear away the rubble and restore their homes as well as rebuild the factories. Meanwhile, the fate of Poland was being decided at the Yalta conference, and politics in faraway Warsaw brought the PZPR to power. Local reconstruction, before the PZPR began mass campaigns of nationalization, involved rebuilding homes, workshops, and factories. There was also the question of who would manage and work in the previously Jewish-owned paper factory, and who would have access to homes and land owned by Jews who had fled or been executed by the Nazis. Because there were no official survivors in Zabłocie, all of this property remained in state hands and was eventually apportioned out by PZPR officials.

The Communist Period

As the postwar communist regime took power in the early years after Poland's liberation, the formerly close ties Żywiec had maintained with northern Czechoslovakia were cut off. The border crossing to Slovakia to the immediate south of Żywiec at Zwardoń was closed to private vehicles, so that people could cross only by train. The border crossing to the southwest to Czechoslovakia (at the town of Cieszyn) was closed to trains, and so could be crossed only on foot or by car. Even though trade was officially open between these countries, restrictions on travel across the border made it difficult at best to organize trade.

The PZPR embarked on a plan of nationalization of all industrial capacity in Poland, and further was devoted to increasing industrial output. The Żywiec Metal Factory was nationalized in 1949 and reformulated as the Metal Factory in Sporysz, Żywiec, National Enterprise on January 1 1951. By 1986, the Żywiec Metal Factory employed about fifteen hundred people. The Żywiec Paper Factory was nationalized on June 21 1947, as announced in the newspaper *Monitor Polski* (number 93) on July 5 1947. On January 2 1951, the Żywiec Paper Factory became the Żywiec Paper Factory, National Enterprise in Żywiec. A whole new line of products was introduced, such as corkboard, napkins, labels, carbon paper, and cardboard rolls. In the 1970s, the Żywiec Paper Factory in Żywiec was combined with the Milowka Paper Factory, the Wadowice Cardboard Factory, and the Czance Cardboard Factory. The consortium employed 1,840 workers by 1986.

Though a substantial increase in industrial output in Żywiec was shaped by socialism, it was rooted in the community and provided many avenues for reinforcement of community ideals. One of the primary avenues for enforcing community norms and reinforcing the Góral identity was through service activities at work. One consequence of the national plan for industry was the formation of a variety of service departments in most large factories. All three of the large factories in Żywiec—the brewery, paper firm, and metal factory—were required to form sports clubs in the early 1950s, and later these service activities expanded to include on-site health clinics, child care, preschools, vacation organizing, help in obtaining potatoes and coal in the winter, and even housing, in the case of the brewery.

Another consequence of the national plan to boost industry was increased investment in machines and equipment for factories, which both expanded their production capacity and created new jobs. To provide enough labor for these jobs, large apartment complexes were built and peasants moved in from the surrounding villages. In the case of Żywiec, the town population grew from a post–World War II six thousand to approximately twenty-four thousand in 1996—a result of both population influxes and the fact that nearby villages were officially incorporated wholesale into the town, inflating population figures.

The Żywiec Brewery was refurbished in 1956 with mechanized bottling lines and began producing beer for export on an industrial scale. As brewery technology advanced, the Żywiec Brewery added more and more equipment to expand production. It became the top producer and most popular beer in Poland, as well as an exporter to other countries. By 1985, the Żywiec Brewery exported 3,791,612 hecaliters of beer annually. In 1982, the brewery bid for and won a Pepsi-Cola franchise, and began bottling Pepsi. The brewery also founded a transport firm, with 92 trucks, employing 115 workers. Trucks with the Żywiec Brewery trademark rumbled constantly through the town and could be seen all over the country. The Żywiec Brewery under socialism was a multifirm enterprise: there were affiliated breweries in Żywiec, Cieszyn, and Bielsko-Biała, as well as the Pepsi-Cola franchise and the transport firm. The brewery also opened a brewpub near the brewery (the one I visited on my first trip to Żywiec) and a cafe in its Góral Sports Club. The primary brewery was the Żywiec plant, which produced most of the firm's bottled beer for export and for the domestic market. The breweries in Cieszyn and Bielsko produced some domestic bottled beer as well as kegs of beer. By 1990, the

Żywiec Brewery employed an estimated two thousand people—a substantial portion of the population of the town.

POST-1989—TRANSITION TO WHAT?

The remainder of this book discusses in detail many of the changes in Żywiec during the first few years of the postsocialist era and the reactions of Żywiec residents to these changes. These changes and people's strategies for reacting to them are inextricably linked to what has come before. The economic changes that have occurred in Żywiec since 1989 are direct results of the so-called shock therapy program instituted by Poland's postsocialist governments. This program, modeled after International Monetary Fund programs of structural adjustment or stabilization, involves privatization of heavy and light industry, housing, public utilities, and much of the public transportation system. Further, government subsidies have been eliminated, there is a general downsizing of the governmental sector, and the currency (the złoty) has been devalued and no longer has a fixed price on the international currency exchange market.

In general, structural adjustment programs have the goal of decentralizing the national economy, reducing or eliminating the state's control or intervention in the economy—that is, replacing the state with the market. The effects of such programs have followed a similar pattern in many countries: privatization of industry is followed by rising unemployment; prices for basic goods, utilities, and housing increase, leading to growing homelessness and hunger, which have incited food riots in many countries.[11] Despite these effects, which have been downplayed by Western advisors, the shock therapy program was embraced in 1990 by Polish politicians as the most effective plan for a transition to free market capitalism. By 1993, the national parliamentary elections were swept by parties promising to slow down the transition and put the brakes on the decentralization programs. In the interim, shock therapy had produced substantial macroeconomic changes, which were viewed by political leaders and international financiers as benefits, but which were experienced by large numbers of Poles as increased poverty and hardship.

The situation in the Polish periphery is worse than in the urban centers of Warsaw, Kraków, and Poznań. Whereas unemployment produced by the liquidation of inefficient businesses is offset in the cities through increased foreign investment, in peripheral areas, the eliminated enterprises are not entirely replaced by new ones. In Żywiec, several factories have shut down, such as the Żywiec Leather Factory. Other enterprises, though not entirely liquidated, have laid off significant numbers of staff. The Żywiec Brewery is an example of a privatized firm that, although a highly successful privatization in terms of profit and production, has laid off a large portion of its work force as a result of mechanization prompted by new investment. The influx of foreign capital in Żywiec has ranged from independent enterprises (such as Gablitzer, an Austrian plastics maker) to investment in privatizing enterprises (such as the Famed hospital furnishings factory and some possible Taiwanese investors, or the Żywiec Brewery and Heineken investors). Neither foreign investment nor local entrepreneurship had been able to make up the difference in employment opportunities from the socialist era. Unemployment in town is high. Personal and family difficulties make it difficult for most Żywiec residents to believe that the transition to capitalism will be personally beneficial.

The association of these socioeconomic problems with "new capitalism" makes it easier for the prewar elite to construct a narrative that castigates "capitalists," while themselves feeling that their small business enterprises that predate socialism are merely part of the community ethos, not "big business" and certainly not capitalism. Because many of the prewar elite were running small capitalist businesses, and thus there was capitalism in Żywiec before the postsocialist era, I call the newly emerging class fraction neocapitalists rather than capitalists. But it is important to remember that townspeople in Żywiec interpret the word "capitalist" to mean big business or global capitalism. For example, in a survey of 393 Żywiec residents conducted in 1994 by a master's degree student at Adam Mickiewicz University in Poznań (himself a resident of Żywiec), respondents were asked hundreds of questions about their responses to local political and economic change (Tłustochowicz 1994). Invariably, the survey questions about the local economy were constructed to gauge opinions about state enterprises and large private enterprises, with no mention of the small businesses that make up so much of the local economy. This category was not even considered by the surveyor as a major index on which opinions might matter. It is significant to note, however, that many respondents to the survey expressed the view that "trade" (smaller businesses) had had really good (40 percent) or rather good (52 percent) effects on the development of Żywiec, with only 4 percent of respondents claiming that trade had had rather bad effects (1 percent claimed trade was bad, 2 percent said it was difficult to say). In considering "industry" (large businesses), only 17 percent thought it had really good effects, and 45 percent thought it was rather good for the development of vwiec, whereas 28 percent actually believed it was rather bad (5 percent said it was bad, 6 percent said it was difficult to say). These results reflect a bias toward local businesses more likely to participate in the client-patron ethic that can be traced back not merely to socialism, but before socialism to the guilds and small businesses of this community.

Town finances were also in trouble in the late 1990s, which led to much local political unrest. National contributions to the town budget were cut. The mayor and the town council decided in December 1994 to try to privatize town public transportation, town housing, and the administration of apartment buildings. Privatization of these services would require private investors to purchase these commodities, however, and through 1997, no prospective buyers had been found. Rents and fees had been raised to attempt to make up the difference between the cost of operating these facilities and the revenue generated by them. After 1989, the first new town administration, elected from a Solidarity slate that included many members of the prewar elite, had much support from the residents. This support quickly degenerated into unrest and suspicion as prices and unemployment spiraled ever higher, and the prewar elite regained homes and businesses. Bitter resentment of the personal benefits and high salaries of politicians fueled a particularly nasty local political campaign in 1991, in which the Solidarity people were voted out.

Those who replaced them, the neocapitalists of my analysis, however well informed of new business opportunities and regulations and equipped (with relatively high state salaries) to take advantage of them, fared no better than their predecessors in terms of their favorable ratings by townspeople—either in townspeople's accounts to me, or in the 1994 survey mentioned above. Neocapitalists were, on the other hand, beneficiaries of a learning curve through which residents realized that their idealistic hopes of a new regime where power would not corrupt and where each individual would have a say in government were naive at best. Townspeople's behavior around their increasing disappointment with the "revolution" followed a pattern of political action that was much the same under socialism—overt withdrawal from the political sphere, claiming they were "not political," accompanied by channeling their energy into alternative political statements such as reentrenchment of ethnic ties, alternative economic strategies (such as gray market activities), and a reliance on family networks.

Privatization in Żyewiec

The Polish Privatization Program began in 1990, and the first sales of national enterprises occurred during 1991. The Żywiec Brewery was one of these initial divestments. From a strictly business perspective, the firm has thrived. Other firms in Żywiec have since begun the privatization process as well, with mixed results. The Żywiec Fur Factory was determined to be too unprofitable even to warrant offering for sale, and it was liquidated in 1993. By 1994, the Ponar factory had closed one of its production wings and was trying to attract capital from a Taiwanese firm to remain open. The Żywiec Metal Factory successfully established ties with German firms and remained a strong enterprise. The mayor of Żywiec was also working hard to convince foreign firms to relocate or establish new facilities in Żywiec. By 1995, the Austrian firm Gablitzer, which produces plastic bottles, was the only foreign firm that had moved into Żywiec independent of a joint operating agreement with a local business.

Many economic strategies that worked for individuals, households, and firms under socialism continued to work under nascent capitalism in the late 1990s. Working on the black or gray market (*na lewo*—literally, "on the left") was as much a part of the postsocialist landscape as it was of the socialist. Other Żywiecers attempted to take advantage of what new opportunities were available. Some tried to start new businesses, to join individualized foreign import ventures such as Amway, or to work abroad. Many economic strategies were household based and tended to be somewhat dependent on factors such as class, gender, age, and education. I discuss these issues in chapter 4.

The growth of new independent businesses in Żywiec was another facet of the new economic structure. Much of the property nationalized by the PZPR was being returned to Żywiec residents. By and large, this was property that belonged to the prewar elite, giving them an advantage in the new era. The reestablishment of the class authority of the prewar elite is the subject of chapter 3.

The large-scale, global capitalism with which Żywiec industries are now interacting has the capacity to pull these enterprises out of the community ethic in a way that the socialist-centered economy never did. This is evident in the community reaction to the brewery's new policies, which have gutted the social services available to brewery employees. The new management has also severely limited the amount of funds it donates to the community, basing donations more on specific transactions, such as permitting the distribution of Żywiec Brewery logo flags during the pope's visit or encouraging special consideration on the issue of the name "Żywiec" as a trademark in the dispute with the Żywiec Zdrój mineral water company. This is a clear violation of the community moral economy and has led to disputes between the town council and the brewery.

In contrast, the Żywiec Metal Factory has managed to maintain many of the auxiliary social services it offered in the socialist era. Many residents do not even know that the metal factory has been privatized, because they associate privatization with liquidation or job cuts and elimination of services. Chapter 5 covers the contrast between these two enterprises, the way they are perceived by townspeople, and how this fits in with community strategies for economic survival during postsocialism.

One major difference on the political scene is that Catholic church authority, such a large part of resistance to national policies in the past, has been undermined since 1989 by the church's attempts to focus on unpopular political and social agendas such as abortion and divorce. Though elderly Żywiecers went to church on all holy days, many people whom I knew who were middle-aged or younger had let their enthusiasm or sense of duty lapse and went to church only sporadically. Jan Kubik (1995) comments:

> The situation has changed since 1989: the tension between the Church and civil society has been growing. The Church umbrella is not needed anymore, since the negotiated revolution of 1989 emancipated the society and lifted all restrictions on autonomy of social forces. On the other hand, in the initial stage of the current transformation the Catholic Church considerably extended its influence, partly because the previous limitations ceased to exist, and partly because some segments of the new political elite stimulated the growth of the political role of the Church. Public-opinion polls show that before the collapse of Communism the majority of Polish society had a favorable opinion of the political role of the Church, while recently the majority declare critical views. As a result, one may notice a significant drop in the authority of the Church over the last years.

The changes in the political economy of Żywiec due to the fall of the communist regime in 1989 are, according to many Żywiecers, to a large extent merely another set of transitions that are similar in scale and effect to the changes that occurred both when the community became a part of Poland and when socialism began. Frustration with the effects of national economic policy in Żywiec, such as unemployment and inflation, have played into the idea of community isolation from the nation-state, which was developed and nurtured during the partition period and during socialism.

Community economic strategies to offset these effects, such as attracting foreign capital or building up a tourist industry, require Żywiec decision makers to emphasize the difference of the Żywiec region within Poland. The invocation of Góralism plays a large part in the Żywiec community strategies for economic growth, described more fully in chapter 4. The push for tourist trade in the form of folk festivals and crafts sales is based largely on the assertion of ethnic difference from other Poles. Żywiec's growing economic trade involvement with Slovakian towns just over the Polish-Slovak border has been allowed by the opening of the border crossing at Zwardoń, several dozen kilometers directly to the south. But the rhetoric surrounding these trade agreements has been that of two Góral communities reuniting and reestablishing ties.

This regional difference was also emphasized during the socialist period. Contemporarily, emphasizing folkloric Góralism gives the town some ideological distance from Warsaw policies, showing that national and local identity do not entirely overlap. It provides additional meaning to the process of pulling together economic ties with Slovak towns and even enables Żywiecers to see cultural ties with other ethnic groups from the Third World. Given that the Góral identity also ties emigrants who have left the region for the First World back to the community, this regional ethnic identity is mapping across the First, Second, and Third Worlds in surprisingly broad and elastic ways.

THE NATION-STATE–COMMUNITY RELATIONSHIP RECONSIDERED

The Polish nation-state is considered by most analysts to be the most relevant political economic context of Żywiec in the postsocialist era. As I have demonstrated in this chapter, Żywiecers historically have had a weak connection to the Polish nation and the Polish state because of their attachment to various other polities over the past few centuries. The Austro-Hungarian Empire had a clear claim on the local political economy, and even on the loyalty of the Żywiecers, through the presence of a Habsburg seat in Żywiec. Even in the interwar period (between the First and Second World Wars), when Poland was reconstituted from the partitions and Żywiec was made a part of Poland, the Habsburg family remained strong leaders in the community. During World War II, the Nazi occupation of Żywiec tied it to the German state. Even after the war, when Poland was again recomposed, Soviet imperialism gave many Żywiecers the impression that the Polish state was not truly independent. During all of these periods, the Góral identity was a source of stability in the community, and local relations were more important in organizing economics.

Chapter 3

◄O►

Elite Class Struggles
and Authority

Exploring the changing social structure of power in Żywiec in volves looking at class conflict around the political and economic changes resulting from the fall of communism—those local changes that are driven by national policies aimed at decentralizing the economy and political system. Rather than just looking at changes in class structure between socialism and the postsocialist era, to understand the current struggles in Żywiec, it is important first to examine the most important class divisions at the end of the Habsburg era and discuss how these social groups were changed in the socialist era. Only then can one understand how the power struggles and changes from the socialist period to the present work, because these power struggles often refer back to presocialist class categories and traditions of community authority. In the current era, then, I explore the interactions between the prewar elite, members of the former PZPR, those involved with the Solidarity movement during the 1980s, and the newly emerging political and economic entrepreneurs, the neocapitalists. I show that throughout these three eras, the classes in Żywiec have formed community organizations through which their conflict is acted out. Finally, I return to the theoretical implications of this multilayered process to discuss class change and conflict through the idioms of traditionalism and modernity.

A central point of this chapter is that the members of prewar power networks and their descendants are reclaiming the identity of Góralism and establishing community authority by positioning themselves as the cultural elite for this ethnicity. This process began during the early socialist era (in the 1950s) but has gained substantial momentum in the post-1989 context, due in part to the breakdown of socialist authority structures and the return of property confiscated during the socialist era. These members of the prewar elite are attempting to recreate the prewar, patronage, social power structure, and, further, to parlay their positions within this older authority structure into positions of authority in the current system. They hope to do this through evoking a sense of traditionalism around the community identity and history—by "tradition," therefore, they would be the most appropriate community leaders.

The rhetoric of traditionalism is counterbalanced by ideas of modernity, which are invoked by global capitalism, the national policymakers, and, at the local level, the neocapitalists. The neocapitalists, who have seized the reins of formal political power in the community, oppose the prewar elite's attempts to regain community authority, touting their skills and familiarity with the new social and political-economic order as a more appropriate basis for authority than the old patronage relationships. Neocapitalists see modernity as a fundamentally new era, where ethnic identity is important only as a folkloric past or to pull in tourists, and tradition is part of the past and certainly should not be the basis for deciding who is a community leader. The prewar elite paint a picture of the modern era as flowing directly from and being still intricately intertwined with their community's past history and identity, not in conflict with tradition. These different ideas about tradition and modernity are used by these two opposing groups in the community to contest one another's cultural authority and support their own positions.

CLASS AND COMMUNITIES

Karl Marx, in *Das Kapital* ([1867, 1885, 1894] 1978), attempts to deduce the basis for classes along the following argument:

> The first question to be answered is this: What constitutes a class?—and the reply to this follows naturally from the reply to another question, namely: What makes wage-labourers, capitalists and landlords constitute the three great social classes? At first glance—the identity of revenues and

sources of revenue. There are three great social groups whose members, the individuals forming them, live on wages, profit and ground-rent respectively, on the realisation of their labour-power, their capital, and their landed property. (441–42)

Class is thus reduced to how a person makes a living—the working class from wage labor, owners of business from their profits, and landowners from rents on their property. Marx goes on to state that this entirely economic definition of class is not satisfactory, because it will result in an "infinite fragmentation of interest and rank"; in other words, that merely having the same economic position would not explain fully the ways that people act together to protect their interests ([1867, 1885, 1894] 1978, 442). More generally, then, he states in *The Eighteenth Brumaire of Louis Bonaparte* ([1852] 1978) that class is composed not merely of economic relations, but of cultural and social relations as well: "In so far as millions of families live under economic conditions of existence that divide their mode of life, their interests and their culture from those of the other classes, and put them in hostile contrast to the latter, they form a class" (608).

A treatment of class that explicitly treats cultural and social relations has been formulated by Pierre Bourdieu (1977). Bourdieu recognizes several kinds of capital, including economic, cultural, social, and symbolic resources. All of these resources, not only economic position, articulate to produce class differentiation. This means that class distinctions, although based in economic differences, have other components that can come to symbolize the class and can even override current economic resources (Bourdieu 1986). This view of the many kinds of capital that make up class is most useful in looking at the history of social groups in Żywiec, in particular because of the functioning of class under socialism.

The economic resources of several elite classes were altered during the socialist period by nationalization of businesses and homes and redistribution of economic power into the hands of the PZPR members, and again in the postsocialist era, when property was reprivatized and new political and economic opportunities became available. In the socialist era, this resulted in the formation of a new class composed of members of the PZPR elite in town and the disruption of ownership for the prewar elite. However, using a strictly economic interpretation of class would overlook the implications of the social relationships that the members of this class had with other members of the community and that allowed them to act as elites in a cultural and symbolic realm. The return of their prewar property in the postsocialist era has meant that the prewar elite have regained their economic capital, but we can continue to trace their actions in other forms of capital. The postsocialist era has also meant the dissolution of the PZPR elite class, because these people no longer have access to state-owned capital, and the emergence of a class I call the neocapitalists. This class contains the new local political elite, most of whom are involved in trying to interest international investors in their community. These two classes, the prewar elite and the neocapitalists, are engaged in a struggle over authority in the community that is acted out primarily in the cultural and symbolic realms through the idioms of traditionalism and modernity, which involves contestation over the meaning and relevance of the Góral identity. In the following section, I first describe the class structure of Żywiec during the prewar and socialist periods and go on to explore the emerging class structure of the postsocialist era.

CLASS DIVISIONS IN ŻYWIEC THROUGH TIME

Prewar Era

The Habsburgs. The wealthiest members of Żywiec society in the prewar era were, of course, the Habsburgs. Though not full-time members of the community, this family, a class unto itself, wielded great influence in the community. They held the economic power of owning many of the largest enterprises in town; but they were also rich in social, cultural, and symbolic capital. The Habsburgs, through dispersing their wealth to members of the community, were patrons of both elite and nonelite classes in prewar Żywiec.

Prewar elite. The prewar elite classes in Żywiec tended to fall into three general categories: small-scale industrial capitalists, large merchants and craftsmen, and managers of Habsburg enterprises. The small-scale industrial capitalists numbered about four families, as can be seen from the description of prewar industry in chapter two. The large merchants and craftsmen ran businesses in a manner essentially similar to that during the height of the guilds, they took on apprentices whom they trained, and they continued to be important in the community. Managers of Habsburg enterprises, according to members of this group, apparently enjoyed high cultural capital due to their proximity to the royal family, as well as high income and some property from salaries and gifts. As a result of their interactions with outsiders, these three classes of necessity spoke standard Polish as well as the

Góral dialect, and many of them spoke German as well. They owned large houses, plots of land, and valuable pieces of art and furniture. These three classes I collectively call the prewar elite, and I discuss them together because they have tended in the socialist and postsocialist eras to have similar fates and act in a unified manner through community organizations.

In terms of evidence of the prewar class status of particular Żywiec families, cemeteries are amazing repositories of knowledge in Poland. The cemetery in which members of a family are buried, the location of their gravesites in the cemetery, and the type of grave decorations all indicate social status. Family plots are a metonym for family status, and cemeteries are an inscribed history of the community. There are many cemeteries in Żywiec, including at least two large Catholic cemeteries, one overgrown and primarily destroyed Jewish cemetery, and a small, well-tended, but sometimes defaced cemetery in which Soviet soldiers who died defending Żywiec during World War II are buried. It is clear when one visits the cemeteries in Żywiec (as everyone does at least once a year on November 1, All Saints' Day) that the old families have more elaborate family plots, which are better located than those of other, less prestigious Żywiec families (i.e., nearer to the chapels on the cemetery grounds, or further away from undesirable locations such as Roma [Gypsy] sections) and, predominantly, plots in Catholic cemeteries rather than Protestant ones.[1] Thus, one can see the status of these families reflected in a vivid, concrete, historical sense by taking a tour of the Żywiec cemeteries.[2]

In Żywiec, because the region did not have local Polish aristocracies (discussed in chapter 2), these "old families" in Żywiec were akin to petty gentries in how they were perceived by other families and how they affected local politics and economics during the prewar period. Although they did not have titles themselves, they formed a sort of local elite.

Several Żywiecers of this class told me that this family class position was reflected in an earlier era through guild leadership, and that members of their families had held prominent positions in the guilds discussed in chapter 2. Many Żywiec residents, whether they were members of the old families or not, could and did list for me the family names that were "old, well-known names in the Żywiec region." In fact, several members of these families suggested to me that I should *only* interview these families, because only they were "real Żywiecers." By this phrase, they meant that these families had held social, cultural, symbolic, and economic capital in the community during the prewar era, and that these particular people were now active in local class politics and Góral ethnic revitalization.

As the guilds declined in importance and independent, small-scale, capitalist-type enterprises arose during the late Habsburg era in Żywiec, these families maintained their positions as first families through their control over key trades and industries—for example, hotels, bakeries, smithies, leather shops, and mills. Some of them had firsthand contact with the Habsburgs, lending an aura of elite, cosmopolitan political status to their families. Several of my elderly informants gave detailed information about their family and personal contacts with the Habsburgs during our first interviews, which served to impress upon me not only how important the turn of the century era was as a "golden age" in the imagination of many Żywiecers, but also the historic status of their families and the legitimacy of their ability to speak for and about their community.

One gentleman told me that he had been at school with one of the younger members of the Habsburg family and had been quite friendly with him, but he had been confused as to whether he should address the young duke using the formal or informal mode in Polish speech.[3] He finally just asked the young man whether he should call him "you" or "your Grace." He reported to me with humor and some pride that the young Habsburg had told him that when they were together informally, they should just address one another informally.

Another member of the prewar elite class, an older woman, told me of her experiences working as the secretary to the manager of the brewery when she was young, in the days before World War II broke out in Poland. She described to me how her father knew the archduke, and how when the archduke called to speak to the brewery manager, he always knew who she was. This particular woman described to me on many occasions how much Żywiec had benefited by the Habsburg presence, how generous the family was to the factory workers and the town in general, and how genteel the Habsburgs were. She dwelled on how beautifully they spoke Polish as well as German (she was fluent in both) and how elegant and paternal the family had been.

A third interviewee, a man who had been a brewery manager during the Habsburg era, also painted a glowing picture of that era and his place in it. He told me about how the royal family had allowed only a few families the right to come onto their property (now the complex of the old castle, the new castle, and the national forest reserve in Żywiec) and how his family had been one of the privileged few. He described the glory of the old royal gardens and how well the managers' families had been treated by the Habsburgs—they had received many benefits from the Habsburgs, from Christmas gifts of clothing and toys for their families to preferential housing, food, and horses.

Nonelite classes: peasants and workers. Peasants and workers made up the nonelite classes in prewar Żywiec. The peasants in the Galician region were some of the poorest in Eastern Europe, in part because of the small size of the plots and their distance from major market towns. They relied strongly on the Habsburgs and the local elite to act as patrons when times were bad, but they also out-migrated at the highest rate in Eastern Europe. Many emigrants sent money home from abroad, and many returned home after several years of "making their fortune." This peasant class made up the majority of those who lived on the outskirts of Żywiec and in the surrounding villages, many of which were later incorporated into Żywiec.

Workers, on the other hand, were made up of two general groups—those who worked as apprentices to merchants and craftsmen, and those who found employment in industrial enterprises. Though economically they gained wages and other benefits through the same relation to production, many Żywiec residents related to me that there had been a strong difference in the social value of their positions. The industrial workers were allegedly thought to be lower in cultural capital (this was expressed as social status) than apprentices, because they were doing work that had no "cultural history" in the region. That is to say, apprenticing at a job recognized as a skill that benefited the community, or that was thought to be traditional, was valued over learning industrial skills that were put into materials that were transferred out of the community. Nevertheless, as the industrial enterprises grew, they employed many of the town residents and even began to construct housing especially for their employees. Thus, at the time of World War I, as many as half of the residents of Żywiec proper were probably industrial workers.

Socialist Era

PZPR elites. During the socialist era, a new class emerged—the PZPR elites. This class was composed of managers of factories as well as local bureaucrats. Because the PZPR in Poland had nationalized business and seized many private homes and other property, all of these resources needed to be managed and distributed. The local party elite had the job of appropriately disbursing these resources, and many others of importance during the socialist era, such as employment opportunities, new housing, travel permits, and even places for students in the different town high schools. In Żywiec, there were few members of the prewar elite who were willing or able to join the PZPR. Community feelings were strongly anticommunist in the postwar years, and as was described in chapter 2, there was even armed resistance to the PZRP, which resulted in clashes between local guerrillas and the Soviet army into the early 1950s in southern Poland. Thus, PZPR members in Żywiec were drawn primarily from the worker and peasant classes.

Prewar elites. During the socialist era, the old elite families lost their wealth and their positions as formal leaders of the community. Their houses and businesses were seized and nationalized, and many of them lived in socialist-built apartments or in just one or two rooms of their homes as other families were moved into their houses. Other people were put in charge of their former businesses, and they were given jobs that had little to do with their former posts. The local PZPR organization was made up of people whose families had no connections to such bourgeois institutions as the Habsburg dynasty. However, despite these outward signs of political and economic disenfranchisement, the families of the prewar elite retained a kind of respect in the community. This can be seen through the way that Żywiecers still referred to them as the "old families," and through their ability to organize cultural events in the community and in schools and, in general, to be seen as local cultural authorities.

The influence of prewar status during the socialist period on the general perception of a family's status can be also seen in Eva Hoffman's 1989 *Lost in Translation*, a biography that begins in her native Kraków. Hoffman comments on a family considered to have high status:

> They belong to the prewar haute bourgeoisie—a status that continues to be respected in Poland's supposedly classless society. In most people's minds, coming from an old lineage[4] counts for more than high position in the Polish People's Republic [PRL];[5] it is certainly better than being an influential party apparatchik,[6] for example— though an apparatchik may have more money, a bigger apartment, and sometimes even, wonder of wonders, a car. Of course, party apparatchiks are compromised from the beginning by their political associations. But even aside from that, lineage gives a solidity, a depth that such newly minted success cannot bestow; it implies a moral uprightness and the dignity of not having to prove yourself, of being somebody to begin with—and being, by the

still preindustrial standards of this particular society, is far preferable to striving. (44)

This cultural capital accumulated by their name and previous stature enabled members of these families to regroup during the socialist era and turn their energy toward a new direction, because they were no longer allowed to wield political or economic power openly.[7] Instead, they positioned themselves as the intellectuals and cultural elite of Żywiec, founding the Friends of the Żywiec Region (FZR [*Towarzystwo Miłośników Ziemii Żywieckie*]), starting a local writers' group (*Gronie* [Grapes]) and a regional literary and historical journal (*Karta Groni* [Card of Grapes]), and founding and working at the Żywiec Cultural Club and the Żywiec Museum and Żywiec Castle Museum.

In the process of focusing on regional culture, this group of cosmopolitan townspeople—many of whom claimed personal contacts with the Habsburgs and who had been to Vienna and Budapest, and spoke standard Polish and sometimes German as well—redirected their energies toward writing about and generally promoting the Góral culture of the rural landscape. This translated into a number of different realms. The writers' group *Gronie* wrote poetry in Góral dialect, and the Żywiec Cultural Club started Góral dance troupes. The FZR gained access to elementary schools to teach Góral crafts. *Karta Groni*, the journal, published Góral poetry as well as articles about the special history of the Żywiec Góral region. The Żywiec Museum gathered examples of Góral art, clothing, and utensils for display. The Żywiec Cultural Club started the Góral Folk Festival, where Góral dance and theater troupes and artists from all over Galicia and even Silesia could come to perform. The Żywiec Castle Museum set up a display of Habsburg furniture and Żywiec guild history in the old castle.[8]

All of this served the community in that it helped people in the Żywiec region differentiate themselves from the Polish People's Republic (the socialist state that was so alienating to them) by asserting that this state was not their nation, and that they had a more complex relationship to the Polish state and to the Polish nation than other people in Poland. The socialist period was not an easy one for this region economically. The Góral region is one of the poorest in Poland (a fact that has led to a higher out-migration rate than in other parts of Poland, as noted previously) and consists primarily of very small-scale farmers. The PZPR government in Poland needed massive revenues to achieve their goal of developing heavy industries, and much of it came from taxing peasants. Góral peasants were the poorest of the poor, and they suffered heavily under this system. At the same time in Żywiec, many of the younger peasants were being moved off

of their farms into the town itself and put to work in the newly nationalized and growing factories, such as the brewery, the metal factory,
the paper factory, and the leather factory. These rural Górals brought
aspects of the Góral culture back into the town in a more insistent way
than when they were merely bringing vegetables to market and buying wares from the town merchants and tradesmen. Clumped together
in concrete apartment complexes commissioned by socialist planners,
these peasants brought the countryside back into Żywiec. They raised
chickens in the yards, spoke primarily in the Góral dialect, and dressed
differently from the other townspeople. People who had been brought
in from the surrounding villages had a very tangible sense of patronage as it was practiced by the Habsburgs. Regardless of the fact that
socialist programs were funding their jobs and housing, rural Górals
looked for moral and cultural leadership to those who espoused those
values of religion and ethnicity that they had held all their lives. The
cultural elite combined the two strands of Catholicism and Góralism,
and wove messages—of resistance to the socialist state, community
solidarity, and their moral authority—into their presentation of Góralism.

Although all of these community-level processes were indeed
part of the result of their actions, the local prewar elite were trying to
maintain some semblance of status and meaning for themselves and
their families. They were the guiding force behind a resistance movement against the socialist state, which was clothed as a resurgence of
local regional identity—something they were arguably barely qualified
to do, given that they were neither farmers nor did they speak the
Góral dialect at home, even if their parents or grandparents may have.
However, appealing to traditionalism and their traditional authority
in the community gave these individuals, and by extension their families, the means to weather the storm of socialism and retain some
authority within the community. The facts (as related to me by many
townspeople) that the regional journal *Karta Groni* had to pass through
government censors, and that teachers of Góral crafts in elementary
schools were occasionally harassed by the local PZPR, only lent legitimacy in the eyes of the local populace to the meaning of Góralism as
oppositional. In true, orthodox Gramscian style, state harassment led
to intensification of local resistance, which was linked to the local
identity. Thus, during the socialist period, the prewar elites cashed in
their chips of political and economic social stature for intellectual and
cultural authority, and, further, they were poised to take advantage of
the dissolution of the local PZPR and attempt to regain political and
economic power in the postsocialist turmoil.

Why weren't these Góral cultural groups censored more by the
PZPR? The answer is a combination of lenient policies and geographic

marginality. The physical marginality of Żywiec vis-à-vis Warsaw was surely part of the equation. Lack of phones (and poor connections where they did exist), a long train journey from Warsaw, and infrequent train service contributed to a socialist Poland in which Żywiec was far from the centers of power and thus far from the eyes of anyone with real power. Another facet of this curious lack of response from the PZPR was the fact that officially, under Soviet state socialism, ethnic groups were allowed to exist and were not to be discriminated against. Though there were no special privileges for ethnic groups (as there were, for example, under Chinese communism), a tolerance for "ethnic" activities such as crafts and dancing allowed people to use ethnicity as a venue for expressing values contrary to the nationally promoted socialist ideologies. There were also fewer socialist constraints in Poland as compared with other states, such as Czechoslovakia, East Germany, or Romania. Many PZPR members continued to attend Catholic masses, whereas in other countries in the region, abandoning religious obligations was necessary to become a party member. Intellectuals in Poland, moreover, were able to publish more freely than their counterparts in other countries. Together, these facets of life in socialist Poland added up to more freedom for Górals in their public expressions of identity.

Another example of a means through which the prewar elite were able to mobilize their social capital and simultaneously reinforce their authority in the community was their involvement in the Solidarity movement in Żywiec. "Solidarity" was the name of the umbrella political organization widely credited with overthrowing socialism in Poland. The role of Solidarity in the history of Polish martial law during the 1980s and the eventual dissolution of the socialist government in 1989 has been extensively discussed, and it is not my intention to engage with this literature to any great degree.[9] However, the Solidarity movement was as important in Żywiec as elsewhere in Poland, and the composition of these prewar activists on this local stage and their subsequent fates are enlightening in the context of this discussion on class. Most of the leaders of the local Solidarity movement were members of the prewar elite. This is probably unique to this region and different from the national composition of Solidarity activists; most Solidarity theorists are taken up with arguments over whether Solidarity was "really" a workers' movement or an intellectualist movement.

In 1989, when the socialist government of Poland (at the time, the Polish People's Republic) agreed to talks with Solidarity, the national umbrella resistance organization was made up of many different groups united by the goal of creating a space for dialogue with the government on labor and civil issues. On the local level, as a general trend, the movement was headed by members of the prewar elite, many of whom I interviewed. Some leaders of the local movement were from nonelite classes, but even they deferred to the prewar elite in decisions. An example of this would be Pan Marek, a local man from the worker class, who had actually attended the 1980 Gdansk shipyard organizational meetings with Lech Wałe̜sa and was active in the Żywiec underground organization throughout the 1980s. He described with great excitement the speeches that Wałęsa had made at the birth of the Solidarity movement. When I asked him why and how he had traveled to Gdansk at that time, he told me that several people, who were prewar elite and leaders of the local Solidarity organization, had sent him to find out what was happening when they had heard through the grapevine that organizing was going on in Gdansk. This grumbling through the grapevine, of course, helped usher in the collapse of the socialist regime almost a decade later.

After the period of national euphoria wore off, these disparate groups realized that they now had disparate goals. Solidarity soon splintered into dozens of different groups: some factions wanted to retain the organization as a labor union only, some were motivated to create political parties, and some were civil groups interested in social issues such as health care and ecology. The result was a dizzying array of organizations, many of which called themselves "Solidarity." As with the national Solidarity organization, what remained at the local level in Żywiec in 1995 was split primarily between Solidarity as a political party and Solidarity the labor union. The most important piece of information for this discussion of class, however, is that as reprivatization commenced and they regained their property, most of the prewar elite dropped out of Solidarity altogether. They declared to me that they were "tired of politics."

An exception was Pani Agnieszka: the woman who was the local delegate to one of the Solidarity political parties (of which there are several) echoed national-level rhetoric in her insistence that the labor union was politically united with the political party. She had been one of the main local conspirators during the 1980s, when the movement went underground, and she continued to believe strongly in Solidarity. She was also one of the prewar elite and involved to some degree in the Góral cultural venues in town.

The head of the Solidarity Teachers' Union in Żywiec, Pani Jola, disagreed sharply with Pani Agnieszka. She felt that the role of the Solidarity union was completely separate from that of the political party, and she told me that her job was to make sure that the teachers got a fair deal from the school, not to fight political battles. In her eyes, the political movement had done its job in overthrowing socialism. Pani Jola did not even really retain ties to other Solidarity unions in town, such as the Doctors' and Nurses' Union, or with other branches of the teachers' union. For her, the Solidarity Teachers' Union was a very local and specific phenomenon, with little power in the face of a national school system and little motivation to attempt to change the system. She told me that the teacher's union did not strike during any of the Solidarity sympathy strikes for coal miners or doctors that occurred during 1993–95, nor did they even strike during the supposedly national Solidarity Teachers' Union strike.

Immediately after 1989, Solidarity people gained community political positions in Żywiec. However, they were largely thrown out of office during a fight over the mayor's position and town council politics in 1991. There were, of course, many different versions of exactly what had happened. After 1989, Pan Marek worked on the Żywiec mayor's administrative staff until 1991. Embroiled in the local controversy over misuse of funds and poor community planning, he was thrown out along with the rest of the community politicians. He could no longer go back to his previous job, which had been liquidated by privatization. He now worked as an hourly wage laborer at the flour mill in Żywiec, which had been returned to its prewar owners (who were also Żywiec Solidarity leaders during the 1980s). Pan Marek and Pani Agnieszka exemplified the tendency, clear among Solidarity members who stayed with Solidarity during the 1990s, to become more and more socially conservative and in line with the Catholic church's views in terms of women's rights to abortion, the evils of divorce, and freedom of religion.[10] In opposition to national-level Solidarity rhetoric, however, they were fiscal liberals and believed that the government should be giving more money to the poor, the elderly, doctors, teachers, and other state employees, as well as providing free medical care and lowering taxes.

Most of the other prewar elite members of the local Solidarity leadership had already gained what they wanted from the Solidarity movement—the return of their businesses that had been nationalized during socialism. These members of the prewar elite were now busy running these businesses, and they claimed that they were "no longer interested in politics" or that politics bored them. Such was the case for the Galunka family, which had had the largest bakery in Żywiec returned to them along with their prewar multifamily home. The Szymierka family, another example of this "antipolitical" phenomenon, had received back the Żywiec flour mill and their large house and

considerable amount of land that went with it. This family took in
poor Pan Marek as an hourly worker when he no longer had any
place to turn, perhaps unconsciously mimicking the patronage system
of the prewar era from which they derived their authority.

Workers and peasants. In the socialist era, the class status of prewar
workers and peasants was fairly undisrupted. Those who worked in
industrial enterprises continued to work there, and because agriculture was not collectivized in Żywiec, those who were peasants continued to farm. This is not to say that there were no internal differences
within the peasant class in the size of peasant holdings, or the number
of animals or other farming resources that peasants owned. There
surely were these differences, and they had an impact on the ability of
peasant families to make a living during the socialist era, particularly
since the Habsburgs were no longer in residence to provide during
poor harvest years. However, the PZPR was a willing patron for some
aspects of peasants' needs, and there was a social safety net for those
whose crops failed. A major change for many peasants was that they
or their children were given jobs working in industry instead of farming. This resulted in an increase in the Żywiec population, because
peasants from surrounding villages were moved into socialist housing
projects in the town. It also meant that former peasant families had
access to better educational opportunities in the larger town of Żywiec.
Workers were assured of employment in theory, even though this
sometimes meant relocating to towns far away from their families.

For some of these peasant and worker families, the socialist era
resulted in massive improvements in their standard of living: they
gained electricity, running water, education, and opportunities for
advancement through the PZPR. They would not otherwise have been
able to afford these luxuries, even had they somehow had access to
these services. But for the nonelite classes, the only way out of their
class during the socialist era was to join the PZPR.

Postsocialist Era

Prewar elite. When I first moved to Żywiec, it was difficult for me to
determine the class of many people with whom I came into contact.
There were, of course, some clear cases of significant contrasts in consumption patterns, which indicated disparities in income levels. The
highest income levels are evidenced by many items of expensive clothing, larger housing (perhaps even a newly built house), and the latest
conveniences and technologies for the kitchen and entertainment,
possibly even Western European or American made. The members of

the community with the lowest income levels lived in tiny apartments, ramshackle houses, and, in the case of elderly peasants who live on farms outside Żywiec, wooden cabins. The poorest people in Żywiec had no telephones, electricity, or running water. They wore home-made clothing of poor material, or the cheapest store-bought goods, and had few garments.

However, consumption patterns and thus income level were not always a good indicator of class status in Żywiec. People at the lowest income level tended to be peasants and/or elderly people with no children living with them. People at the highest income levels tended to be (a) managers working for the brewery and other internationally linked businesses; (b) politicians who had been able to get good bank loans and start lucrative businesses and/or were managers or new owners of town businesses that had privatized;[11] (c) prewar elites, many of whom had had socialist-nationalized businesses returned to their families; and (d) entrepreneurs who had expanded businesses that existed illegally during the socialist era, most of whom were members of prewar elite families. Not all of the high-income families were considered by other Żywiec residents to be "upper class." This designation went far beyond mere income level, and it seemed to be based primarily on the family's prewar position in the community. Thus, in the postsocialist era, the class of prewar elites has been cul-turally afforded the category of "upper class," even though income and relation to the means of production meant that there were other elite classes, just as in the socialist era.

Neocapitalists. There are few truly new well-to-do political and eco-nomic entrepreneurs in Żywiec, that is, people who now have political positions or run new businesses and whose families did not have similar positions in an earlier era. As a result of the role the prewar elite played in the Żywiec Solidarity organization, in the first several years after the end of socialism local politicians tended to be chosen from among the Solidarity activists and, thus, the local prewar elite families. In the past several years, however, after the glow of over-throwing socialism had worn off, dissatisfaction with shock therapy policies instituted by the Solidarity-led governments backfired on these initial local politicians, and they lost their bids for reelection.

The newly elected politicians had a vision for the future of Żywiec. This vision involved creating ties with international business and in-teresting them in investing in Żywiec businesses or creating new ven-tures in Żywiec. These politicians believed that the infusions of international capital would create jobs in Żywiec, thus attesting to their business prowess in the postsocialist era. They drew relatively large salaries, and they also had direct knowledge of opportunities for investments or loans in the new era. Another group of people who benefited from this vision were those who had positions as managers for the international businesses investing in Żywiec. Together, these politicians and managers made up the emerging neocapitalist class.

The neocapitalist politicians lost no time in commandeering resources for themselves and their families, making it possible for them to start new enterprises. One enterprise that was bitterly resented by many of those with whom I spoke was the town gasoline station, which was run by the mayor's family. Accusations of misconduct in the licensing of the station and the loan that was secured to pay for it ran rampant, and some Żywiecers were convinced that the station was making a huge profit that the mayor could use to bribe people into electing him again. They may have been correct about the potential for a large profit, because it was the only gasoline station in town.

These neocapitalists were procapitalist because their businesses were doing quite well in this "not really free" market system. They tended to believe that the best future for Żywiec was to attract investments from outside businesses, even international businesses. This strategy runs directly in opposition to the one favored by members of the prewar elite, many of whom were now small-scale local business owners. Neocapitalists saw the involvement of Heineken in the Żywiec Brewery as a step in the right direction, and they worked to get other multinationals interested in Żywiec as a location for investment, both as partners in privatization efforts and as stand-alone enterprises. In 1995, they had managed to attract an Austrian plastics producer, Gablitzer, which set up a small factory on the outskirts of Żywiec, and they were working on a deal with a Taiwanese company that was considering investing in another privatizing Żywiec business, the hospital furnishings factory. The chief benefit this class saw in Góral "tradition" was that it provided a quaint backdrop against which to cement business ties. Thus, Góral bands and dance troupes were sometimes taken along on trips to sister cities, as goodwill performers and to demonstrate the pastoral past. But to this group of Żywiecers, and unlike the prewar elite's vision, Góralism was a part of the past, and Góral revitalization was to be used only to attract tourists and businesses to enjoy modern facilities, not to provide real moral guidance or authority.

Ex-communist leaders. The fate of former PZPR members has been mixed. All of the local PZPR members lost their political positions in Żywiec after 1990. None of them have been able to regain a position on the town council, the mayor's office, the regional council, or similar positions. Most of the larger enterprises in town have been privatized, and the PZPR members who were in charge of any of these privatized enterprises lost their positions. In fact, there has been a pattern in Poland that communist managers have only retained their positions when their factory was likely to be liquidated during privatization.

Such was the history of the Żywiec Leather Factory, which produced hats, coats, boots, and gloves. This factory began the privatization process but ended in liquidation. In 1995, two years into the privatization process, it was still not considered a closed case because the committee in charge could not even find a buyer for any of the junked machinery or the factory building itself. However, the factory had shut down, and everyone who worked there (primarily women) had lost their jobs. Rumors blamed the manager for alcoholism and womanizing, especially approaching young women who worked for the factory for sexual favors, instead of trying to make the factory a success. Officially, the story was that the factory simply was not profitable and could not be saved.

However, some PZPR members have been able to regain some influence in local politics. The head of the former local PZPR organization, for example, now runs three intertwined ecological groups, which are focused on running a recycling program, preserving the national forest, and teaching ecology in the schools. He is working closely with the town council on these matters, and retains some respect and influence in the community for his work. He appears to have thrown himself wholeheartedly into these projects, and once lectured me for three hours on the necessity of taking care of the environment. I pointed out to him that environmentalist politics have been taken up by many new Polish parties since 1989 in an attempt to show their opposition to PZPR policies, which were destructive to the environment, and I asked him how he positioned himself politically on this point. He denied that the growing environmental movement in Poland was in any way ideologically driven by anticommunist feeling, and he told me that it was, in fact, "outside of" politics. This claim of being politically neutral has served him well in regaining access to community politics, and the town council is allowing him more and more responsibility for running town ecology programs. Ironically, he really did seem politically neutral, at least in the local sense—he had developed good ties with both neocapitalists and the old elite.

Nonelites. The workers and small-scale farmers (still known colloquially as peasants) had not changed much in their class composition by 1995. Despite high unemployment (official estimates by town employees were around 15 percent, unofficial estimates by those same employees rose to 25 percent), workers continued to be the largest class in the community. Full-time peasants were mostly older people, and their farms would not be worked full-time by their descendants. These classes had neither more nor less access to different kinds of capital now than they did under socialism. However, a new underclass of permanently unemployed and underemployed was emerging, which was attributable to the privatization and downsizing of community firms to improve their profitability. Thus, some people, particularly those who fell outside family networks and who were old or disabled in some way (including alcoholics), were unable to regain permanent work after being laid off, and they did not have social ties to maintain themselves. These people attempted to find temporary jobs in construction, cleaning, or other gray market activities, or they were effectively reduced to begging from their neighbors and friends for resources.

CLASSES AND COMMUNITY ORGANIZATIONS

Members of these different classes tend to gather in community organizations, many of which have overlapping memberships, and work through those organizations in planning events and policies and implementing programs. Thus, class is concretized, and class actions are taken, through organizations that are ostensibly formed for the purpose of promoting culture, education, or business. For example, the members of the committees that run the FZR, the Metal Factory Culture and Sports Club, and the town library staff all overlap substantially with that of the Żywiec Culture Club. Members of these organizations tend to be part of the cultural elite. The town council and mayor's office are another nexus, running events through town bureaus and through related organizations such as the ecology groups mentioned earlier, with ties to new businesses and to outside businesses that are investing in Żywiec.

These organizations are resources for the classes as different strategies for representing and contesting community authority are played out in part through the offices of these organizations. The organizations are in return affected by the classes' decisions about strategies.

The Habsburgs Are Coming! Privatization of the Żywiec Brewery

An example of class conflict around community responses to national-level policies was the reaction to the news that the Żywiec Brewery would be privatized in 1991. In the decision about which kind of privatization plan would be followed for the brewery, the issue of the

Habsburgs as the prewar owners surfaced. One kind of privatization plan was for property to be returned to its prewar owners, and many Żywiec residents began to wonder if this would be the plan for the brewery. The possibility of a return of Habsburg heirs to Żywiec seemed to answer many fears about privatization and lack of patronage in the community, now that the political and economic realms were being decentralized.

The characterization of the Habsburg era as a golden age for Żywiec was not relayed to me only by members of the cultural elite. Many residents of Żywiec, particularly those older than forty-five, repeatedly told me how wonderful the archduke was. On one occasion, I was taking a bus to a tiny village near Żywiec to see the national forest and a small cultural center there, when I became engaged in conversation with a quite elderly peasant woman who lived in that village. When I told her that I was going to the cultural center in her village, she replied that I should really visit the church, because it was one of the few remaining old, wooden churches in the region, and she was very proud of it. I asked her how old it was, and she had no idea. What she could tell me, however, was that the archduke had paid for some renovations on it when she was a young girl, and that his wife had personally obtained the altar cloth for the village and hired foresters to take care of the wild national forest near the village proper. During the course of my fieldwork, I heard so much of this motif of the "kind but stern patron" and his "gracious and beautiful wife" that I jokingly dubbed it the "archduke was such a great guy" motif. For some time, I doubted that I would ever persuade my older informants from the cultural elite to tell me about anything other than the archduke and their position during the Habsburg era.

The local identification with the Habsburg family, however, had ramifications in the postsocialist period far beyond mere "golden-oldie-ism." When the time came to privatize the Żywiec Brewery in 1991, local Habsburg sympathy erupted and contested the national-level plans for the privatization.[12] A group of Żywiec residents apparently believed that the privatization certainly should have been carried out as a return of the brewery to the previous owners (the Habsburg descendants) rather than as a public stock sale. They contacted the remaining children of the archduke to encourage them to contest the Polish state's plan. Only one heir was interested enough to become involved, and he reportedly hired a Polish attorney to sue the state for the right to reclaim the property under the law about return of nationalized property to the previous owner. This lawsuit failed because the brewery was seized during the war by the Nazis, and it was never in fact returned to the Habsburgs after that. Technically, therefore, it was not seized and nationalized by the socialist Polish People's Republic—it had passed straight into the hands of the Polish People's Republic from the Nazis and was not eligible to be reclaimed by prewar owners.[13]

The privatization went through in 1991, with the effects Żywiec residents feared: many benefits to employees were cut, and many employees were laid off as a result of mechanization of work that previously required employees. However, the reputation of the Żywiec privatization as highly successful financially could be used by neocapitalist town planners in their attempts to bring more foreign investment into Żywiec. In 1994, when Polish laws changed to allow foreign investment in alcohol-producing companies, the Heineken brewing company immediately purchased 25 percent of the Żywiec Brewery's stock. This introduction of foreign capital was exactly what neocapitalists had in mind to bolster their reputations as people who could bring Żywiec into the international economic scene.

TRADITIONALISM AND IDENTITY

Local class conflict over tradition and identity in response to national political-economic change is a widespread phenomenon both inside and outside the postsocialist countries, and there is a wealth of literature on revival or re-entrenchment of traditional identities in the face of encroaching global capitalism.[14] It is true that in many ways, the re-entrenchments in Żywiec in the eras depicted here are comparable to Third World responses to colonial and neocolonial forces: several national polities over the past few centuries have attempted to drain the local economy for the benefit of the core; armed resistance has been futile; local political elites have had an advantage in shaping the community's relations with the outside forces, and they have been in a position to shape the ethnic re-entrenchment to suit their own pursuit of power. Furthermore, in both the Second and the Third Worlds, power conflicts between existing and newly emerging classes are often framed in terms of tradition versus modernity. What makes this case of class conflict different from many others, however, is the preexistence of small-scale capitalism, the particular European context of political economy, and the context of ethnicities of whiteness.

Both inside and outside Eastern Europe, there are many discussions of ethnic-regional versus national identity and political-economic change that compare closely to the Żywiec case. Many case studies of ethnic identities used to resist nation-state policies come from the literature on the Third World or involve the movements of members of Third World ethnic groups to First World nations. Because of the distinctive place of race in these discussions, they are not entirely suitable in discussing this community in Poland, which is not "racially" different from other Poles. Additionally, Poland is within Europe (though a part of Europe that has been radically "otherized"), and geographic placement can have substantial influence on political, economic, and cultural change. We may be moving toward a world where imagined communities (Anderson 1983) and spaces of representation (Lefebvre 1974) are just as important as physical communities and physical space, but we are not there yet, and the underlying importance of positioning and proximity has not yielded entirely to postmodern pastiche. The globalizing logic of supranational entities such as the European Union and NATO affect both core and peripheral nations in Europe, and Poland is subject to these same forces.

Thus, I believe that the most appropriate comparative cases of community identity versus the nation-state would come from elsewhere in the European periphery, from such places as Spain, Portugal, Greece, and Ireland, as well as from other postsocialist regions. There are similar processes underlying the sweeping changes in the concepts of the nation in the Western European experience with the establishment of the European Union and, in the Eastern Bloc, the casting off of ties to the former Soviet Union. The merging of political and economic boundaries associated with the European Union in Western Europe, such as currencies and passports, has produced anxiety over patrolling political, ethnic, and linguistic borderlands. Ideals of linguistic purity have become prominent as populations attempt to delineate their national identities in opposition to the integrating tendencies of the European Union (Coulmas 1991, Irvine and Gal 1994, Albert 1996). Eastern Europeans must reconstruct national identities that were maintained in opposition to socialism into forms that resonate with current national ideals and, on the cultural landscape, construct forums for displays of identity, such as performances of folklore that claim an ancient past (Maners 1996, Cahalen 1996). Some common themes that can be traced in both Eastern and Western Europe are changing collective memories and national identities, counterhegemonic discourses attempting to manipulate mass historical consciousness, and the affects of changing attitudes toward authority and freedom under different historical circumstances (Galbraith 1996, Hendry 1996, Lefkowitz 1996).

The Żywiec case opens a window to view how elite class change happened during socialism in the Polish countryside and how it is happening in postsocialism. This case can also provide information on how smaller identities, ethnic and regional, were related to nationalism in socialist Poland and how surviving smaller identities are faring in the post–Cold War era. More interestingly, this case study sheds light on how these two processes interact—how class change affects or effects changes in ethnic and regional identities. In examining this interaction in the Żywiec case, it is important to understand the extent to which the interaction of class and identity in this community will be similar to that in other places in the world. Two major factors might make the Żywiec case radically different from communities elsewhere in the world—the history of socialism and the fact that Żywiec is in Europe. The history of socialism in Eastern Europe, though differing widely in the countries there, has had some similarities with regard to class change outside the major cities. We need to understand these similarities to start to compare Eastern European cases with cases elsewhere.

Anthropologists have undertaken some revealing studies of the maintenance and reproduction of Eastern European class and community during socialism in Eastern Europe. Just as I have done in the Żywiec case, small village studies have consistently highlighted the ways in which presocialist class relations were maintained during socialism. The method of participant-observation has been essential in allowing scholars to understand and portray the complex relations of class and capital under socialism. The sometimes extremely subtle effects that presocialist social, cultural, and symbolic capital have on the balance of power in socialist villages is strikingly similar in descriptions across the region. For example, in a Romanian village, Kideckel (1993) shows that some members of the village, the presocialist wealthy peasants, continued to have the ability to mobilize the labor of their fellow townspeople and villagers. In part this was based on differential retention of economic capital, and in part on differential access to jobs that provided excellent resources for some families under state socialism.

Taking a different tack in her investigation of class processes in a peasant village in a southern Polish region not far from the Żywiec region, Carole Nagengast (1991) agrees that presocialist class distinctions continued through into socialism:

> Much of the class stratification among peasant farmers in place on the eve of World War II still remains. In villages, the overt links of class to economic capital have been partially reproduced but have also been supplemented and transformed by other forms of capital, today as in the past. During

the forty-five years after the advent of the socialist state, these relationships were disguised as simply natural differences among farmers in individual ability, ambition, educational achievements, and success in accumulating social, cultural and occupational prestige. The veiled process of stratification, the political struggle over meaning, masks the symbolic nature of cultural capital. Further, it accentuates the necessity of examining the accumulation, transmission, and reproduction of all forms of capital such that social identity and class relations have been continuous even when they appear to have been disrupted. (19–20)

Nagengast is able to show how presocialist village elites deployed a range of kinds of capital that had carried over relatively intact from the presocialist to the socialist era. In urban core areas in the Eastern Bloc, however, where the state socialist apparatus was able to more fully penetrate the population, it is entirely probable that some class relations were disrupted under socialism. Nevertheless, I agree with her contention, certainly for peripheral areas such as Nagengast's Wola Pławska and the subject of this study, Żywiec, that "the saliency of capital, class and class domination has been upheld in a superficially altered but fundamentally unchanged fashion. Therefore, in spite of a split between the possession of economic and cultural/social/symbolic capital between 1944 and 1989, the apparent complete break with the pre-World War II class structure in Poland was largely chimerical" (1991, 20).

This case study of Żywiec builds on these previous works on class in Eastern Europe, investigating not only how presocialist elites brought class relations forward into the socialist era, but also seeking to understand whether and how these local elites have been able to maintain their class status in the postsocialist era. Class change in both the socialist and the postsocialist eras can be compared to cases in other parts of the world, if we understand the basic principle that class change is being driven by changes in national economic policies that are themselves the results of large-scale political change. Class change in socialist Poland is not very comparable to, for example, class changes in Western Europe during the Industrial Revolution. It would be fair, however, to compare the ways that class changed in socialist Poland (as a result of a foreign power directly influencing governmental structure and policies) to class changes in countries under European colonialism when "native" individuals were being used to run the government and economy, but all policies were designed to serve the needs of a foreign power.

Turning to ethnic identities during the socialist era, researchers have shown that there was a great deal of variability in whether ethnic identities were strengthened or weakened under socialism, depending on the way nationalism and socialism interacted. Several studies have shown that in the former Soviet Union, the creation of ethnic-nationalist states as socialist republics, as well as other Soviet policies, actually increased the expression of ethnic identity because they were associated with Soviet-sponsored nationalist states.[15] This was despite the fact that official Soviet rhetoric stated that nationalist identities would disappear as socialism advanced. Similarly, in Eastern Europe, the Romanian identity was strengthened vis-à-vis other ethnic identities in that country after the creation of Romania. Evidence is ambiguous in Yugoslavia, where some blurring of ethnic lines under Tito, especially in urban areas, is balanced by evidence of strong retention of ethnic differences in the countryside, most strikingly by the post-Tito wars. This is, of course, in part because ethnic differences were linked to religious differences among Serbs, Croats, and other Yugoslavs, a difference difficult to erase.

In Poland, the Polish identity was strengthened relative to other ethnicities after the recreation of the Polish state after World War I. One important study by Chris Hann (1985) investigates the interaction of a number of ethnic groups in a region in southeastern Poland after World War II and charts changes in their identities during socialism. In this study, ethnic groups that had no link to a nationalist state tended to gradually disappear as people found the identities less meaningful than the Polish national identity. Hann focuses on class to some extent, stating that

> the Ukrainian ethnic minority is by no means as satisfactorily integrated as official sources claim, although there are signs that in the long run the ethnic cleavages will weaken, as regional differences within the Polish population have weakened already. It was also suggested that new cleavages might appear in village society as a result of recent economic policies; the present divisions between occupational groups and a potential for class differentiation within the private sector could be followed by a polarisation of sectors, a situation in which class distinctions were more conspicuous within the socialist sector than amongst the successors to the peasantry. (1985, 156)

Hann sees the importance of occupational positions in maintaining distinctions among ethnic groups, but he believes that these distinctions will fade over time. Perhaps because he is drawing a "big picture" of the differences between groups, he does not thoroughly problematize class relationships within these ethnic groups and how these might play a role in the maintenance of ethnic identity. Instead, he focuses more on differences, such as language, religion, and cultural practices, and on state ideologies.

These issues raise questions as to how ethnic identities that retained some strength through the socialist era might be maintained or weakened in the postsocialist era. Bruce Grant (1995), in his study of Sakhalin Island on the Soviet Union's far eastern perimeter, shows in a similar fashion to the Żywiec case how the Sakhalin identity changes and adapts to changing Soviet nationalist policies over nearly a century and how the identity continues to have meaning in the post-Soviet era. Though the Sakhalin ethnic identity was not linked to a nationalist one, it provided the islanders with a sense of difference during various eras of Soviet identity policies. The Sakhalin and Góral cases raise the question of why these particular identities were able to be retained when other local, nonnationalist ethnicities clearly faded in the face of strong nationalism. It is possible that the fact that both identities were geographically on the borders of their nations played a part—as Donnan and Wilson (1999) point out, nationalism is always weaker on the margins of modern nation-states.

Somewhat in contrast to the Sakhalin Island case, though, in Żywiec, the community identity is not strongly unified, and the class indicators of identity remain strong. In a strikingly similar case to Żywiec, Richard Maddox (1993) looks at the entrenchment of "traditional" Andalusian culture during the political and economic changes brought by the new post-Franco regime in Spain, in which the community's response to the national economic policies was to become economically insular while marketing their folklorized identity to outsiders. The Andalusian identity and the meaning of tradition in his study have been reworked in various historical periods in Aracena, a small Andalusian town. Maddox examines the transformation of old elite from feudal landowners to prominent businessmen in the context of Spain's transition in the late 1970s and early 1980s from authoritarian dictatorship to liberal parliamentary democracy. He sees class interests as responding to changes at the national level and influencing, but not determining, the construction of identity. Traditional authority, in the Andalusian case, masks the class position of local elites and their role as mediators with outsiders and national institutions.

Maddox's study, like this one, points to the particularistic character of subnational communities: the power of government policy fades in the face of local resources available to accomplish objectives, and family, class, and community techniques and strategies for accomplishing some semblance of those objectives may differ radically from the government's stated policy as to how efforts were to be organized. This is true for Żywiec during both the socialist and postsocialist eras. For Maddox (1993), following Antonio Gramsci and Raymond Williams, traditionalism is "a set of strategies that involve using cultural materials from the past to authorize contemporary relations of domination [within the community]." He explains that in the community he studied, "even though promoting Aracena's reputation as a highly traditional community helps attract tourists and serves to incorporate the town into the contemporary Spanish and European socioeconomic order, traditionalism for most townspeople continues to be the primary means to assert cultural distance and difference [between the community and the nation-state]" (259). These different purposes of class politics, economic benefits of tourism, and establishing regional difference from the state is evident in Żywiec as well. In Maddox's case, the use of traditionalism as resistance to the contemporary nation-state fails: the community is still firmly integrated into the nation-state. In Żywiec, the case is more complicated. Under the Nazi occupation and Soviet socialism, we can see the success of traditionalism as community resistance to the nation-state's political and economic policies. In terms of the so-called shock therapy of postsocialist Poland, traditionalism (the retention of the sense of ethnic difference between the community and the state) has had some limited success, but the impact of globalization on the community cannot be denied or reversed, and changes in class structure have been eroding support for the contemporary meaning of the Góral identity. The Góral identity still has meaning for the community's *past*, however, which means that traditionalism in Żywiec can also be understood to include using cultural materials from the past to contest and negotiate the community's place in prior political economic systems, as well as in contemporary relations of domination between the community and the contemporary Polish and global political-economic order.

Traditionalism has in some sense an opposite—modernity. Both traditionalism and modernity are idioms through which elite class conflict is enacted in Żywiec, and both are visions of what the future of Żywiec's relation to the nation-state and global capitalism will entail. The class conflict is between the pre–World War II elite, who are now (again) owners of small community businesses, and the newly emerging (postsocialist) class of neocapitalists in Żywiec, who are the intermediaries between the community and international capital. Of course, some of the former prewar elite have gained neocapitalist employment, so there is not a clean break between these two classes. The neocapitalist class fraction is forming as the prewar elite fraction is changed by postsocialism. Traditionalism, in Żywiec, means ethnic re-entrenchment, but in the hands of the prewar elite, it also stands for community insularity (resisting the penetration of international capital). Modernity, in the hands of the neocapitalists, stands for encouraging international investment in Żywiec. Both the prewar elite and the neocapitalists are interested in weakening Żywiec's ties with the Polish nation-state, because the state has been a declining source of funds and an increasing burden on the community.

When the prewar elite use the cultural/traditional as a frame for response to change, this use is hegemonic; the elite's assumption of authority, use of traditionalism, and shaping of local action and local identity to benefit their own class position is below the level of consciousness. The feeling of loss of tradition is genuine to them, and evokes responses that to an outsider might seem solely self-interested because these responses differentially benefit local elites. Though events that emphasized the local identity, such as folk festivals, arts festivals, and attempts to renovate or preserve buildings with historical meaning, certainly did reemphasize the traditions in which prewar elite had a great deal of influence and authority in the community, the prewar elite also seemed to take real pride in their community's history.

Local elites, both the prewar elite and neocapitalists, are restricted in that they are working through a cultural frame of traditionalism and identity. The frame is hegemonic in that the classes are situated inside it in a community that is steeped in it. Even the neocapitalists in Żywiec must somehow deal with the frame of traditional ethnic identity and deal with those who are the bearers of authority within that frame. Those groups who have had authority for many generations are also the groups that have in the past shaped the identity to best suit their needs and bolster their position in the community authority structure. Likewise, the new meanings of tradition that they can create exist in only a few general configurations, because these new meanings must be negotiated within the community. Though issues of power mean that some members of the community have more influence than others, it is still not possible yet to completely refigure the identity, no matter how beneficial it might be to class interests.

These issues link to larger themes of the interaction of national or even global political economy and local identity, the articulation between local customs of authority and strategies of adaptation, and the ties between ethnicity, class, family, and the national agenda. The prewar elite are trying to simultaneously recreate their prewar ties of patrimonial authority in the community and relying on them to bolster their positions of authority as small business owners within a community that is newly capitalist, or at least newly interacting with global capitalism. In commenting on the influence of local elites over local affairs in Aracena, for example, Maddox (1993) states:

> Local businesspeople, officials in the town hall, and professionals are taking a leading role in cultivating local customs. In their efforts, they are especially eager to encourage the young and underemployed men and women who are anxious about their futures to become involved in the cultural life of the community. This enables the members of the leading group to present themselves as persons with the collective interests of the community at heart and to assume the role of mediators between the townspeople and the outsiders who are imagined to have primarily self-interested motives. Thus, in reanimating traditional rites, celebrations, and images of personhood and community, the leading members of the community have occupied the high ground of patronage and once again managed to maintain their influence over local affairs. (261–62)

The Żywiec prewar elite, though a part of what might be considered Żywiec's "civil society," were nothing so simple as a "government in waiting" in Żywiec during the socialist era, ready to take over local politics after the PZPR left power. True, some members were able to obtain bureaucratic positions in the new town government after 1989. Their authority could not survive the disillusionment of Żywiecers with the new regime, however, and this group needed to reestablish the justification for their power and authority. The prewar elites ultimately failed in their continuing attempts to parlay their traditional patronage authority into bureaucratic positions of authority as politicians, because the Solidarity town government (made up primarily of prewar elites) was replaced by the neocapitalists. The result was a face-off between two local classes with differing economic priorities: the neocapitalists interested in bringing in foreign capital and the prewar elite interested in preserving some measure of community autonomy. The prewar elite and the neocapitalists also had differing bases of authority: traditionalism versus expertise in understanding global capitalism. Without Żywiec's industrial base, it is likely that community change there would have looked much more like that in Maddox's Aracena, in which elites were able to parlay their patronage authority into bureaucratic authority as local businesspeople, town hall officials, and other professionals. The classes in Żywiec also represent a basic split between local and national political and economic viewpoints.

Ideas about tradition and modernity are another cultural resource intertwined with Góral identity, which Żywiec classes (particularly the neocapitalists and the prewar elite) maneuver and manipulate. These two classes use ideas about tradition, modernity, and local identity to characterize themselves through various arguments to other Żywiec residents and also to outsiders as the "true" inheritors of authority in Żywiec. The classes have different ideological bases of support and recourse to different claims of moral authority, and they weave these two together in contrasting ways to support their claims to bureaucratic authority in this community. The prewar elite espouse a "traditionalist" approach to Góral identity, claiming that the meaning of Góralism is both fixed and relevant in the contemporary era. The neocapitalists, however, claim that "modernity" (the capitalist era) has made the Góral identity part of the folkloric past. Currently, the particular meaning of Góralism is in flux, with no clear hegemonic fixity, because the different classes represent different relations to a constellation of outside forces. They fight over the Góral identity as it is intertwined with defining the community relationship to these outside forces.

The formation of the neocapitalists as a distinct and competing class fraction to the prewar elite is a process that needs to be explained. Given more or less the same social resources, one might think that *all* of the prewar elite could have become neocapitalists in the new era. One of the major differences between Aracena and Żywiec, for example, is that in Żywiec, the neocapitalists are challenging the role of the old elite as community mediators with the outside, whereas in Aracena, the whole old elite seems to have retained their authority. The penetration of large-scale capitalism injects the outside directly into the Żywiec community, thus creating a different power base, which the old elite opposed bringing to Żywiec and over which they have not gained direct power. The Heineken brewery and other sources of international capital can penetrate directly into the town, affecting the lives of employees and other residents without going through the old elite. They thus are not easily swayed by the desires or the authority of the old elite. This leads to a different style of interaction (Foucault would call it a different technology of discipline). The old elite cannot appeal to the representatives of international capital on a personal basis infused with community cultural values of authority. Instead, they have to find some way to "talk their talk"—threaten them in a

business-oriented way if they want power or influence over these
businesses. The point here is to realize that there are multiple and
complex meanings of behavior in the postsocialist context: culture,
community, and tradition have become conversant with class interests
to produce a polyvalent identity struggle.

The neocapitalists are forced into a more complex strategy for
building their authority because they have no access to traditional
authority as it is recognized in the community. These businessmen
(and some few businesswomen) in some senses have broken away
from the mode of distinct community and moral economy, and they
are interested in creating links with international business. They are
drawing on their belief that those who know how to operate in the
new political economy of Poland will gain authority (both political
and cultural) and will gain power. Thus, through attempting to bring
in foreign capital, the neocapitalists wish to be seen as power brokers.

In Żywiec, both bureaucratic and traditional authority structures
exist in an uneasy balance. Economic and cultural capital also coexist
and interact uneasily. People in Żywiec are wary of bureaucracy, wary
of political and economic change that moves away from tradition and
toward global capitalism, and wary of the encroachment of Western
European and American culture on their way of life. In short, one
might state that they are wary of the coming of modernity. Yet this is
the very idiom the neocapitalists are attempting to use to counter the
traditionalism touted by prewar elite. Despite their misgivings, many
Żywiecers are drawn to the idea of modernization, and, thus, the
neocapitalists are able to use images of modernity to bolster their
claims to authority.

Ferdinand Tonnies (1957 [1887]) perhaps best captured the general sense of the modern versus the premodern in his descriptions of
gemeinschaft and *gesellschaft*—the organic moral unity of small-scale,
close-knit communal groups pitted against the impersonal, instrumental, compartmentalized ties fostered in more institutionally complex
settings. More than one hundred years later, Coleman (1993a) repro-
duces this argument perfectly when he states that modern organizations use "rules, laws, supervision, formal incentives, and sanctions by
designated agents" (9), whereas premodern organizations are based
on "coercion, constraint, and negative sanctions, under the oppressive
blanket of closed communities" (14). Even though a strict Durkheimian
distinction between simple premodern societies and modern complex
societies has been rejected by most social scientists as theorists delve
more deeply into the cross-cutting ways in which power is expressed,
maintained, and built through the social structures that depend on

differences of gender, ethnicity, age, and other hierarchies, there remains a fundamental disjuncture between bureaucratic and affectual strategies of authority. The premodern situation is generally conceived of in terms of interpersonal ties, which are traditional, communal, personal, and family- or community-oriented; modern ties are more impersonal, contractual, and bureaucratic, including rational rules and associations. Modernity and rationality have even been seen (in a return to the nineteenth century fin d'siècle attitudes) as end states that will result in the best of all possible worlds and the "end of history" (Fukuyama 1992).

These conceptions of tradition and modernity construct a false dichotomy about community leadership, and they misunderstand both modernity and tradition. I have already discussed to some extent the role of community leaders in shaping identity. The current, "modern" period is no different from other periods in that different kinds of capital get mobilized in different ways, such that almost anyone can create meaning within families, but only leaders have the resources to actively institute changes in communities. Many people will attempt to create meanings for themselves, their families, and their communities in the face of or in support of encroaching rationalism and modernity, and the family, civil society, and state are battle sites where attempts to construct common meanings will be fought out. Even in the premodern there has always been a role for leaders in creating community meaning. The political, economic, and social projects that are part of modernity do seem to result in some loss of meaning, some loss of community feeling, and in Żywiec, this translates into both neocapitalists believing that the Góral identity is part of the past and nonelites believing that they are not "real" Górals because they do not speak entirely in dialect or wear "traditional" clothing. But as globalization progresses, local and even national leaders have proportionally less influence, resulting in new possibilities for meaning and new kinds of definitions for communities. In modernity, the meaning that is produced, whether by leaders or organically, is more fragmented and mutable.

A theorist of modernity who focuses this multivalent meaning of modernity is Néstor García Canclini. In contrast to other theorists of modernity, he states that modernism "is not the expression of socioeconomic modernization but *the means by which the elites take charge of the intersection of different historical temporalities and try to elaborate a global project with them*" (1995, 46; italics in original). In Żywiec, the process is riddled with class conflict over which elites should or can do this. I argue that in Żywiec, the idea of "modernity" is a cultural resource; elite Żywiec classes maneuver and manipulate to character-ize themselves as modern in different ways, and, hence, through vari-ous arguments, as the "true" inheritors of authority in Żywiec. Just as García-Canclini argues for Latin America, modernity in Żywiec does not mean just a move toward bureaucracy—it is an attitude and a capacity for mobilizing power differently. An exemplar might be the PZPR leader who had adopted a new crusade (the environment, with which few take offense) and had successfully built ties with both elite classes in town to recoup his political losses.

Another example of a new venue for mobilizing power is the new regional newspaper, the *Żywiec Gazette*. The founder of the news-paper, Pan Jan, began this project immediately after the 1989 elections. He was able to expand his distribution to communities of Góral emigrés living in several countries abroad, including the United States. Górals who had settled in New York, Chicago, and San Francisco were pur-chasing this regional newspaper, which seemed to be a child of de-mocracy—a direct demonstration of the fact that they could now get information about what was going on in their old home community. Previously, during the socialist era, they knew that letters they wrote to and received from relatives would probably be opened and read by government agents, and they could never be sure how their relatives were censoring their own letters so as not to get in trouble with the state. Now they could find out just what was going on, and, more important, they could see how democracy and capitalism were shap-ing up on their home turf. Even better, parts of the paper were written in the familiar Góral dialect, with amusing folkloric cartoons that ro-manticized the "old country" for them.

This audience from abroad turned into a political wedge for Pan Jan when he decided to run for public office. His candidacy was strongly supported by emigrés, who wrote to the *Żywiec Gazette* to tell local people that Pan Jan was an exemplar of the new era, a neocapitalist, obviously a man with business sense, and generally someone for whom they should vote. With such strong foreign sup-port (which at the time was convincing to many Żywiecers who were confused about the implications of the political and economic decen-tralization), Pan Jan was able to mount a strong campaign in 1991 among those who were procapitalism. Intriguingly, he was listed officially as a candidate for a communist-successor party. Thus, he was also able to portray himself as a leftist candidate, in touch with the pain of those who had suffered from shock therapy, which would be most of the town. Finally, in a last postmodern touch, when I inter-viewed him, he declared that he was not a member of the communist-successor party. He said that he was in fact a member from a party that represented the concerns of retirees and other elderly people who were suffering from the reforms.

What is certain is that during previous eras, Pan Jan would not have had such luck in playing all sides. A political playing field that seemed more starkly defined during the martial law period in the 1980s (are you for Solidarity or for martial law?) has turned into a chaotic melee where individuals are able to adopt and combine rhetoric from different sources, draw on conflicting audiences, and still manage to gain political power. Pan Jan was elected to the national parliament and was active on the local scene as well.

Conclusion

In Żywiec, the prewar elite class is trying to create authority by drawing on premodern claims, such as ties to the Habsburgs, their prewar positions as community leaders, and their socialist era position as community intellectuals, in particular as keepers of the history of the town and of Góralism. This class took on the task of running different town clubs and organizations, many of which were concerned with preserving Góralism within the community. They also, by virtue of running these clubs, had the authority to present this ethnic identity to outsiders and insiders in specific manners and position themselves as the appropriate representatives of that ethnicity. This demonstrates the ability of politics and class to interact with senses of peoplehood in a hegemonically intertwined way.

By drawing on the strength of this authority to convince local businesses to give them money, the prewar elite class provided an argument and a reflection of their authority, which could only add to their authority if they succeeded. Alternatively, if they failed, they were in a position to proclaim that it was not their authority that was lacking. Rather, the businesses had lost their sense of Góral responsibility to the community.

In opposition to this, the neocapitalists have drawn a picture of their political and economic expertise in the new era. They too engage with the idea of Góral identity, but they are attempting to relegate it to the historic past. For them, folk festivals are opportunities to expand publicity about Żywiec, bring in tourist dollars, and (as I show in the next chapter) cement ties with sister cities that will bring economic cooperation to Żywiec. They see themselves as the bridge to the future for Żywiec, the ones who have the outside contacts and the skills to draw foreign capital into Żywiec to create jobs. Their problem is to control the effects of foreign capital once it is introduced to Żywiec.

The two classes remain locked in a struggle for community authority at the moment. There is some possibility, of course, that the prewar elite will begin to believe that their way of life would not be threatened by more interaction with the outside and that they will give up the struggle for community isolation and autonomy. Analyzing the class underpinnings of their situation, however, shows that this is not a likely outcome as long as their authority is threatened by the neocapitalists. With no other way to maintain their power in the community, the ideas of Góral ethnicity and community moral economy may be the only resources they have to work with.

Chapter 4

◄○►

Nonelites, Family Networks, and Identity

The restructuring of the Polish political-economic system since the end of the Cold War has had a great impact not only on the large-scale factors of the national economy, such as state enterprises, and on the scale of communities and classes, but also on the microeconomic strategizing of individuals and families. In Żywiec, as in most of Poland, the ways in which people respond to the effects of these structural changes are mediated largely by family units. There are tensions and tugs in this relationship between the familial self and the individual self: individuals are shaped by families, and families in turn are reshaped by those individuals. Other factors, such as gender, age, and education, are also manifested within the boundaries of family decision making. Through the lens of family, we can understand how class works in the community. Unlike elite classes, the members of nonelite classes in Żywiec have little capital—economic, cultural, social, or symbolic—they can mobilize to strategically position themselves in times of change, or even just to "make do" when times are hard. Family networks are thus of major importance for survival for nonelite families, to an even greater degree than for elite families. Family is a key to understanding nonelite class structure in Żywiec.

This chapter is a counterweight to the previous chapter, in that it focuses primarily on nonelite classes. Through case studies, I show

how family strategizing works as a response to the economic changes resulting from state restructuring policies, that is, the changes in the job market in Poland and the effects of new economic policies on the different classes in Żywiec. I explore the way economic strategies are generally differentially accessible to individuals based on their gender, education, language abilities, and age, but all within the structure of class and family networks. However individualized the strategies themselves, they are never acted on solely by individuals, but are developed and implemented within the context and boundaries of family groups, which can aid or constrain individual efforts.

Unlike in other parts of Poland, the ideal of Góralism is a symbolic resource available to families in the Żywiec region. When there are disputes or differences within nonelite families in Żywiec about appropriate economic responses, Góral ethnic identity can be used to bolster one or more competing claims by couching the proposal in terms of traditionalism. Ideas of proper Góral conduct are closely intertwined in family networks in this region of Poland. I show in a variety of cases how individuals use the idea of Góral ethnic identity to aid them in their attempts to embed new economic strategies with traditional meaning, thus making these strategies more palatable to others in their families.

The distinction between a felt, or hegemonic, sense of Góral identity and a folklorized, contested, ideological sense of Góral identity is central to understanding why nonelite classes in Żywiec are willing to go along with elite class struggles around the identity. In this chapter, I explore the hegemonic sense of Góral identity as it is expressed by the nonelite classes in Żywiec, and I show how this unspoken sense of identity is in the process of change in the postsocialist era. I distinguish it from the ideologically contested "public" face of Góral ethnicity that is the target of elite class conflict.

HOUSE HUNTING

The importance of networks of family and friends, even (or perhaps especially) in the postsocialist era, is illustrated by my own search for a place to stay in Żywiec. I had been warned by other researchers that it was particularly difficult to find accommodations in Poland outside the cities, and it had even been suggested to me that I find an apartment in Kraków, purchase a car, and drive to Żywiec several times a week to conduct interviews. I was determined to find a place in Żywiec, however, and optimistically hoped that my contacts there would allow me access to the information network on housing. I knew that there was no local paper listing apartments for rent and that there were likely to be few available prospects for me. I soon learned just how hard it can be to accomplish tasks in Żywiec without close kin and friends.

The bus ride to Żywiec from Kraków takes two and a half to three hours. You almost have to take the bus, because there is only one train a day. As it leaves Kraków, the bus travels along one of the few highways in Poland for a half hour, until the highway runs out and turns into a two-lane road that winds up from the broad plain through the foothills of the Beskid Mountains. The bus stops in Kalwaria Zebrzydowska, where one can see the huge, famous monastery, home of a Good Friday pilgrimage where thousands of people spend the day praying in a pilgrimage through the Catholic stations of the cross. Next, the bus stops in Wadowice, the birthplace of Pope John Paul II. As the bus continues on up into the mountains, it passes back and forth over the dams on the Soła River, which flows back into the Vistula River. Finally, it pulls into the Żywiec bus station, on the south side of town.

When I took this bus ride in the beginning of the fall of 1994, the weather in Kraków was turning frosty, and I knew that it would be even colder higher up, where Żywiec was situated. I was hardly prepared, however, for the way the rain turned into snow as the bus pulled into Żywiec. Fortunately for me (or so I thought), I wasn't going far in this weather.

During the summer, I had written to Pani Morawski,[1] the former director of the Ethnographic Museum, asking for help in finding housing. She was an elderly woman who was a family friend of the Sicińskis, a family I knew and was staying with in Kraków. She had been very encouraging about my project and promised me a great deal of help. I had also written to the current director of the Żywiec Castle Museum, with whom I had had a meeting the previous spring, and who had told me that the museum would help in any way it could. Pani Morawski had sent a postcard to the Sicińskis, saying that she had not yet found an apartment for me, but that I could rent a room at the youth hostel in Żywiec for a few weeks until I found some place more permanent. Before setting off to Żywiec, I had been trying to phone Pani Morawski for three days, but the phone lines from Kraków to Żywiec were not working. Finally, I had just decided to take the bus down to Żywiec, hoping that I could talk to her there and that I would be able to rent the hostel room on the spot. I got into town around noon and headed for the bureau where Pani Morawski volunteered.

When I got there, it was closed, so I went looking for her apartment. When I realized she wasn't home, I left a note saying that I was in town and would be staying at the hostel.

At the hostel, the manager told me that she had not discussed this with Pani Morawski, but that she could rent me a room that I would have to share with other travelers, at a rather expensive rate because I was a foreigner. This wasn't very useful for me, because I didn't want to have to worry about leaving my possessions in an unlocked room every day. I asked her if she knew of any other options for me, explaining that I was looking for long-term housing, but that I would certainly settle for short-term housing for the present. She at first said that there was nothing but the town hotel and a hostel at a sports facility, but then, after a few minutes of more talk, she gave me the name and address of a woman, Pani Babiuch, who was running a semilegal (unregistered) boarding house just two blocks away. As I was leaving the hostel, the cleaning woman curiously asked where I was from. I chatted with her for a few minutes, telling her my story and asking if she knew of a place to rent and if there were real estate agencies in town, as there are in larger Polish cities. She asked me what a real estate agency was (though I was using the Polish word, it was obviously unfamiliar to her), and when I explained, she assured me that such "modern" things weren't to be found in Żywiec.

I left my things in a locker at the hostel and walked over to talk to Pani Babiuch. I found her house, down a dirt lane behind the bus station, amid a collection of ramshackle buildings, some of which looked as though they had never been reconstructed after the destruction from World War II. Pani Babiuch, whom I interrupted as she was feeding her chickens and gossiping with her neighbor, looked at me dubiously and listened to my story. She told me that she could rent me a bed in a room with two other girls for several weeks, and suggested that perhaps when the girls left, I could rent the room for myself and my husband, who would be joining me in several months. I thanked her and told her that I would need to think about it, because she was willing to grant only limited cooking privileges and there was no telephone, which I thought I might need.

Next I dropped by the Castle Museum and talked to the director, who told me that he had not had any luck in locating a place for me. (I was certain that he had given no thought to it, though I had sent him several letters asking for help on the off chance that he might give it.) He suggested that I check with the tourist agency on the main town square, which handled private room rental in family homes during the summer tourist season. Again I brought up the possibility of my going to a real estate agency in town, but he told me that these agencies in Żywiec only handled sales and rental of business properties. By this time, it was three o'clock, and both the tourist agency and the real estate offices were closed. Considering my options, I decided that it would be best for me to stay at the boarding house for the time being and try the bureaus after a good night's sleep. At the boarding house, I met the two other young women who were staying in the room, who told me that they were from a village about an hour away by bus and lived in Żywiec during the week so that they could work in a knitting factory. They were the only ones in their families with paying jobs.

It wasn't possible for me to take out a newspaper ad to find housing because the town newspaper was printed only once a month. Most Żywiec residents rarely bought a daily newspaper in any case, so no one would think of listing rentals in one. Another option the Sicińskis had suggested was to put up posters advertising that an American couple was willing to pay American dollars for a year for housing—which, in retrospect, probably would have obtained quick results, but I was wary of distributing my address and apparent wealth all over Żywiec.

The next day, I set out in quest of more information about housing. I visited the tourist agency first, but the women there said that most people who rent out housing during the summer were not interested in renting out for long periods where they would have to share their cooking and bathroom facilities. Nevertheless, they said they would check around, and I left my name and boarding house address. Next, I went looking for real estate agencies. I found three, one of which was closed. At the other two, the owners explained that they primarily handled sales of apartments, not rentals, and at the moment they did not have any rental requests on hand. They suggested that I come back in a few days, to give them time to look around. Knowing that the informal gossip network was likely to be more fruitful for me, I talked to the curious secretaries at these agencies on the way out, told them who I was, who my contacts were in town (for the purposes of legitimization), and what I was looking for, and again left my name and address.

In the meantime, Pani Morawski returned to town and found me in the boarding house, spending most of my time on my hunt for housing. She suggested that she had a few friends who might be able to rent me housing, but she would need some more time to set it up, and she had to go out of town again. It was not until several days later, when I was rechecking one real estate agency that had actually found two possibilities, that I had any luck. The two "apartments" that were officially offered to me were rooms that were far out of town, tiny, and had no cooking facilities. However, a secretary called me to her desk after this and said that a friend of hers was thinking about renting part of her house, if I was the "right sort" of person. I told her that I would like to meet her friend, so the secretary got her coat and told her boss she'd be back soon. Out we went toward the main square, where I discovered that the friend was an elderly woman, Pani Zofia, who worked in the kiosk on the main square. Kiosks in Eastern Europe are combination newsstands, drug stores, and bus ticket vendors, as well as sellers of various other merchandise. They are often neighborhood—or in this case, town—gossip centers. Pani Zofia, the woman I was about to meet, had ruled her roost with Swiss precision for more than a decade.

Zofia grilled me about whether I was married, whether I had children yet, and if I could afford her price. The rent she requested seemed a little steep, but she promised my own entrance, kitchen, and indoor bathroom, which even had an electric hot water heater. She also said that she had a phone I would be able to use. It seemed perfect, so I agreed to meet her when she got off work. Later in the afternoon, I passed the kiosk again, and she invited me inside to talk more, asking about my family, my research, and my contacts in town. She was particularly pleased to hear that I knew the emeritus director of the Żywiec Castle Museum, Pani Morawski, who, as she put it, was "from one of the oldest families in town." Then she took me home, introduced me to her family, gave me some dinner, and finally showed me the apartment. It turned out to be an addition on the side of her house, with a furnished kitchen, bedroom, and bathroom, which she had purchased from the owners several years previously and renovated. I agreed immediately and said that I would move in the next day. I paid her the first month's rent, she gave me the key, and it was settled.

Over the following year, I was periodically invited by people I came to know well to move into apartments owned by themselves or their families. Almost all of these opportunities were offered to me by members of the prewar elite. Personal contact is the most common way of finding an apartment in Żywiec and in most of Poland, that is, renting an apartment from a family member or a friend of the family. Sometimes a couple and their small children, or an elderly person alone, will move in with other family members and rent out their apartment to raise cash. But it is very rare outside of large cities for people to rent apartments to or from strangers. Most people find housing in as idiosyncratic a way as I had. In fact, near the end of my stay in 1995, another researcher starting a project in Poland asked my advice on the subject of finding housing, and I felt unable to provide any that would be helpful. I described my experience and told her that the best way seemed to be through networks of family or friends, and if one did not have access to this, it seemed rather difficult to find housing outside the cities.

One of the striking aspects of this episode is how few results I obtained by going through official channels. In retrospect, part of this is a result of lack of supporting structure (i.e., local newspapers with rental advertisements available, rental agencies, chamber of commerce listings) for doing things such as renting apartments to people who are outside one's network of family and friends. Żywiec is in a position in which neither "communist" nor "capitalist" institutions could help me in my search for short-term housing. The official state channels for obtaining housing are more or less intact, but this only serves the interests of those looking for permanent housing. The new real estate agencies handle primarily business property sales and rental. It appears that either there simply is not enough demand for apartment rentals in Żywiec to warrant a rental agency, or so few people even consider the possibility of listing an available apartment publicly or looking for one through a public agency that third-party handling of apartment rentals would not create enough business to bother with. Indeed, as Pani Zofia explained to me both at the time and a year later as I was preparing to leave, she was not looking for just any renter and would not go through official channels to find one. She was looking for a childless married couple of good income, or a professional unmarried man, or even a small business to rent the property. She had decided to take a chance on me, because she knew Pani Morawski was an esteemed member of the community, because I was married but childless, and because I was a foreigner who she felt would definitely move out if there were too many problems.

I, on the other hand, at first attempted to use unofficial channels in house hunting, which did not work very well for me because my social networks were neither very strong nor wide, and I did not have much time to wait to see what might become available. I wanted to find something and move in within a matter of weeks, not months or years (the time that most people seeking housing are able to wait). Official channels yielded few results as well. In the end, I found suitable housing through unofficial channels, which was overpriced and not well appointed by the community standards. As my network of friends grew, I was made aware of several other opportunities for housing, should I want to move, or should I return to the community for another stint of fieldwork.

This anecdote illustrates the importance of family ties in day-to-day life in this community. We can also see how family works as the key through which class structure is reinforced for both elites and nonelites. Had I not been vouched for through my acquaintance with Pani Morawski, Pani Zofia might have hesitated in offering housing to a stranger in the community. But more important, if I had been on closer terms with members of the prewar elite, I would have had several choices of apartments to borrow or rent in Żywiec. These people clearly had greater housing resources available within their family networks. For the nonelite in Żywiec, finding housing was a major undertaking, in which family networks were essential to finding information and even raising the cash to afford the new place to live.

FAMILY AND THE REPRODUCTION OF CLASS

Class plays an important role in determining the possibilities for families in Żywiec in the postsocialist environment. Families who are members of different classes have different kinds and amounts of resources, which results in the reproduction of class through family structure. Families of the prewar elite class in Żywiec have been likely to value higher education and likely to try to get their children accepted into the most competitive high school in Żywiec, but this was true in the socialist years as well. Today, a major advantage to membership in the prewar elite is that reprivatization laws have resulted in the return of property, including homes and businesses, to those from whom it was confiscated by the Polish state for nationalization after the end of World War II. Other important variables, such as age and gender, also tend to structure the possibilities available to many Poles, and I show how these are mediated in important ways through class and family networks.

Most theorists agree that the importance of family networks in economic strategizing has hardly changed in the past one hundred years in Poland, although the organizing basis for the economy has gone from prewar feudalism to emerging capitalism to socialism to global capitalism. Carole Nagengast (1991) notes that there "is no reason to expect rural economic structures or class membership to be stable over generations" (78) but then goes on to explain how families reproduce their class standing: "A family seeks to keep its position, its standing in the social world through various strategies: procreation, education as a tactic of cultural placement, or more purely economic measures, such as investments, savings and so forth" (80). She states that in the village in which she did fieldwork, in eastern Galicia, "class differences associated with economic and social differentiation occurring two generations ago have been maintained to this day through the elaboration of various strategies of reproduction. Further, the method of family case studies reveals some of the mechanisms by which families keep their place in the community over time" (81). The same links between family strategies and class pertain in Żywiec.

The family serves as a support network, a resource bank, and a "back door" (as opposed to the official front door) contact through which goods and services can be procured when official channels are slower or unworkable, which is the normal situation in Poland. Christopher Hann (1995) notes that although significant modernization had taken place during the socialist period in Eastern Europe, "specific socialist patterns of development have invested the extended family with continued significance as a residential grouping and a primary group in society" (104). Two of these socialist patterns of development were a serious shortage of housing and the requirement that almost all women work outside the home. Inside the home, however, the sexual division of labor has remained the same, with women responsible for child care, elder care, and housekeeping. Three-generation households were a solution to this problem during socialism, because the grandmother could perform much of the tasks at home. Hann states:

> The official retiring age was younger than is usual in the west, and older persons generally had more time available. Younger couples did not earn enough to be independent, and there were other, very basic reasons in most socialist economies for not aspiring to any high degree of household economic autarchy. Recurrent shortages dictated dependencies: whenever a deficit item appeared, you bought as much as you could in order to have resources to exchange for other deficit items which neighbours and friends had managed to acquire. (1995, 106)

Thus, for many people under socialism, and Żywiec is no exception, individual strategizing was inextricably linked with family networks and family strategizing. Many people expected to live out their lives in the same house in which they were born, never leaving their parents. Eva Hoffman (1989), in comparing the Polish sense of family to the American one, states that Americans tend to imbue their mothers with a gothic sense of doom, attempting to escape from them as soon

as possible and viewing mothers as the source of many of their problems, but for Poles, a mother is "as familiar as the old slippers in
which she shuffles around the house." A young woman in Żywiec
even remarked to me that one of the problems with Americans is that
we do not feel that we truly have become adults unless we have
moved out of our parents' homes. She felt this meant that Americans
never dealt with their parents as adults. Whether or not this is true, it
demonstrates that for her, families and particularly the family home
are primary places where life occurs. The utilization, sharing, and
passing on of family resources—not just of housing but of education,
access to jobs, and symbolic value of the family name—are major venues
through which class is reproduced through families in Żywiec.

In the postsocialist era, residual problems for Polish families are
a lack of housing and the fact that women still need to get jobs but are
being laid off in greater numbers than men. What has changed after
socialism is the ways in which people can and do draw on those
family networks to create economic advantages for themselves. Changing economic and social conditions—including the scrambles for land
and capital during privatization, the forced return of many working
women to the home in the face of disproportionate layoffs and cutbacks in state-funded child care and health care, the continued housing shortages, and the limited information market about scarce job
opportunities—may make people even more dependent on family and
friends in the postsocialist era. Despite the hope that many Żywiecers
had held that under capitalism one could "do whatever you wanted,"
the reality for members of nonelite classes was that they still had the
same meager resources and were still either dependent on the rest of
the family or had family members who were dependent on them.

In this chapter, I look at the postsocialist effects of the return of
private property, variation in education, privatization of industry,
gender, and age. Through anecdotes and examples of actual strategies
that people in Żywiec have reported to me, I show how the effects of
these characteristics are mediated in important ways by family structure and family networks.

Postsocialist Return of Private Property

The reprivatization of homes and businesses in Żywiec that were
nationalized by the communists after World War II is another important factor in tracking strategies that Żywiec families are able to employ. Only properties nationalized by the Polish communist government
are eligible for reprivatization to individuals; property seized by the

Nazi occupation and never returned by the communist government cannot be claimed by prewar owners. If a business or home was large enough to be nationalized, it was certainly owned by an upper-class family. Families who have regained these homes and businesses generally find themselves in possession of major resources they can deploy to gain even more economic capital.

Some examples of prewar elite families who have benefited from the reprivatization program are the Galuskis, the Morawskis, and the Sablonskis. Maria Galuski's family owned the largest bakery in Żywiec in the prewar era, as well as a very large home in town. Both were nationalized when she was a young girl. In 1991, they were returned to her, because she was the sole heir to these properties. She and her husband, past retirement age, took over running the bakery and moved into the house. As a result of taking over the bakery, she was able to move her daughter, now a middle-aged woman, back to Żywiec from the town to which she had been moved by the communists. Her daughter took over as the main manager of the bakery, and with her new salary, she was able to renovate an apartment for herself and send her daughter to college at the prestigious Jagiellonian University in Kraków. Maria was also able to move her son and his family into her regained house, thus saving them the expense of renting an apartment.

Another family who regained large amounts of property in 1991 was the Morawski family. Before World War II, they had owned a large hotel and restaurant in downtown Żywiec, which later had been nationalized by the communist government. When they regained their property, the only heirs were elderly Magdalena Morawski, an intellectual leader in Żywiec, and her nephew, his wife, and two young children. The nephew and his family took over the management of the properties, which by 1994 were obviously thriving. Magdalena, who previously had been making do with a small retirement stipend, found her standard of living raised considerably by her share in the profits.

A third family success story was that of the Sablonskis. Jolanda Sablonski's father had owned the town flour mill (an extremely lucrative business in a mostly peasant community) and a large house attached to the mill. Jolanda's mother regained the mill in 1991, and the family moved into the attached house. Jolanda's husband learned the work necessary for running the mill and took over the management. In 1995, the household consisted of Jolanda's mother, Jolanda and her husband, their daughter, Ola, and her husband, and their one-year-old daughter. Ola had been able to attend the University of Katowice with a major in English, and was soon to finish her *magisterium* (five-year university degree equivalent to a bachelor's or master's degree). She told me that she hoped to find work teaching English in an academy in Bielsko-Biała. When I asked her in her mother's presence what she would do if she could not find a position in Bielsko, her mother replied confidently that she thought they might be able to start an English school in Żywiec—a plan that would never have been possible without their newly acquired capital.

Education

For the majority of the population, educated and employed before the post-1989 economic and political reforms, the economic changes are like playing the slot machines at a casino: very few people have big wins, some win a modest amount, but the house odds mean that most lose. Class plays an important part in determining who "wins," however, so the element of chance is much reduced. Foreign enterprises prefer to hire educated young people who speak English or German, the business languages of Europe. In Żywiec, most of the schools are not able to offer sources of study in these languages. Many of the prewar elite families spoke German, however, and by teaching their children how to speak it, they have passed down this resource through the family. Children of the prewar elite are also more likely to gain entrance to the one high school in town that teaches English, because they tend to have a higher standard of education within the family. Nonelites are at a major disadvantage in this process, because they have neither prior knowledge of a foreign language, nor a history of higher education that would help them prepare their children for placement exams, nor social ties that allow them to "pull strings" to get their children into the desired high school.

Class is strongly linked to educational opportunities. In the Polish educational system, there are several different kinds of high schools, including technical schools, vocational schools, economic schools, and general education schools. Only the general education high school could grant the *matura* diploma, which was in turn required for entrance to colleges that grant *magisterium* degrees. Possession of a *magisterium* degree was an important tool for political and economic advancement in socialist Poland. In an interview I conducted with a class in the Żywiec General Education High School, many students expressed the opinion that a *magisterium* was no longer as useful, because the real key to advancement in their eyes was to find a job working as a manager for a foreign enterprise or in the newly burgeoning computer industry in Poland. Rather than a college degree, these students believed that knowledge of English and computer skills would stand them in better stead. Again, in Żywiec, the general education high school was the only school that offered English classes and some computer technology to the students. Elite-class parents were themselves likely to have the educational skills to tutor their children to be able to pass the entrance exam for this high school, because they probably attended it in their day. Members of the lower class in Żywiec more often went to technical or vocational high school, and they did not attain the knowledge necessary to tutor their children.

Privatization of Industry

The impression most U.S. citizens have received through press accounts of Poland is that the transition to capitalism is flowing smoothly. People in Poland supposedly are quickly able to adapt to new economic structures that are put in place; the new structures work, and the positive economic indicators, such as increased gross national product (GNP) that are often cited by U.S. newspapers reflect an underlying reality of improved quality of life for individuals in Poland. Even as early as 1991, the *Wall Street Journal* was discussing the "Polish Boom." In 1994, *Gazeta Wyborcza* reported that Poland led the Central and Eastern European countries in growth in GNP and percent of GNP represented by activities of the private sector (Zagroszka 1994). The news for 1996 was that unemployment rates were still dropping. Certainly it is true that in Warsaw, there are many employment and educational opportunities for Poles; luxuries and services are available, and the standard of living for a significant part of the population has gone up since 1989.

In a rural country such as Poland, however, in which 30 percent of the population is small farmers and their families and a majority of the population lives outside the urban areas, it is vital to look beyond these superficial optimistic portrayals that are biased toward urban experiences to discover the actual prevalent patterns of adjustment to the economic changes. The ideologically driven picture of a new model of the citizen acting individually within a democratic civil society and a fluid capitalist economy does not hold when the nature of change and responses is examined in the countryside.

Żywiec is an example of an intermediate community in many senses. It is neither a small village nor a city, and as a medium-sized town, it is not entirely dependent on any one industry. The impact of privatization has been mixed: some enterprises have been liquidated, some have flourished. But even when a privatization follows the "successful" model of a large factory that survives the sale of its shares on the stock market, as with the Żywiec Brewery, there can be a hidden shadow. In the case of the brewery, the large-scale layoffs and cutbacks in services can cast doubt on the criteria of success that are used to evaluate economic change.

Privatization of state-owned enterprises entails large-scale layoffs. Most of the population is too old and well established in their jobs to change careers to take advantage of the possibilities for private ownership of businesses, or even to find work in foreign enterprises about which they know little or nothing. Lack of start-up capital is a major barrier to starting an individually owned or family-owned business, and lack of foreign language skills bars many from employment in foreign companies. The privatization program, which is designed to affect eventually all state-owned firms in Poland, very rarely results in expanded employment opportunities in businesses; layoffs are most often the result. Under these circumstances, most Poles rely on their family networks to support them, and families strategize together to make the best of their situations. Members of the elite classes (the prewar elite and the neocapitalists) have more capital to share throughout their families, and they also have access to employment opportunities, because they are owners and managers of businesses.

Gender

> Women generally earn less than men [in Poland], because their incomes have disproportionately shrunk in the last four years. Almost three quarters of women and 56 percent of men make less than the mean. —Danuta Zagroszka, "Polskie tempo"

Partially through selective hiring and firing practices, and partially because of initial gender and age biases in job distribution, the workplace in Poland is becoming more and more dominated by younger, male workers. The decrease of women in the Polish workforce has several causes. During the communist regime, women worked in positions with less authority, made less money, and held lower positions in political office (Hauser 1991, Drakulic 1993). In general, women have been especially vulnerable to losing their jobs as Polish enterprises capitalize more heavily, because women are concentrated in jobs that are likely to be reduced by automation. As Polish businesses privatize, they frequently "downsize" (as the current U.S. euphemism puts it) to increase their profits. As in the United States, the first to feel the results of this downsizing are the lower-paid, primarily women, workers.

One of the particular problems that women face in the new market situation, especially if they are working in a privatized industry, is that their jobs are no longer held for them while they take maternity leave, childcare leave, or any other time off to deal with family crises. Thus, for an employed woman, an unplanned pregnancy can spell financial disaster, because she will almost certainly lose her job and receive no maternity benefits. The Polish state still provides a small stipend or benefit for women who are caring for young children, but it is less than before and the duration is shorter. When they wish to return to the labor force, women have no guarantee that they will be able to find work, and they have access to only one year's worth of unemployment pay.

Most of the women who have been laid off will not find permanent work easily. They face consistent discrimination, not only from men, but from other women as well. As one older woman, the owner of a small business in Żywiec, told me, "women are better workers than men, but it's better to hire them after their children are grown. Women can't keep their whole minds on their work—they're always thinking 'what are the kids up to?' and being interrupted; they have to take time off when the kids are sick. You'll see when you have children. They never call to Dad, always to Mom." Several teenage girls were working for her, and she anticipated that when they married and began to have children, they would leave the workforce until their children were old enough to do without their constant care. She also had a number of older women employees, whose children were grown-up enough not to need a great deal of care. This woman's outlook was more liberal than many businesses in the present era, because she was willing to hire women at all. This can be explained in part through the nature of her business, a bakery—cooking is considered women's work.

Women who have remained in the workforce in Poland are likely to face this problematic double bind: their husbands expect them to care for the household, children, and any older relatives who need care, and their employers expect them to act as if they have no additional responsibilities beyond those of male employees. A woman who was the head of the sampling laboratory at the Żywiec Brewery described to me her difficulties in fulfilling her job obligations and caring for her husband and two children (ages nine and twelve) in their apartment. She told me that even though she and her husband enjoyed having their own place (not living with any extended family members), this produced problems when she needed to work long hours or when the children needed extra care. To compensate, the children ate their midday meal (the largest meal of the day in Poland) at her mother's apartment, and they often stayed there several nights a week.

Some strategies for making money that are equally available to men and women are nevertheless dominated by women. Small-scale marketing in Żywiec was primarily the province of women—setting up a table at an open-air market with whatever goods one has to sell, usually fruits, vegetables, and small, domestically produced items such as nylon pantyhose or shampoos. I noticed, however, that if significant amounts of foreign merchandise were displayed, usually the sales-person was a man. (I heard several stories of significant cash being accumulated by men smuggling merchandise—usually vodka or ciga-rettes—over the Slovak or German border and selling it in Poland. Sometimes these men had ostensibly traveled to Germany for migrant agricultural labor, and, thus, even had a cover explanation for where they had acquired the money.)

This kind of small, informal marketing usually requires transpor-tation and a card table, or just a car with its trunk open and goods displayed. Given access to a car (not an easy matter), this is an option for women or men of any age, class, or educational background. It is significant that this small-scale activity cannot always be monitored by the unemployment office, and, thus, one popular strategy is to collect unemployment for as long as possible while also engaging in small-scale sales. It is usually more profitable, for both men and women, to collect unemployment pay and work on the gray market for a few days a week than to work for an average salary in Poland.

A more systematic version of the small sales strategy has re-cently become available in Poland. Multilevel marketing-type sales organizations, such as Amway, and investment schemes, such as Glo-bal (a pyramid savings and investment scheme with no merchandise involved), have made an entree into the Polish market and are par-ticularly popular among women. In the case of Amway, this is partly due to the type of products (cooking and cleaning materials and cos-metics) and the fact that women can sell them to their personal net-work of friends, neighbors, and relatives. Additionally, women continue to earn money for as long as they are trying to work, cannot be fired, and can adjust their hours to fit their families' schedules. I attended an Amway recruitment seminar at the Kosinski home, described in the case study later in this chapter, and the woman who gave the recruit-ment presentation (who lived in a village not far from Żywiec) cited all of these reasons for why women should try Amway home sales. The relatively high cost of Amway products, however, can make them difficult for Poles to afford. Though Barbara Kosinski tried to make the work profitable, she found that she was not able to sell enough to make a concerted effort worthwhile.

One low-paying option for women's home work that continues to be available from the socialist period is to make traditional craft goods at home and sell them to the Cepelia, the State Organization of Artists and Craftspersons stores. In Żywiec, there is no Cepelia, but there is a handicrafts store that caters to tourists who come for the large festivals. At the folk festivals, some families have their own handicrafts booths with traditional Góral products such as woodcarvings, bird-shaped ocarinas and whistles, paper cuttings and paper wreaths, and even articles of clothing. This type of home craft work is low-paying, but has the advantage of usually being a transaction that does not affect women's unemployment pay, because it is not permanent work. Additionally, women can do this type of work whenever they have time, so that it can fit around other duties of child care, elder care, and housekeeping. Similarly, of course, women can bring goods to outdoor markets as their schedules permit.

Most women do not travel abroad to work, though ironically, many people told me that it is easier for a married woman with dependents to obtain a visa to travel abroad for long periods, because the authorities think that it is more likely that these women will return to Poland rather than permanently relocate illegally. It is rare that a woman does this, although several young girls with whom I spoke suggested that they might like to try being an au pair or domestic servant abroad. It is unlikely that those particular girls would be able to work abroad, because these positions usually require minimal English or German skills, which they did not have. Also, horror stories of Polish au pair girls who were overworked and abused by foreign families almost have the status of rural legend, which serves to discourage girls who might be offered an opportunity. Because of the close-knit nature of families and the fact that few women move away from their families, the very idea is unthinkable for many Polish women. In an interview with one young woman in Żywiec who was nearly finished with a degree in English from Katowice University and who had an opportunity to travel to England for six months, she expressed intense distaste for the idea of being so far away from her mother and husband for such a long time. In all my interviews in Żywiec, I was told of only one married woman (with two children) from Żywiec who, a decade or so before, had gone to the United States to work as a maid for a year and returned home "a princess" because of her hard currency wealth. The woman I was interviewing considered this particular case extraordinary, and she said that it was only because the woman had a very understanding husband, whose own mother helped with the children, that the woman was "allowed" to go abroad for so long.

In sum, women have been much more likely than men to be laid off in the postsocialist period. They frequently have a harder time finding jobs, because no allowances are made, as they were during the socialist period, for the fact that they bear the majority of the family responsibilities. Their families, by and large, need whatever income every adult in the household can contribute. Therefore, women need to employ different strategies from men to make up for their lost income. Frances Pine has suggested (1996) that women in rural areas in Poland are more likely than women in urban areas to be able to mobilize family networks to enable them to adjust for the severe changes that have affected their ability to participate in the formal workplace. In Żywiec as well, many women of childbearing age rely on their parents or in-laws to help out with child care and housing for themselves and their nuclear families, thus providing them with the flexibility to pursue income opportunities.

Age

For men, age is a factor that affects their chances of employment. Men who are in the middle range (between age twenty-five and forty-five) have had the least problems with layoffs. Those who are in the position of having virtually no seniority, or being old enough to seem like "dead wood," have suffered disproportionately when firms are looking to cut costs by cutting labor.

Aside from women, the group that has been most disproportionately laid off since 1989 is older people (older than forty-five years old). It is particularly difficult for this group to obtain new employment. They often do not have the resources to retrain for different jobs, and new jobs are likely to advertise for young applicants anyway. Western businesses such as McDonald's and Pizza Hut, which account for many new jobs in Poland, even put an age limit on their recruitment advertisements. In calls for résumés for managerial positions at McDonald's, for example, applicants are told that they should be between twenty-one and twenty-eight years old and that they should send a photo with the résumé (*Grabowski* 1995). In a newspaper interview with a McDonald's district manager, she claimed that there is in fact no age limit, but that the tiring nature of the work (". . . the first week is the worst. Everything hurts—your entire body") makes it more suitable for young, strong energetic employees (*Grabowski* 1995). This attitude is typical of large enterprises and Western businesses, both of which seem to want as new employees workers who are young enough never to have worked in state socialist enterprises.

In Żywiec, the plight of older people who have retired or lost their jobs very much depends on their family situation. When they live with their children and grandchildren, especially if they are women, they often are able to make contributions to the household through their labor—housework, cooking, and child care— and in turn are supported by the other wage earners in the household. Elderly Żywiec residents who live by themselves and are unemployed are likely to find themselves in dire straits, because their pensions usually do not cover housing, utilities, food, and the medicines they need. (Medicines can be extremely expensive, especially if they are imported from Western Europe or the United States.)

Older people have few options available, depending on their age. Formerly, women could retire with full pension privileges at age sixty, and men at age sixty-five. For many firms that were privatizing, the age was reduced to fifty-five for women and sixty for men who were forced to retire as part of the downsizing efforts. This is a relatively young age in Eastern and Central Europe, and these payments have become a burden on the state. Thus, the age has been increased again to sixty and sixty-five. Of course, the state pensions are not large, with full pensions in 1995 averaging about 300 new złotys (Zl), or approximately U.S. $120, a month. Private pension plans do not yet exist. Average pay hovers at around Zl 400 a month (U.S. $160). So, instead of immediately retiring, it is preferable to claim unemployment benefits for as long as possible. Some older people are able to find work off the books as small-scale marketers or cleaning women, or by providing services such as painting or home repair, or by taking in boarders if they have space available at home. But the sad reality is that many older people in Żywiec are living in extreme poverty and distressing conditions, some with no electricity or running water.

Probably the poorest person I met in Żywiec was Hania, an older woman who was living in just such conditions. Hania was about sixty years old and had been unemployed for many years. She had epilepsy and was not able to afford, with her disability check, the medication that would have controlled this condition. During the socialist period, she would not have had to pay for the medication if there were supplies of it available at the state hospital. However, if she had to look on the black market for the medication, she could not have afforded it during socialism either. She quoted a common saying regarding the scarcity of goods during socialism and the current plethora of goods but massive inflation to explain this: "Under the socialists, we had full pockets and empty shelves. Now, we have full shelves and empty pockets."

Hania's children had all left her and her husband had died, so she lived alone. When I asked her if she could find work as a cleaning woman on the gray market, she replied that she had tried that option several years ago, had had a seizure while cleaning a window, and broke the window, severely injuring her arm. She said that she could not gain a higher rate of disability pay because the employment bureau would not list her as completely unable to work. At the time of the interview, she was earning a pittance by collecting cardboard boxes from town businesses, carrying them around town on a cart, and selling them to other businesses that needed them. She explained to me that she could earn about Zl 50 a month if she worked very hard at collecting boxes, and her disability check was Zl 100. To supplement this income, she sometimes did odd jobs, such as weeding gardens, and friends often invited her to dinner, because they knew that she could barely afford food.

For young people, however, an ideal scenario suggests that the possibilities seem limitless in postsocialist Eastern Europe. They are able to study foreign languages such as German and English, and they can take advantage of the boom in business due to the investments of foreign enterprises, joint enterprises, and privately owned firms. Restrictions on travel are greatly reduced from the socialist era, and the free market has extended to the labor market, which means that workers can themselves decide where they would like to be educated, in what area they will specialize, and in which cities and to which firms they will apply for jobs. No longer will the state have influence in these matters.

This utopian script presumes that their parents can afford to send them to superior schools and retain private language tutors, and that jobs and housing will be available upon completion of these plans. Relatively few families, however, have the resources to gain access to private education, foreign travel, and high-paying jobs. Most of the families that do have such resources reside in urban areas. In Żywiec, as in most rural areas, young people follow a scholastic path similar to the one they would have followed before the fall of communism: they attend the state schools in which they can enroll for free, where Russian is likely to be taught because the schools can neither find nor afford German or English teachers. Then they look for a job, though this is a difficult task with the high unemployment rate in Żywiec and without the help of a socialist state guarantee to find them a job. Instead of signing up on a state list for housing (which guaranteed a decades-long wait under socialism), families try to save up enough money to buy or build their own, with approximately the same success—that is, they live with their parents until they are well into middle age.

In comparison with women and older men, however, younger men in particular have a range of possibilities for economic strategies. Most important, men have not experienced the same degree of layoffs and salary cuts, and so a significant number have retained their jobs. Additionally, young men have the advantage of being the most sought after workers, especially if they have any English skills. Military service still removes many young men from the job market for two years after high school and provides them with some work experience and skills and a small stipend.

The job market in Żywiec is such that there is reasonable doubt that students who have recently finished their education will find jobs; however, young men are more mobile than women and older men. They are most likely to travel to Germany, France, Scandinavia, England, America, or Australia for seasonal work, a few years of nest egg building, or to try their chances at finding permanent work there. Most of these men rely on networks of kin and friends who have already emigrated to these places and "know the ropes" as well as the language.

Another possibility for younger unemployed men is to look for day work at construction sites, loading trucks or trains, and other manual labor. For most men, this can allow them to double-dip from unemployment benefits, because this is not legally registered as income. The construction work on Pani Zofia's house was performed by unemployed men who were willing to work for a small salary plus meals and vodka.

Age restricts the possibilities for women as well. Particularly, young women are not customarily supposed to travel away from their families looking for work in the way that young men may. One way in which some young women in Żywiec got around the problems of traveling alone was to participate in a group trip. About ten high school girls were organized by the father of one of them to travel to a farm in Germany to pick fruit for a month during the summer of 1995. I was told by one of the girls that this trip took place every year. The fact that they were all going together and under the direction of a Żywiec father apparently calmed the fears of the girls' parents, and this allowed the girls to earn a relatively large amount of money for their ages. The girls also told me of a similarly organized group of girls who worked as maids at a German resort for two months in the summer.

Another unusual instance of young women traveling for work was the case of the girls I shared a room with briefly at the boardinghouse in

Żywiec. Having just finished their education at a technical high school in a distant village (perhaps an hour away by bus), they shared a room in a boarding house in Żywiec during the week so that they could work in a knitting factory. Every weekend, they went home. These women knew that this was a short-term solution for them, but it was a way to earn a little money that their families desperately needed. The one factory near their village had been liquidated, and, according to them, the unemployment rate in their village was near 100 percent. Although this may have been an exaggeration, it surely was an extraordinary case for two such young girls to be traveling so far and living out of their homes to work. In general, in the unusual cases in which women travel to find work, they are usually unmarried, have no children, and are chaperoned by adults.

The Importance of Family Networks

As shown in the following case studies, family networks are a crucial element of the Żywiec economic terrain. These family networks are not taken into consideration by the Polish state policymakers, who have absorbed much Western rhetoric about individuals "pulling themselves up by their bootstraps." The dimensions of the effects of national economic and political policy in Poland are measured in most discussions in terms of their effects on members of groups differentiated along the lines of age, gender, class, education, and even resources, such as former PZPR membership. These are certainly dimensions that have real social effects. The context in which these effects are significantly shaped, however, is families.

The International Monetary Fund (IMF), World Bank, and Organisation for Economic Co-operation and Development (OECD), three of the major lenders to Poland, have economic policies that focus on individual entrepreneurs. I have tried to show that most people are not culturally, geographically, and financially set up to assume this role. Individuals who wish to become entrepreneurs are likely to have to deal with family networks to obtain sufficient resources to start a business, and families may feel that they have a say in that individual's decision making. Few individuals are in positions where they are able to make decisions without considering their family networks. Two of the pillars of international and domestic policy for the transformation in Poland, large-scale entrepreneurialism (in comparison with the "card table" variety) and joint ventures, depend heavily on connections, prior resources, and much time investment. Few Poles are likely to have the resources to become major players in these enterprises. These jobs may also depend on language ability to some extent, especially for upper management positions. German or English is a prerequisite for entering into joint ventures, because few Western businessmen or-women speak Polish.

These government policies of encouraging (or sometimes just hoping for) large-scale entrepreneurialism and foreign investments in joint ventures are also unworkable for most Żywiec residents, because they are designed for people who live in more urban areas. The economic geography of socialism emphasized developed industry throughout the country, in small towns as well as urban centers, even though the available infrastructure made remote locations less profitable than centralized ones. There was some labor migration during the socialist period, but it was regulated by state planners.

In contrast, the geography of capitalism is such that capital tends to concentrate in areas where there is good infrastructure. Poland's communication and transportation technology is heavily concentrated in a few cities. Most foreign investments and joint enterprises are concentrated in cities such as Warsaw, Poznań, and Kraków, and, thus, the unemployment rates there are the lowest. The closing of any enterprise, layoffs, and other negative side effects of privatization have a differential effect in the provinces, such as in Żywiec, because employment options are so severely limited there already.

Migration to cities, widely practiced in the First and Third Worlds, is not as feasible in Poland. For most Poles, not just for Żywiecers, simply moving to another city in Poland to look for work is not possible. The housing situation in Poland is such that affordable housing for individuals is either not available or not easy to find. Even in cities, where there may be rental listings in a metro section of the newspaper or real estate agencies that list apartments for rent, it may take months to find housing. Żywiecers are used to using a personal information network in searching for new housing, and many Żywiec residents would have no idea how to find housing or negotiate a housing contract in a city. Most Poles tend to stay where they already have a place, even if they can no longer pay the rent, and where they have family to help them out.

In the next section, I show through two case studies of particular families how these strategies interlock when they are placed within the context of households, and how notions of traditional Góral identity are used by individuals within families to justify their decisions about what family strategies should be.

Nonelite Family Strategies: Two Case Studies

Family households in Żywiec have a fluid and flexible structure. Family members may move in and out of the household depending on their needs and circumstances, whether they are getting married, having children, going abroad, being laid off, or saving up money. Even deciding who is "in" a household and who is "out" can be difficult. Different families have different systems of dividing up expenses and incomes, but in general all families, elite and nonelite alike, try to maximize and diversify their household strategies, depending on who is living in the household at that particular time, to provide a broad base of resources and hedge against disaster.

The two household case studies that I have selected to discuss in detail provide contrast in terms of the impact of economic change on their situation. I do not mean to suggest that they are representative of some "typical" family in Żywiec; there is no one norm. They are, however, both typical examples of the diverse strategies that Polish households use to minimize their losses should any one strategy not be productive. Both families are from the worker class in Żywiec, and both attained that class position in the socialist era, having previously been peasant families. Some aspects of the family strategies discussed in this section existed during the socialist period and perhaps before (Thomas and Znaniecki 1927), whereas others are uniquely a product of new circumstances. These two households highlight the different ways in which age, family structure, class, and gender affect choices and outcomes in the current, rapidly changing environment. They also both show the ways in which Góral identity is felt and contested within nonelite families, and they suggest some ways in which individual members of nonelite classes in Żywiec would benefit from the elite classes' struggle over the meanings of traditionalism and modernity in the community. This provides some insight as to why nonelites would not reject, and even accept and participate in, the ideological conflict over the relevance and content of the Góral identity.

The Porzyńskis

The first household, that of the Porzyńskis, was also the place I lived during my stay in Żywiec. When I first moved into the Porzyński household, the other residents consisted of Pani Zofia; her elderly second husband, Franciszek; their divorced daughter Malgorzata (thirty years old); and Malgorzata's son Lukasz (five years old) (see Figure 4.1). Franciszek, bedridden with a tumor for the past year, received some pension money from the state, which was barely enough to cover the cost of his medicine. Malgorzata worked as a secretary to a small business in Bielsko-Biala. Because of the constantly increasing cost of daily train fare to Bielsko, her take-home salary hardly covered her commuting expenses, yet there were no options for better work in Żywiec.

For the Porzyńskis, the rent I contributed was thus a great boon. For example, it enabled Zofia and Franciszek to get the superior private, rather than state, medical care and medicines for Franciszek, and it allowed them meet the expenses of having their daughter and grandson living with them. In reality, Zofia was the sole bill payer in the family; although her daughter earned a small paycheck, she did not contribute to most household expenses, only paying for outright purchases for herself and her son. Thus, the Porzyńskis had a diversified strategy for making ends meet. Franciszek had retirement pay. Zofia earned a paycheck for working in the kiosk, and a half payment of social security–retirement pay because she was past retirement age. She also grew roses on about half of the property, which she occasionally sold both directly to consumers and to her sister's family, who owned several florist stalls in town. The rest of the front yard was a conventional Polish vegetable garden, which provided much of the family food, and in the backyard, they raised chickens for eggs and occasional meat. Renting the side house to me made the household income relatively high for what was primarily a single-income family, and they were able to start renovations on another very small addition (which was truly dilapidated when I arrived), with the intent of possibly renting that out as well.

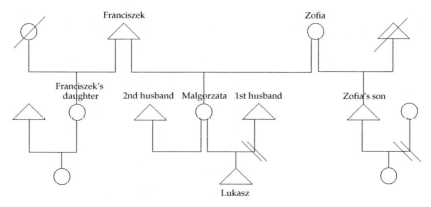

FIGURE 4.1   The Porzyńskis and Related Individuals[2]

This diversified strategy weathered a few storms in the year that I lived with the Porzyńskis. Several months after I moved in, Malgorzata remarried. In most cases in Żywiec, the newlyweds would have moved in with the bride's family, both because the community is generally matrilocal and because, in this case, Malgorzata's family had more room than her new husband's. This did not happen with Malgorzata. She and Pani Zofia fought about the wedding because of Malgorzata's divorced status (under Catholic doctrine, divorced Catholics may not remarry) and Zofia's dislike of the groom. As a result, Malgorzata and Lukasz moved in with her husband and new in-laws, who had an apartment in the town and who expected them to pay much more of her salary toward household expenses. (I came to suspect during the course of this feud that Zofia had rented the apartment to me in part to spite her daughter and ensure that she would not be able to move into it.) Malgorzata's husband was unemployed, and this caused much friction between Malgorzata and her in-laws. Zofia, meanwhile, was determined not to contribute to her daughter's upkeep, because she felt the new marriage was illegitimate.

The death of Franciszek several days before Christmas sent the family into a turmoil. Zofia's son from her first marriage and his young daughter came into town for the funeral and stayed through several weeks of the holiday season. Malgorzata came back to the house to help prepare for the funeral. By midwinter, however, her son and daughter had returned to their own households. This left Zofia alone in the house, except for me. Yet it did not mean that she stopped strategizing in terms of her family. Zofia had to change her will to reflect Franciszek's death, which soon embroiled her in a family legal dispute: Malgorzata filed a lawsuit against her mother to obtain rights to part of the house and the land Zofia owned.

Because she judged Malgorzata unable to deal responsibly with any property she might inherit, Pani Zofia revised her will so that upon her death, her property was to be held in trust for her two grandchildren, untouchable by her son and daughter. When her daughter discovered this, however, she sued to gain control over part of the property, claiming that her father would have left her property and that agreements he signed before he died had been coerced by her mother. Pani Zofia, however, argued that the property had been hers before her marriage to Malgorzata's father and, thus, was hers in entirety to dispose of. In the meantime, Franciszek's daughter by his first marriage also tried to claim part of the property, using the same argument as Malgorzata—that Franciszek would have left her part of the property.

Zofia, beset on all sides, fought the lawsuit on several fronts. First, she tried to get her son to intercede on her behalf with his half-sister Malgorzata. When he refused to become involved, she took to complaining to her friends, neighbors, other family members, and me that her children had no shame—and that no real Góral would drag her mother into the public view like that. She claimed that real Górals would not shame their families by this public contestation and would stick with their families against outside forces, sacrificing their claims in the name of what was best for the entire family. Only as a final resort did she consent to talk to a lawyer about the matter.

Malgorzata, on the other hand, claimed that her mother was unnaturally trying to deny her her birthright and her land. She argued that real Górals are independent and that her mother was denying this to her and her husband by withholding the land. Land is particularly important, in both an economic and an ideological sense, in this community. Many of the current inhabitants of Żywiec (such as Zofia) moved there from the surrounding peasant villages over the past fifty years, and their connection with their family land (of which they usually retain ownership) is part of their sense of belonging to this region, of being Góral. It is also an economic advantage to farm the family land, or at least plant a large garden, as part of a family strategy for subsistence.

Zofia actually had rights to family land in the village from which she originally came, but her brother and sister-in-law there cared for that land. The property she owned in Żywiec was a relatively recent acquisition, and the inheritance of that land was contested because of the intricacies of her and Franciszek's several marriages and the unusual nature of her will in cutting out her daughter, who would traditionally have lived with her and inherited her house. The land was particularly important to Malgorzata, because she had isolated herself from the resources that family networks would otherwise provide by quarrelling with both her mother and her in-laws.

Zofia and Malgorzata eventually worked out an interim agreement in which Malgorzata was able to plant and harvest in the vegetable garden. This was an important asset for Malgorzata at that time, because she and her new husband were embroiled in a second lawsuit. They were moving into a different apartment because they could no longer get along with her new in-laws. Her in-laws were suing them for most of the furniture and appliances they owned, some accumulated during their marriage and some that Malgorzata had owned prior to the marriage. The newlyweds' impending need to pay rent, in addition to the possibility of needing to repurchase furniture, gave an extra importance to the ability to obtain food from the family garden plot.

This case shows the importance of family networks in constructing and supporting households, especially young ones, and the disaster that can strike if a young couple tries to circumvent the family hierarchy of authority. There is also an element of attempted control over the family's decision-making process by both Zofia and Malgorzata introducing arguments about who or what represents "real" Góralism. Family and household strategizing failed for Malgorzata because she was not willing to deal with the complications of her lack of authority in a three-generation family; thus, she was cut off from two sets of family resources. If she had mellowed on this point, she and her husband and son could have possibly moved back in with Zofia in the future, thus saving money and pooling their resources.

Zofia was an anomaly in the sense that at that point, she as an individual could support herself—most households consist of several adults, all attempting to bring in what resources they can to contribute toward meeting the household expenses. Pani Zofia did not have to make any rent payments, she had a steady job, a half pension, a garden, a paying tenant, chickens, and occasional flower sales to her sister and brother-in-law's florist business. Her children were grown, and after her daughter moved out, she was not helping to support them or her grandchildren.

Up to this point, her position had not really been affected by the political-economic changes in Poland: she was still employed, and there was no one else contributing to her household income who was at risk of unemployment. She had, of course, been affected by the rise in costs for everything from coal to food, but her plethora of strategies had given her some economic resiliency. As a former peasant and now elderly member of the working class, she felt no need to bolster her class position by purchasing newly available luxury goods that would drain her budget. Though her actions were intricately intertwined with her children's, in this case, the family strategies they used did not work very well as a result of a variety of personal factors.

The Kosinskis

Other families have been more directly affected by the changes in Poland's economy. The second case study is about the Kosinskis, a family deeply embedded in kin networks (see Figure 4.2). This had kept them financially afloat and able to plan for future improvements despite severe setbacks in the new economy.

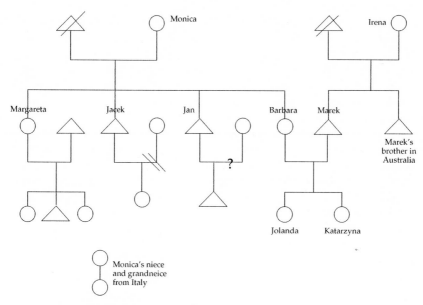

FIGURE 4.2   The Kosinskis and Extended Family

The immediate Kosinski family consisted of a husband, Marek (aged thirty-seven); wife, Barbara (aged thirty); and two daughters, Katarzyna (aged nine) and Jolanda (aged seven). Marek's mother, Irena, lived on an adjacent property with a small farm and a barn with cows, chickens, and pigs. The Kosinskis lived on the second floor of Barbara's mother Monica's house, in an addition they had built themselves. Monica lived downstairs, and one, sometimes two, of her sons lived with her. Barbara's older brother, Jacek, had divorced his wife, and his toddler daughter sometimes came to spend several days with him. Barbara's younger brother, Jan, had a stormy relationship with his wife, so he lived sometimes with her and their infant son at her mother's house, sometimes alone at Monica's, and sometimes his wife and son would stay at Monica's house. Barbara's sister Margareta's children (young teenagers) would also come to Monica's for meals or to stay the night occasionally, and Monica's niece and her daughter would come from Italy for a time during the summer. This house had only two rooms plus a kitchen and bath on the ground floor, and it was sometimes very crowded! At such times, the family members would spill out into the other households available to them in the community until the space crisis was over.

The Kosinskis had a complex strategy for meeting their family needs. Marek had been employed at the Żywiec Brewery as a manual laborer, but he lost his job when the factory mechanized after privatization. As a result, he collected unemployment compensation for a year, the full period allowed. During this time, he worked for cash as a day laborer at various odd jobs in the Żywiec community, and sometimes he could work offloading trains in Katowice (an hour's train ride from Żywiec), when a friend told him that there would be work there. Because these jobs were not licensed by the government, they did not interfere with his receiving unemployment checks. After his unemployment period ran out, his mother, Irena, registered him as a worker in her tiny, self-owned business, which provided office work for local businesses. This allowed him to build up time toward being able to collect unemployment again. He helped Irena manage the farm and care for the animals, and, in return, Marek and Barbara were able to share the vegetables and animal products, such as milk and eggs, as well as house some of their own pigs. In June 1995, Marek was trying to organize several men for a summer trip to Germany to earn money as illegal fruit pickers. The necessity of having one member of the group be fluent in German caused problems, however, when their fluent friend backed out of the deal.

Barbara managed to keep her job as a secretary at the Brewery Sports Club, though there were constant rumors that the club was going to close. Her salary for this job was considerably less than the average national the equivalent in 1995 of around U.S. $90 a month), but there were some other benefits that she explained to me: her boss was understanding when she was late or had to take time off to care for her children or her ill mother; there was a health clinic at the brewery (although this closed in July 1995); and the brewery ran a care center for the children. They had also invested in several shares of the brewery's stock during the 1991 privatization, and she felt that the brewery was doing well financially and she wanted to keep working there for reasons of stability. To supplement her income, she also worked occasionally for her mother-in-law's typing business, and she attempted to earn some money as an Amway saleswoman.

Planning for Katarzyna and Jolanda's future caused the most heartache for Marek and Barbara, because their own income was hardly enough to pay the family bills. Their greatest hope was to be able to open their own store. Because a road built next to their property in 1992 had become a major throughway for traffic going to Slovakia, they felt that they could build a small store on the corner of Marek's mother's property and have enough drive-by business to become profitable. Irena agreed to this plan and was financing the building of the store. She in turn earned money from her small typing business and received remittances from Marek's brother, who had moved to Australia. Marek and a friend were taking care of the construction of the store themselves. They were not exactly sure what they would sell in the store, but Barbara was arguing for including at least beer, soda, and hot dogs for travelers. Marek argued that he did not want to cook hot dogs, and because he would be running the store, they would then have to hire someone to cook. Barbara countered that her sister Margaret's daughter would soon be old enough for that sort of work and would work for free or very little because she was part of the family.

Marek's mother was very concerned about the education her granddaughters were receiving, and she constantly pushed Barbara and Marek to involve them in activities that would raise their community status and also their chances for employment. Irena paid for the girls to attend Góral dancing lessons for several years, and then she changed her mind and determined that they should be learning English. This was an expensive proposition and rather difficult to arrange, because few people in Żywiec spoke English. However, she was able to find students who had studied English at the university level, or cousins from abroad visiting their families in Żywiec, who were willing to tutor the girls for several hours a week. This was certainly a coup for the family, because English lessons were otherwise available only at the most competitive high school in town, which the girls were unlikely to attend for a variety of reasons, including the fact that they were not from the upper class.

In the family network to which the Kosinskis belonged, they were certainly the recipients of many benefits. Because they were having economic problems, their families pitched in to help them. In some matters, however, they were able to contribute their own resources to the other members of the family. One of the incidents that stands out most vividly in my recollection of my time in Żywiec is the Kosinski's pig-slaughtering, which I attended in the spring of 1995. The Kosinskis decided that they would kill one of their pigs, which was newly matured, to provide meat both for themselves and to celebrate their youngest daughter's First Communion. They were not having a good year economically, and an adult pig could provide pork for a family of four for at least a year, because every bit of pig is used in making various dishes.

The occasion of a First Communion is a major event in Poland, and it requires a large celebration and dinner to which family and friends are invited. The young celebrator receives large gifts of cash

($25 to $50 is not too much) from friends and family. Jolanda received a bicycle from her parents; this was very expensive but not out of proportion to the "miniwedding" feeling that First Communions command. By slaughtering a pig, the Kosinskis provided enough cuts of meat to host this party. Katarzyna, who had had her First Communion the year before, asked within my hearing why a similar pig-slaughtering had not been performed for her ceremony. She was clearly disappointed that this exciting honor was associated with Jolanda's ceremony and not her own. The answer from Barbara and Marek was a mixture of the facts that no pigs had been fully grown and that they had had more money in the previous year.

Meat from the slaughtering also went to a variety of other people. A professional butcher was hired to supervise the butchering and the preparation of some of the pork, and another man, a family friend, came to help as well. They were both given prime cuts of meat, such as hams and ribs—the best part of the pig. Other products included pork sausages, bacon, various kinds of pâtés, and several other recipes. Neighbors and friends were given portions of the latter out of goodwill. The pig was formerly housed and was slaughtered at Marek's mother's farm; because Irena also stored the resulting meat, she had access to it as well. Many members of their extended family and some neighbors, perhaps twenty in all, came to the slaughtering to sample the parts that were immediately cooked and distributed, and most of them took home some portion of the less prestigious meats. (I was also given some of these products, which I then redistributed to my landlady and some neighbors, because I could not store or use all that I was given.)

This will seem to anthropologists a fairly classic example of reinforcing social ties through food exchange. But pigs and pork are important in Poland, and Góral Poland especially—not only for subsistence but also as an expression of identity. Poles in general consider pork to be a staple at religious holiday meals, and it reinforces a major boundary of religious difference with Jews, for whom pork is forbidden. The Góral identity is expressed through the kinds of kielbasa that are made—Żywiec- and Góral-style kielbasas are regional varieties that are famous throughout Poland—and distinctive secondary products involving mixtures of, among other things, bulgur wheat, pig blood, and organ meats. Recipes for making these are important family and regional traditions, and arguments erupted during the slaughtering party as to whose recipes would be used and why. Some of these arguments concerned disputes over who had the most "authentic" or "traditional" Góral recipe, and some were in-law disputes between Irena and Barbara as to who had the authority to use her recipe.

Because they were a close-knit family, it was ironic that the Kosinskis were also involved in a family lawsuit. The dispute was over who owned the land and house in which they lived. The land had originally belonged to Barbara's father, and because his widow and their children had lived in the house for more than twenty years, they believed that the right to use of the house and land belonged to them. However, they did acknowledge that the father's siblings, who were dispersed to Russia, the United States, and several cities in Poland, had some share in the rights to the house. When Barbara's sister, Margareta, and her husband saved enough money to want to build a second house on the land, Margareta contacted her aunts and uncles to see if they would sign their rights over to her. Most of them did this without qualm, except for an uncle in the United States and an aunt in Katowice. The aunt decided that she wanted half of the property for her own children to build on, and she contacted her brother in the United States to ask him to send her a letter giving her his rights in the land. Her rationale, as it was conveyed to me by Barbara, was that the family land should not be given over to only one branch of the family, because that would cut the others off from their roots as Górals. She filed a lawsuit stating that Barbara's mother and her children had no right to own any of the land or the house, because it should have passed to Barbara's father's siblings upon his death. Barbara's mother told me that she believed that her children should own the house and land, not only because they were the ones who had truly kept up the family tradition by living there, but also because they had the legal precedent of having lived there for more than twenty years. The family eventually won over the uncle in the United States, and without his support, the aunt withdrew her lawsuit.

In the case of the Kosinskis, the location of their home was actually in a village on the outskirts of Żywiec, which had been incorporated into Żywiec in the 1970s. Thus, they were still living on land their families had farmed for many years. The desire of other family members who had moved away from Żywiec to retain their connection to that family land, and thus to the region and the Góral identity, sparked the feud over its ownership. If Barbara's mother and her family had lost the ownership of the house and land, they would have been hard pressed to find a place to live and pay rent there. In the case of Barbara's sister, Margareta, who wanted to build the second house on the property, she certainly would not have been able to purchase land on which to build a house. So both economically and ideologically, by virtue of remaining in the community and making use of the property, the Kosinskis claimed rightful ownership over the land and house.

Marek and Barbara's strategies were influenced by their age, gender, class, parental status, and education, and they were enacted within the context of their family networks. Marek's age made it difficult for him to obtain full-time employment after being laid off by the brewery. As a result, he pieced together a variety of other options: temporary labor on the black market (meaning that it was not registered with the government), unemployment benefits, and farming. He was approaching the age at which men no longer make an effort to seek migrant work in Germany, that being considered a young man's province. Barbara, at age thirty, also feared that she would not be able to obtain employment as good as that she had at the brewery, should she be laid off. Her part-time work as a typist for her mother-in-law was the type of work for which Marek, though he was legally registered as working there, would or could not perform because it was gender-typed as women's labor. Her involvement in Amway was also gender-typed, because it allowed her flexible hours and products to sell that were within a woman's realm of responsibility (soaps, cleaning products, cosmetics, etc.). It was considered especially appropriate for a mother, because she could work around child care. Because both Marek and Barbara belonged to the working class, they had attended vocational high school. This gave them no chance to attend college and aspire to higher-paid management positions or to learn languages such as German or English, which would have allowed Marek to travel more easily to Germany to find work or allowed either of them the opportunity to look for work at new, foreign-owned businesses in the county seat, Bielsko-Biała. Without the support of their family networks, Marek and Barbara would not even have been able in 1995 to keep a roof over their heads or food on the table.

Nonelite Classes and Traditionalism in Żywiec

There is a great deal of articulation between the class structures outlined in chapter 3 and family strategies as discussed in this one. Class position means that families of different classes have differential access to loans for opening new businesses and to education and opportunities abroad, and some have better resources for handling unemployment than others because they have more widespread family networks. Even obtaining information about new political and economic change has class aspects, through overt mechanisms, such as whether or not a family can afford a television, and through self-selecting mechanisms—such as purchasing national newspapers or not, watching television news and debates or not, and participating in local politics through attending town council sessions or talking to the mayor. As a result, community strategies as implemented through various civic groups and through the town council will almost always affect family strategies, but class differences mean that not every family has the resources (economic or cultural) to have an impact on community responses to national policy changes. Families and individuals who compose the upper classes certainly have access to power in terms of influencing factors that will affect the entire community.

What sorts of politicking has this resulted in, in the wake of postsocialist changes? The broad answer to this is relevant to far more than the postsocialist era in Eastern Europe. In a wide variety of historical times and places, an important class difference can be drawn between active and responsive political and ideological roles in a community. Resistance must be led by those who have the resources to effect change. The average peasant, worker, or other member of a nonelite class does not have the resources (whether that means economic, cultural, social, or symbolic capital) to become actively involved in local politics, and can only respond to arguments made by those who do have resources by accepting or resisting their political agendas. Lynn Stephen (1991) discusses a similar case in which she shows how local elite families in a Oaxacan village were able to influence the meaning of the local ethnic identity while solidifying their class position during the integration of the community with global markets. Richard Maddox's case study in Andalusia (1993), to which I have already made reference, shows how this same process of ethnic re-entrenchment and class entrenchment articulated in Spain.

The dividing line in Żywiec involves both economic and cultural capital. Because the new class of neocapitalists has access to economic resources—in the form of high salaries, employment opportunities, and distributive power over community funds and cultural resources—through their interpretation of modernity and their place as knowledgeable community authorities, they are able to challenge the hegemonic power of the prewar elite. The prewar elite in turn have responded by attempting to further entrench their authority in the community and return to their formerly hegemonic place in the reproduction of community meaning. The new resources available in the postsocialist era have resulted in the emergence of a new class, which has been able to effectively resist the prewar elite's traditionalist rhetoric through creating a counterideology of modernity. This points to far greater possibilities for resistance than were presented, for example, in Maddox's study.

Members of both the neocapitalists and the prewar elite in this analysis are likely to have greater economic capital in comparison with others in the community—the neocapitalists because they have recently obtained it, and the prewar elite because businesses, homes, and other resources that were nationalized during the socialist period have been returned to them. Both groups have access to some kind of status or cultural capital: the old elite can draw on claims of ethnicity and traditional cultural authority, and the new entrepreneurs can claim that they are the bridge to the economic future of the community because they best understand how to cope with and profit from capitalism.

I focus on these two groups with high status and economic power to understand class struggle in this community, not because I do not understand or see the "tools of the powerless," such as withdrawal from the system and involvement in the black market, but because strategies for dealing with the changes in national policy (privatization, links with different countries, foreign capital) on a *community* level are driven by the strengths and tactics of these two classes in the town. The two elite classes have differential access to resources and different kinds of resources (cultural as well as material). The conflicts between these classes, involving hegemonic and ideological meanings of the Góral identity and the vision of the town's future, have had an impact on community adaptations, because they have been played out on the level of community strategies.

What of the nonelite classes, then? If they are not able to create new possibilities for resistance, how are they able to affect community strategies? One way is through participating in local political elections. The ousting of the prewar elite from the mayor's office and town council seats in the 1991 election was a clear example of the members of the nonelite classes in Żywiec siding with the neocapitalists. It is not a case of community members consistently taking the side of one elite class over the other, however. The nonelite classes have felt the downside of the neocapitalists' program for the future through the effects of privatization and investments from international capital. Unemployment, rising prices of community services such as transportation, and the possibility of losing housing through the privatization of town-run apartment buildings have not sat well with Żywiecers. Members of nonelite classes can show support for the prewar elite in the present through their attendance at cultural events and their involvement in community cultural groups organized by the prewar elite. In the future, there will be local elections again in Żywiec, and these elections will provide some barometer of which class is winning the struggle for the hearts and minds of the nonelite classes in the community.

The greater question is why the nonelite classes would come down in favor of either the prewar elite or the neocapitalist class. How do the strategies of traditionalism or of modernization benefit members of the nonelite classes? Some of the nonelite can benefit from the traditionalist approach of the prewar elite. The folk festivals and other cultural events bring in tourists, which means that local businesses, such as hotels and restaurants, profit. Though the owners of these venues are likely to be members of the prewar elite, nonelites employed by these businesses benefit in a trickle-down way from the extra hours of work they are paid for, as well as the tips they make. This is a small benefit, but at the very least, it means that when these businesses are doing well, they do not mechanize and cut their work force. The prewar elite, like the flour mill owners who have employed the former Solidarity leader, tend to take on aspects of the prewar patronage system. This means that they are likely to provide some stability and fringe benefits for employees, such as health care, that international businesses in the area are eliminating. The nonelite classes also benefit from travel opportunities provided by cultural folkloric groups, as I will explain in chapter 5, which can be networking opportunities to find migrant labor work.

In all of these ways, traditionalism and the re-entrenchment of folklorized Góral identity benefit nonelites in Żywiec. However, the vision of the future provided by neocapitalists is beneficial for those community members who have retained their jobs in privatized businesses, who manage businesses for international capital, and who are drawn in by the rhetoric of modernity. Not every family in Żywiec has been adversely affected by the influx of international capital into Żywiec, and some see this as a positive development that yields employment for nonelites and stability for the community.

Chapter 5

—◄o►—

The Community,
the Nation-State,
and Globalization

Thus far, I have shown how traditionalism is an idiom through which elite class conflict is occurring in Żywiec. The prewar elite and the neocapitalists are struggling over the emphasis on and interpretation of the Góral identity, and their visions of the contemporary relevance of the identity correspond to their visions of the economic future of the community. These discussions and conflicts focusing on traditionalism are linked to discussions and conflicts over the relationship between the community and the nation-state, over which local economic and political strategies will benefit the community, and over how the community should best regulate its incorporation into the world system in the light of globalizing processes.

This interpretation of conflicts over community, regional, and ethnic identity contrasts with that of many observers of Eastern Europe, who view entrenchment of ethnicity within the former Eastern Bloc as evidence of "backwardness," as a threat to the newly emerging democracies, and as an impediment to economic change.[1] I contend that rather than a desperate attempt to cling to outdated tradition, a renewed emphasis on ethnic identity is a forward-looking product of the political and economic changes in Eastern Europe, the postsocialist transition to market economics. The re-entrenchment of the Góral identity can be used to mediate outside influences, emphasize cohesiveness, and suggest community-positive courses of economic action within Żywiec, as well as create bonds with other communities and nations.

The decentralization of the postsocialist economy (such as, in Żywiec, privatizing industry and housing) is a product of national structural adjustment policies designed to strengthen the economy. But these policies also weaken the power of the postsocialist state, because the state is giving up control to others, both domestic and foreign investors. The postsocialist states of Eastern Europe find their political power undermined as well, because national policy decisions are subordinated to decisions made by supranational entities such as NATO and the European Union, which the Eastern European states would like to join. These processes, which emphasize supranational entities (either political, such as the European Union, or economic, such as large transnational corporations) at the expense of the power of the nation-state, are an aspect of globalization as it is occurring in Central and Eastern Europe. The declining importance of the nation-state in running either the economic or political arena under globalizing political and economic structures increases the likelihood that peripheral areas within these states, such as boundary regions like Żywiec, will begin to act outside the boundaries of the nation-state. We would expect subnational and transnational peripheral identities such as that of the Góral to have the opportunity to gain importance under these conditions.

Almost all facets of current national plans to privatize the economy in Poland will have the effect of alienating people in peripheral areas such as Żywiec, because these plans are based on the idea that when the government pulls out of funding some business or service, someone else will step in to buy the business or provide the service. Of course, there are cases in which businesses clearly make products that few people want (such as the fur factory in Żywiec, which made traditional fur and wool garments), and those businesses would fail even given private investment. But given a desired product or service, this idea presumes that people will have the resources to buy and run a business or provide the service, overlooking the fact that most of the infrastructure in Poland is concentrated in the cities. If a factory in rural Poland makes high quality sweaters, for example, but train service is slow and the phone lines are erratic, few investors would think of this as an ideal buy. Many small factories in rural Poland have been liquidated under such conditions, leaving high levels of unemployment among the very people who are least likely to be able to find other work. In Żywiec, the official unemployment rate was approximately 18 percent in 1995 (in reality, as I learned from interviews, it was closer to a third of the townspeople).

In a large city with good transportation and communications infrastructure, perhaps that fictional high-quality sweater factory would have remained open. But even if it had been liquidated, the former employees would have had a much greater chance of finding work than their country cousins. Simply by virtue of their better transportation and communications lines, cities are by definition the places where domestic entrepreneurs will find it easier to start businesses or buy former state businesses. Just as important, cities are primarily where foreign investors invest. The logic of capitalist investments dictates that places where there are large labor pools and good infrastructure are the most profitable places to invest in. The logic of investment under socialism was not driven as much by profit, since there was also an ideological commitment to developing industry in the countryside. This leaves a socialist legacy of industrial development in rural areas with low population and minimal infrastructure, and this development is being actively shut down by national policies focusing on profit. In other words, socialist development is geographically dispersed, and capitalist development is relatively geographically focused. Because capital and infrastructural investments are focused on urban centers in postsocialism, decentralization in Eastern Europe is leading to the active underdevelopment of peripheral areas and the alienation of people living there.

In the Żywiec case, traditionalism (the promotion of folk festivals, folk art exhibits, poetry readings, and other public expressions of Góral identity) is used by both the neocapitalist and the prewar elite classes in Żywiec in the struggle between their visions of appropriate community strategies in the postsocialist era. In both their visions, however, traditionalism downplays the importance of the nation-state in community-level processes, and it relies instead on political and economic ties forged directly between the community and some other (foreign) place or business. The conflict between the elite classes lies in their specific approaches to the relationship between Żywiec and the world system. It is clear that the prewar elite's vision of Góral traditionalism relies on an insular notion of Góral community moral economy that would reduce ties to international capital, thus benefiting the small-scale businesses owned by the prewar elite. The neocapitalists, in contrast, are interested in attracting international capital to invest in Żywiec and increasing Żywiec's trade ties with communities in other nations. How can the promotion of a subnational identity generate

transnational political and economic ties? The answer lies in the possibilities of using ethnicity as a resource to capture the interest of
potential international investors, to establish cross-border alliances with
Slovak communities that also identify as Góral, and to provide a trope
through which they can relate to other European communities. This
process exemplifies some of the ways in which globalization simultaneously leads to both fragmentation (within the nation-state) and integration (with other sociopolitical and economic entities).

In this chapter, I examine various strategies of community responses in Żywiec to the national economic and political policies of
transformation from socialism. These responses are all based on traditionalism; however, they divide into strategies that emphasize insularity, associated with the prewar elite, and integration, associated with
the neocapitalists.[2] The results and implications of the solutions are
intertwined with elite class conflict, but also open to multiple interpretations by the nonelite (workers and peasants). I first discuss public
performances of Góral identity, in historical and contemporary contexts and on small and large scales, to show these multiple interpretations. I examine the ways in which these performances are co-opted
for class purposes, the features that are oppositional to the nation-
state, and the features that privilege insularity or integration into the
world system. Next, I turn to the topic of the discourse of these community strategies. Using Arjun Appadurai's (1996) formulation of the
importance of the local imagination in mediating globalization, I examine the underlying themes of patronage, the moral economy of the
community, and the encroachment of global capitalism. I discuss the
class realities of who benefits from the community strategies as they
are currently enacted. Also, I show that the promotion of ethnic re-
entrenchment and community solidarity by elite classes enables some
members of the nonelite in Żywiec to benefit from these strategies,
and thus both the prewar elite and the neocapitalists gain support
from this group of nonelites. In general, however, the elite classes are
the primary movers behind public political expressions of ethnicity
and the primary beneficiaries of these strategies. Finally, I analyze the
performances of class, identity, and community in relation to the nation-state. This discussion juxtaposes models of global political
economy, local identity, and modernity, to show how local ideals of
authority and community-based economics result in various strategies
of adaptation to a globalizing political-economic environment. These
strategies help the community, as well as classes within it, negotiate
the relationship with the Polish nation-state and with the larger global
system. Ideas of local identity and contrasting views of modernity

play a large role in the development and implementation of these strategies, and it is clear that the transition to a market economy, or globalization, can be effectively dealt with through traditionalism.

PUBLIC PERFORMANCES, PUBLIC CONSUMPTION

There are many different facets of Góral identity at work today in Żywiec. Góral traditionalism is publicly and self-consciously performed at folk festivals, poetry readings, art exhibits, and other artistic events. These symbols of dress, dance, and songs are objectified parts of an older experience of Góral identity. Contemporary Góral identity is an unselfconscious facet of home life, work, sports, language, and many other parts of life. The self-image of Górals that is more fully and hegemonically integrated into the community is not one of "neutral" folkloric images, but of resistance and defiance toward outside forces— as the community has resisted the domination of the Nazi occupation, for example. Additionally, Żywiecers have other practices that many of them do not even realize are different from the way most Poles live, and thus they do not consciously associate these practices with Góral identity (though outsiders do).

Folk Festivals, Exhibits, Poetry Readings

It is important to note that the notion of *traditional* Góral identity for many Żywiecers is that it is an unchanging identity, set of ideologies, and way of relating to the world. Numerous Żywiecers told me that "real" Górals these days could be found only in Zakopane, a mountain town well set up for tourists who want to see people dressed in old-style clothing and speaking completely in Góral dialect. Góral identity has been reified in public representations to mean certain clothing, songs, dialect, and crafts. This ideology can be successfully used by the elite classes to reinforce old lines of authority in opposition to new ones. However, the practice of Góral identity has changed with the times, as all identities do, and the very notion of traditionalism and regional identity or difference has helped the community to negotiate its relationship to different economic systems and different national authorities in a dynamic way. Thus, as I discussed in chapter 4, Góral traditionalism can be used by individuals within family relations to justify new strategies and kinds of authority as simply different interpretations of precepts that follow from "traditional" identity. Both the prewar elite and the neocapitalist

classes can use the idea of traditional identity to bolster their positions of authority in the community.

That the Góral identity is seen as positive at all is somewhat
ironic, given the history of the town as related in chapter 2. To outsiders, it would certainly seem that Żywiec Górals have been dominated
over the centuries by different state powers, and that the community
has never had autonomy. Insiders in Żywiec, as well, sometimes feel
a sense of resignation about the fact that outside forces have had and
continue to have such determining effects on them and their community. They have to compromise, "lie low," draw away from national-
level politics and economics, and rely on their families to get what
they want. How, then, is traditionalism a powerful force for mediating
change? The answer is that Żywiecers focus not on the failures of
Góral communities to attain independence, but on their essentialized
reputation for being tough and subversive. A core of the internalized
Góral identity is that a Góral is fiercely independent, resists outside
forces, and will win in the end through either guile or perseverance.
The legend of Kapitan Ogień, the Góral resistance fighter who organized guerrilla companies against Soviet troops long after World War
II was over and through the 1950s, is an exemplar of this kind of
stereotype. So is the cartoon by the artist Mlecho, a sort of Polish Gary
Larson: a sign on a mountain that says, "*Witamy na podhale*" (roughly,
"Welcome to Góral territory"), beside which lies a body with a traditional Góral ax–ice pick sticking out of its back. In the same vein
would be naming community sports teams the "Górals." This meaning—that Górals are fiercely resistant to outsiders coming into their
territory and win in the end—subverts the coexisting stereotypes that
Górals are less educated, primitive, and ruled by others. The idea of
a Góral community as being wily and resistant to outsiders is not at
all threatened by the self-folklorized image of dancing peasants presented to outsiders.

There are a variety of behaviors that many Żywiecers do not
realize are specific to them. Grammatical constructions within the
dialect, which they carry over into their "standard" Polish conversation, are one example of this. Even though standard Polish is taught
in the schools, small grammatical differences slip through the linguistic cracks. Sometimes Żywiecers will think of these speech patterns as
Polish slang usages that are not specific to the Góral dialect, when in
fact they are not used by other Poles. Another example of an unreal-
ized cultural difference might be the particular style of barbeque to
which I was exposed several times. This involved making a fire; filling
a three-legged cauldron with chopped cabbage, bacon, chicken, and

onions; screwing a lid down tightly on the pot; and driving the kettle legs into the ground so that it sat over the fire. After several hours, the cauldron lid would be unscrewed and the meal served out. Poles in other areas of the country, hearing my description of this, assured me that this was a "gypsy barbeque," which was a Góral practice. When I in turn questioned Żywiecers as to whether this was a Góral activity, every person I asked stated that this was not particular to Góral communities and was widely practiced throughout Poland.

These unselfconscious expressions of Góral identity are not politicized. However, both the hegemonic sense of Góral identity as resistance and the self-conscious enactment of traditionalist Góral arts and crafts are specifically political statements, although on different levels. Taking the latter first, the public activities that make up traditionalism in Żywiec include Góral folk festivals, arts and crafts clubs, writers groups, dance clubs, instrumental and choral groups, and artisan displays. The prewar elite uses traditionalism to reinforce their authority in the community and thus to recreate their class position. Traditionalism is also an attitude about important characteristics of the community and region that mark them as different from other parts of Poland at present, and have served in the past, under other regimes, to mark this ethnic difference and thus mediate between the community and the national state. Several Góral folkloric programs involving traditionalism began in the period preceding World War II, continued through the socialist period (1947–89), and continue to encourage particular community strategies in the present era. Each of these programs has played a role in keeping the idea of Góral cultural difference alive in the community throughout these periods of incursions by outside forces: the Austro-Hungarian Empire, the German and Russian armies during World War II, the Soviet political and economic system during the socialist period, and the current influxes of large-scale foreign capital.

The interwar period in Żywiec (the era between the end of World War I and the beginning of World War II) was one of renegotiation of national identity. The entire region of Galicia had been ceded from the Austro-Hungarian Empire to Poland as Poland was in the process of reconstructing itself from the three partition areas: Galicia, under Austro-Hungarian control; the German partition; and the Congress Kingdom of Poland, under Russian control. Żywiec, though it lay in Galicia, was less than thirty kilometers from the new Polish–Czechoslovakian border. Comparatively, the distance to the new capital (hundreds of kilometers) was immense and untravelable. Meanwhile, the Habsburg presence had not declined in Żywiec. They still controlled the brewery, a major employer in the community, and family members continued to live in the New Castle and wield considerable political, economic, and cultural influence in the town. In fact, the new government of the unified Poland had seized control of the brewery at first, but the massive political and economic problems involved in creating a new state overcame the new government. In the 1930s, the new Polish government asked the Habsburgs to resume control over the brewery and act as a politically and economically stabilizing force in the region.

As the Nazi menace toward Poland increased in the late 1930s, the Habsburgs began to leave. When Hitler's army invaded Poland in 1939, the last Habsburgs in Żywiec fled, leaving a vacuum of authority. At the same time in the late 1930s, a writers' group was formed, which consisted primarily of the wives of local community leaders. The group, named *Gronie*, wrote poetry about the Żywiec region and Góral life, some of it in the Góral dialect, and they published several issues of the regional journal *Karta Groni*. At the same time, on the eve of World War II, *National Geographic* published an article by an American woman about her bicycle trip through southern Poland, which focused heavily on the Górals of the Tatras Mountains (Hosmer 1939). The Nazi invasion of Poland in 1939 and the subsequent occupation put an end to this local and international exposure of the Góral identity as fighting swept through the Żywiec area. German troops took over the town and industry and set up an industrial base there to provide themselves with metal-working capacity in southern Poland. Resistance fighting in the region was bloody and tense, and many Góral fighters were captured and executed or sent to prison camps.

In the 1950s, after the reconstruction of Żywiec homes and industry was well under way and the socialist government was beginning to nationalize industry, a new Góral writing group was formed. This group also took the name *Gronie* to evoke continuity with the previous group, and it served similar purposes—to emphasize the difference of the community and entrench Góral identity in the face of socialist-internationalist ideologies of unity and sameness. This time, many men contributed to the new regional journal *(Karta Groni)* to write about their wartime experiences in the resistance. These articles frequently dwelled on the image of Górals as fierce fighters who would never give in to outside oppression. It is especially important to note that Poland as a whole succeeded in convincing Soviet planners that there were too many complicated regional differences in Poland for their system to succeed without certain locally oriented adaptations, and they thus averted some of the programs that were such bones of contention in other socialist countries.[3] Poland never collectivized agriculture, for example, which meant that a mainstay of the Góral identity—independent ownership of small farms—went relatively untouched during the socialist years. Also, the Catholic religion was never suppressed in Poland to the same extent as religions were in many other Eastern Bloc countries, and Catholicism was a strong component of the Góral identity as well. In sum, though ethnic diversity was not left unchecked, ethnicity in and of itself was not considered threatening by socialist leaders in Poland, and thus community groups that celebrated ethnicity were able to plan public programs.

Small-Scale Groups

During the socialist period, Żywiec abounded with groups that celebrated their ethnicity. The writing group *Gronie* was one of a number of Góral-identified community organizations founded at the same time. The Żywiec Culture Club (ZCC) and the Friends of the Żywiec Region (FZR [*Towarzystwo Miłośników Ziemii Żywieckie*]) were foremost among them in terms of influence. It is important to realize that this was not simply spontaneous activity: encouragement of cultural groups along nationalist and ethnic lines was part of Soviet policy in all parts of the Eastern Bloc. In fact, to satisfy socialist regimes, some scholars and performers were threatened into wholly fabricating folklore (Zemtsovsky and Kunanbaeva 1997). Anthony Shay (1999) argues that through subsidizing folklore, even if fabricated, the governments of the former Eastern Bloc made the political point that they "respected and protected the primordial traditions of their many peoples, unlike the West, which the Soviets claimed had as an aim the eradication of the arts of the colonized peoples they politically dominated. This point of view resonated in countries like Egypt, Mexico and the Philippines" (41).

During the socialist period, the major factories in Żywiec took advantage of the directive to form sports and cultural organizations through workplaces. The Żywiec Brewery, Żywiec Metal Factory, and Żywiec Paper Factory all formed soccer teams, ran sports clubs, and founded culture clubs. These organizations all contained Góral themes: the sports teams and new sports arenas were named "The Górals" or other Góral names, Góral icons were adopted, Góral-style furnishings were added to the cultural clubs, and Góral-oriented crafts and dance clubs met there.

People in Żywiec were able to use the nationalized industrial workplaces, themselves bastions of socialism, for their own purposes to resist socialism. They emphasized their particular ethnic identity, their difference from other parts of Poland, and, by extension, the community's difference from the rest of the Soviet sphere. This mediation of what socialism meant to them by reinforcement of the ideals of traditionalism was channeled in part through the workplace, which ironically was considered by Soviet planners to be a primary site of socialist ideological transformation. Additionally, community groups such as the ZCC and the FZR provided a variety of programs to reinforce Góral identity in the community: folk festivals, programs for schoolchildren, publications, and cultural artisan displays. The programs for schoolchildren included primarily dance and arts instruction by women who volunteered at the ZCC and the FZR.

Some of these programs faced censorship by the socialist state because of their references to Catholicism. Socialist leaders were attempting to stamp out religious practices in Eastern Europe, and they knew that Polish Catholicism in this region conveyed the double sense of Polish nationalism and ethnic regionalism. Government censors saw references to Mary, Queen of Poland (or even worse from the socialist point of view, Mary, Queen of Galicia), the miracles of the Virgin of Cze.stochowa, and Catholic holidays as antisocialist messages, and they pressured these programs to disband or censor themselves. Volunteers who had run these programs told me of their censor's decision to keep them out of the schools at times. Even years later, they protested to me that in teaching about Polish priest-martyrs they were "only teaching about Polish history," and that in showing children how to make Góral-style "palms" for Easter processions they were "only teaching Góral crafts." What the socialist government perhaps did not understand was that in censoring these programs, they created more local interest in Góral identity and resistance to giving it up. The highly politicized folklore produced under socialism paradoxically took the form of prepolitical, apolitical, or innocent aesthetic forms, which allowed it to be used against socialists in the nationalist causes (Shay 1999, 35). In censoring these women (many of whom were from the prewar elite), they inadvertently called attention to the prewar elite families and lent legitimacy to their status by casting them in the role of dissidents who were important. By censoring the activities, which many townspeople viewed romantically, the socialist government was cutting off its nose to spite its face by generating more dissatisfaction with socialism.

These reminders of Góral identity were also reinforced by sections of books on local history and Górals at the two main libraries in Żywiec for schoolchildren: the Teachers' Library and the Public Library. The head librarians at both of these were involved in community Góral organizations and promoted a Góral sensibility to the libraries through Góral-style decorations, displays, and furniture. Sections in the libraries focused on the history of the community and Góral folklore. The libraries also provided space for community events for children and adults, such as crafts days for children, when the public schools were not allowed to host the ZCC or FZR events.

Large-Scale Góral Productions

Large-scale involvement in the public production of Góral traditionalism began when the town of Żywiec began holding Góral folk festivals in the 1950s. The main festival (now called the Week of Beskid[4] Culture) occurred in midsummer and involved Góral dance, instrumental and choral groups from around the Żywiec area, and displays by craftsmen. Various Góral groups also came from nearby regions to perform skits, dance, and play music. This festival was in competition with another Góral folk festival in Zakopane, the next valley to the east and at a distance of about a two-hour bus ride. Górals from Zakopane are considered by many Żywiecers (most of whom have never been to Zakopane) to be "real" Górals who continue with an "unchanged" way of life.[5] Hosting a competing festival served to convince Żywiecers that even though their town had been changed by socialist economic development, there were still real cultural differences between themselves and other socialists. The festival and other traditionalist activities also served as an outlet for expressions of Góral independence, reinforcement and creation of local history and memory, and community ideals.

Soviet directives formed similar dance companies at local and national levels throughout the former Eastern Bloc. By the early 1950s, every state in Eastern Europe had state-sponsored companies. This practice spread to the Philippines and Mexico in the 1950s, and to Turkey, Iran, and elsewhere in the 1960s and 1970s. The genesis of this activity was the Moiseyev Dance Company, which was founded in 1937 in Moscow, but whose effect in the postwar period cannot be overestimated. Anthony Shay (1999) argues that it was this troupe that inspired not only the many state-sponsored dance companies in the Soviet Union and its satellites, but also state-sponsored dance companies around the world. The performance of these companies, which ranged from highly stylized professional companies to relatively untheatricalized village dance troupes, was meant to symbolize the happy life under socialism's achievement (Giurchescu 1994, 17).

Michael Herzfeld (1997) notes that "visual and musical iconicities have been especially effective in rallying entire populations" (27). Turkish dance scholar Arzu Ozturkman (1994) likewise argues that "the idea of folklore [including dance] provided the emerging nation-states, and their devoted intelligentsia in particular, with ample opportunities to mobilize their subject populations toward the construction of a national identity" (83). In the same vein, the socialist sponsorship of famous national dance troupes such as the Mazowsze in Poland and the State Folk Ensembles in Bulgaria, Serbia, Georgia, and Croatia served to reify national cultural identities in those countries.

But while the intended meanings of these dance ensembles was to show the national folk as idealized under socialism, other political and representational issues could lurk below the surface, particularly in the village- or regionally oriented troupes. To Polish intellectuals, the essentialist portrayals of the pure, rural soul of the Górals meant the imagined *volksgeist* of Poland. But to residents of Żywiec, the portrayals could also reinforce their geographic imaginations of themselves as separate from the Poles.

The largest Żywiec festival, the Week of Beskid Culture, began as a one- or two-day Góral festival, extended through a long weekend in the socialist era, and after 1989, developed into the largest international folk festival in Europe. The festival now lasts about ten days and includes an initial Góral Festival that lasts several days and a separate International Festival in which groups from all over the world perform. There is a preponderance of groups from other postsocialist Eastern Bloc countries, but groups also attend from Togo, New Zealand, Canada, Mexico, and India. There are now many different kinds of activities: performances on a main stage in Żywiec, others on the town square during the day, ceremonies at Bielsko-Biała (the county seat), a finale procession through Żywiec, local and international vendors of food and clothing, and artisan displays in various other small villages surrounding Żywiec. Though the prewar elite are primary organizers of the festival, neocapitalist politicians are also prominent, making speeches, garnering sponsorship money from large businesses, and welcoming the international groups.

The Góral and international segments of this festival are kept fairly separate in time, with the Góral portion occurring during the first three or four days and the international groups performing during the last six or seven days. An exception to this rule is that Góral groups from Slovakia and the Czech Republic can be put into either part of the festival, on the grounds either that they are Góral and therefore in-group members, or that they are from another country and therefore out-group members. Czech Górals, however, have not been involved in the recent attempts by the neocapitalists to expand trade ties among Górals, as Slovak Górals have.

The shifting meaning of the participation of Czech and Slovak Góral groups contributes to the extension of the beginnings of the festival further back in time. By this I mean that although the "Góral and International Folk Festival" as a whole is a recent addition to the town's calendar of activities, a Góral folk festival was been held throughout the socialist era, and Slovak and Czech groups have attended the festival in the past. Thus, during a 1994 interview with the director of the ZCC, which has a leading role in planning the festival, I was told that the festival had been in existence for three years. The brochure produced for the festival in 1995, however, stated that the festival was in its fifth year. Other posters referred to it as going back further, to the original Góral festivals in the 1950s. Explanations offered by various residents were that some of those previous Góral festivals were certainly international, because Górals had come from "abroad" (Czechoslovakia).

Thus, these Żywiecers seemed to be altering their concept of history to include international ties, where previously they had conceived of these groups only as other Górals. On the other hand, they were highlighting international ties, where they previously did not see them as important. This two-pronged approach to reworking the meaning of their history importantly bypasses the Polish nation-state, by being both locally particularistic and globally inclusive, but not nationally specific. This serves the needs of both the neocapitalists and the prewar elite by emphasizing the importance of tradition while drawing attention to the new importance of international ties.

A closer ethnographic look at the festival reveals how these processes work out on the ground. The festival begins with the Góral groups from Poland, Slovakia, and the Czech Republic performing skits, music, and dances. The Góral groups who perform in this segment of the festival participate in a competition judged by university ethnographers who study Góral folklore. In 1995, the master of ceremonies for this portion of the festival was a television personality who was also a famous Góral imitator. He dressed up in the objectified "traditional" Góral costume from Żywiec and bantered with each group while announcing them. The people at the festival, mostly Żywiecers and others from the immediate area, seemed amused by his jokes for and about Górals, performed in a perfect Góral dialect. Townspeople whom I interviewed did not express irony over the fact that actual Górals, dressed in jeans and "heavy metal" T-shirts, would pay money to watch a non-Góral dress up and talk like a Góral. Perhaps some of the reason for this was that he was a truly funny comedian and a wonderful showman, but I believe that a more important aspect was the nature of the jokes he told and the banter he invented. All of his repartee seemed to reflect the sense of Góral traditionalism as resistance, of Górals as smart and wily. He therefore effectively combined the overt, reified symbols of Góral identity with the internalized sense of what it was to be a Góral, and presented an image of themselves to them for their delighted consumption.

Another aspect of this portion of the Góral and International Folk Festival was the schedule of separate receptions for town dignitaries. These events were run by the neocapitalists for the express purpose of welcoming politicians from other towns. When I expressed an interest in these receptions, I was warmly invited—perhaps as a kindness, but I also believe that I was a town oddity who could be used to good effect by being introduced as "an American scholar who has taken such an interest in Żywiec that she is writing a town history." (Members of the prewar elite, on the other hand, tended to emphasize that I was writing a cultural history of the region.) In any case, talk at these receptions tended to focus on politics and economics and what marginal towns could do to save their businesses or attract businesses from outside.

The business aspect was also relevant to which firms would sponsor the festival and which of these would get top billing as advertisers. (The involvement of the Żywiec Brewery, a major sponsor, raises complex issues that will be discussed later in this chapter.) By 1995, a shift had taken place in which the major sponsors of the festival were large, outside businesses and media such as the largest Polish radio and television stations, which merited prominent signs displayed by the stage and arena, where they would draw the most attention. Businesses internal to Żywiec, which had contributed smaller donations or even no donations, responded to this by moving in with their own advertising. A particularly enterprising example was a new and struggling Żywiec-based car dealer, who hired teenagers to walk through the crowded arena distributing leaflets advertising his business. The security workers were obviously unprepared for this move and could not think of a good reason to eject those leafleting.

Many town vendors set up booths to sell food, especially during the evening performances. These vendors include both established businesses, such as restaurants and butcher shops, as well as once-a-year enterprises selling such specialty items as Góral gingerbread cakes and chocolate-covered ginger snaps, a delicious traditional Żywiec specialty (which Poles outside Żywiec sometimes commented on when they learned I was living in Żywiec). Some of the cultural groups in town ran these small, seasonal businesses, and they also sold items such as Góral arts and crafts, and even cassette tapes of Góral songs. Non-Żywiec food vendors set up shop as well, including popcorn and candy vendors and sellers of more substantial food, such as baked potatoes. Foreign concerns were also represented, such as Coca-Cola distributors and a distributor of T-shirts featuring the logos of American heavy metal bands and sports teams.

During the Góral and International Folk Festival, groups from cities with economic ties to Żywiec performed on the main square in town for all to see. These free performances in front of the town hall also featured small-scale local vendors of Góral arts and crafts, as well as international commercial food items. The familiar red and white Coke trucks selling expensive soda were parked on the corners of the square, lending a surrealism to the scene that is familiar to development theorists. In this case, however, it is the class conflict that is providing a venue for both the self-folklorization of these towns and the entree of global capital into this developing Second World region. Richard Maddox (1993) discusses a similar event in his Aracena case, where, however, the uses of traditionalism seem to be less contested, because there is less class conflict:

> While the character of the site and some of the ritual aspects of the celebration reanimated traditional images of religion, honor, and patronage, other dimensions of the event tended to cast traditional culture in a nostalgic light. For example, the display of regional costumes and the self-conscious cultivation of the folkloric by performers and commentators served as a reminder that many local customs and crafts were being supplanted by modern products and fashions in music, literature, and dress. Moreover, the explicit rationale and keynote speeches of the celebration were progressive in tone and designed to promote rural development. . . . Similarly, [the festival] enhanced the prestige of the marques [local elites] and his associates because their sponsorship and support of the event enabled them to represent themselves both as enterprising private individuals whose voluntary initiatives demonstrated a practical concern for the economic prosperity of the region and as honorable and devout patrons conscious of the religious and moral burdens that their heritage placed on them. (118)

In Żywiec there is also a dual character to the folk festivals. Themes of patronage, religion, identity are traditionalist in nature, and thus tend to privilege the authority of the prewar elite. The conscious self-folklorization of costumes, dances, and other consumables, however, juxtaposes the "modern" community with the "past," thus adding fuel to the neocapitalist fire. Why did this dual character not disrupt the authority of the old elite in Aracena, as it does in Żywiec? In Aracena, there does not appear to be a major conflict over the investment of transnational capital in the community, as there is in Żywiec, with the accompanying split into prewar elite and neocapitalist classes. The Aracena old elites made a smooth transition to become the local capitalists, using traditionalism to justify their authority in the community and to draw money into their community by attracting tourists. In Żywiec, however, the uses of traditionalism are contested through class conflict between the prewar elites and the neocapitalists precisely because traditionalism benefits these classes differentially.

The more "exotic" performance groups (those who had come from farther away) were all scheduled on the Żywiec amphitheater stage during the evening performances for the international portion of the festival. People had to pay for tickets to see these groups, as opposed to the free performances on the town square during the day. The prices for these tickets were more expensive than those for the earlier Góral portion of the festival. These international groups (by and large) had no particular ties to Żywiec—they were there because they were spectacular and exotic and lent an air of cosmopolitan internationalism to the festival. Many of these groups were from other Eastern Bloc countries and thus both the people and their costumes looked familiar to Żywiecers. A number of groups, however, came from farther away and differed significantly from Slavs in their music and costumes. Most people in Żywiec have had little to no experience with people from other racial groups, and the mere sight of Africans, South Asians, and Native Americans causes quite a stir. On one occasion, I watched a group of Indian girls clad in saris walk through the downtown open-air market in Żywiec, with a crowd of curious children tagging along behind and adult heads swiveling to watch their progress. I overheard a small Polish boy ask his father who they were and why they were there, and his father replied that they had come "all the way from India, just to show us their dances." The general air of acceptance with which Żywiecers greet these groups contrasts with their treatment of other groups in Poland whom they consider to be racially different, primarily Jews and Roma (Gypsies). Especially when entertainment groups came from poor Third World countries, Żywiecers expressed a sense of solidarity with them as fellow members of the periphery in the global economic system. Racialized groups within Poland, on the other hand, have specific economic roles as scapegoats and are seen as unsympathetic Others.

The presence of these international groups lends a sense of legitimacy to the neocapitalist program of fostering political and economic ties with communities in other countries, because the neocapitalists are the ones who have pushed for the inclusion of these foreign groups. The original Góral festival lent legitimacy only to the traditional elite, because it emphasized an identity in which they had pride of place. Neocapitalists, however, benefit ideologically from the international festival. The more exotic groups represent international ties and show that neocapitalists understand the global political economic scene, that they are capable of establishing international relations and can pull groups in from abroad. The tourist money that flows into the town during the festival is certainly important to a few local vendors, and the sponsorship from major national enterprises such as Radio RMF/FM (national Polish radio) pulls in additional funds to finance the festival. However, for neocapitalists, even if the net profit is small, they recontextualize the meaning of the festival by adding an international section. This portion offsets the Góral part of the festival, and thus neutralizes the ideological capital that would otherwise flow only to the prewar elite.

Emergence of Other Festivals

The success of the festival, both in terms of local interest and drawing tourists to town, has spurred the emergence of other festivals, such as the winter festival known simply as the Góral Wedding. This festival was held throughout the socialist period and is primarily a post-Christmas caroling festival. In Poland, the Christmas holidays extend at least through Three Kings' Day (January 6, twelve days after Christmas) and even up to Candlemas (in early February). This period of traditional celebration includes caroling for sweets at people's homes, as well as special skits that invoke the themes of Christmas and the Three Kings mixed in with regionally specific, pre-Christian and non-Christian imagery and archetypes such as witches, devils, Jews, death, rebirth, and fertility images. For example, traditional pre-Christian costumes with straw masks symbolizing death, rebirth, and fertility are sometimes donned by actors who perform mummery. Another tradition at this time is for people to mark their doors in chalk with the initials of the Three Magi, while a priest goes around the neighborhood blessing their homes.

Because Christmas celebrations were censored in socialist Poland, the festival was named the Góral Wedding in an attempt to give
it a folkloric rather than a religious cast. But Catholicism, as has been
mentioned previously, is a strong aspect of this ethnicity and was
considered oppositional to the socialist state. Thus, the existence of the
festival was polyvalent under socialism: it stood for celebrating
ethnicity, celebrating Catholicism in a somewhat covert way, and criti-
cizing the socialist state. This two-day event now consists of a children's
caroling contest, skits by adult Góral acting and dance troupes, and
displays of Góral Christmas-related arts and crafts. The entries are
judged by a panel of "community leaders," who generally turn out to
be members of the prewar elite. It has continued into the postsocialist
era, but the name has not been changed to a more religious one.

Another emerging local event of particular interest is a festival
that was added in 1995, the Days of Slovak Culture (DSC). The DSC
features the same kinds of groups who frequent the Góral portion of
the Week of Beskid Culture, except that they are all from Slovakia.
This festival has a kind of pan-Góral theme to it, as Żywiecers redis-
covered how many similarities of language, clothing, food, dance, arts
and crafts they have with "their neighbors on the other side of the
Beskid mountains" (across the Slovak border to the south). This festival is also a symbolic public occasion for community leaders from the
towns along the road that crosses the newly opened border to the
south of Żywiec to make speeches about the new era of trade relations
that Polish and Slovak Góral towns will achieve due to the new border
opening. The Polish and Slovakian languages are mutually intelligible,
and code switching into Góral dialect makes them even more so to
Górals. Local politicians and cultural elites thus were able to subtly
emphasize their points about how easy it is for Polish and Slovak
businesses to work with one another (as opposed to "foreign" businesses) by making their speeches in their native languages without
translators, with the crowds understanding both.

A number of these new festivals that have been developed in
the past few years take advantage of the tourist-drawing capacity
of Żywiec by drawing out the traditionalist themes. The Days of
Old Music festival is held in the Old Castle in Żywiec, consisting
primarily of medieval and Renaissance musical groups in period
costumes, interspersed with the occasional Góral artist. This festival draws few tourists and is organized by the prewar elite and
associated groups.

In contrast, the town council is working on the possibility of
starting a new jazz festival, and they believe that they can garner

enough sponsorship money to promote the festival and attract people from out of town. Jazz is clearly not a Góral tradition, and the mayor explained to me that the town was trying to show that they can encompass new, modern activities as well as traditional ones. The association of each class with these two newer and smaller festivals demonstrates their general attitudes toward the other, larger festivals: they are involved for different reasons and interpret the festivals differently. The prewar elite believe that the purpose of the festivals is to celebrate their living heritage and pull the community together. The neocapitalists see the festivals as opportunities to cement political and economic ties with other communities and show their power by convincing multinational corporations to donate money to the festivals.

Sister Cities, Parent Companies, and Family Ties

Since the opening up of Polish borders, Żywiec has gained several sister cities in Slovakia, Germany, and France, with whom the town is building trade ties and cooperative information exchanges. One of the ways in which these relationships are publicly celebrated is for the towns to arrange cultural exchanges of their folklore groups; thus, there are always representatives of the sister cities at the folk festivals in Żywiec. These festivals thus cement political and economic ties with towns in other nations, which benefits the neocapitalists who are working on building these ties. The troupes the sister cities sent to the Góral and International Folk Festival mainly performed for free during the daytime, on the town square in front of the town hall.

One of the sister cities is a French town, Rhien, of similar size to Żywiec, which had a regional hospital much like the one in Żywiec. Cooperation between the hospitals for educational and administrative benefits is the aim of this sister city relationship. In my interviews with the vwiec hospital administrator and other hospital workers, they were very hopeful that Żywiec workers would be able to gain important information about how to run a provincial regional hospital under a capitalist system and provide decent health care with minimal state funding. Exchange visits were planned between administrators and doctors of the two hospitals. To cement this sister-city relationship, though, more than mere administrative decrees were necessary: the two cities tried to connect via imagined folkloric ties as well. Thus, Żywiec Góral dancers had traveled to France, and in return Rhien sent a dance troupe, which performed traditional French clogging to a musical accompaniment on Renaissance-era French folk instruments, to the international portion of the Week of Beskid Culture.

Another sister city in Germany, Unterhagen, was a recent relationship, and this city sent no group to the folk festival. However, when the ceremonies celebrating the sister-city agreement were held in Germany, the town representatives took along a Żywiec Góral dance troupe to perform at the festivities, as well as a large quantity of Żywiec beer. In interviews, hospital administrators and health workers alike focused on the economic benefits of creating ties with sister cities. The relationships, however, were symbolized through folkloric ties.

In the case of the Slovak sister cities, more than folkloric ties are involved. It is certainly true that Slovak groups frequently send dance and musical troupes to the Żywiec festivals. However, the fact that many of these groups also claim Góral identity results in symbolism around pan-Góral ties as well as ties of kinship. Many of the Żywiec residents have kin across the border in Slovakia. Since the closing of the border after World War II, these people have had their ties to their Slovak relatives disrupted, and they are only now, fifty years later, able to freely travel to see Slovak kin. The fact that this Polish–Slovak border placement was contested in the post–World War I era, when Poland was reconstituted from the Russian, Prussian, and Austrian partitions, is partially explained by the fact that this single ethnic group spans the border in its present incarnation. The mayors' rhetoric at the DSC festival about the Polish and Slovak Górals being one people referred in passing to these previously severed kin ties. One of my neighbors, an extremely elderly woman, had in her youth actually married into Żywiec from a town that was now in Slovakia. She and her children were considered Polish, because they were living within the new borders of Poland at the time that the partitions were reunited. Unfortunately, she had had restricted contact with her Slovak relatives during the socialist period. This woman, who remembered all of the national political changes that Żywiec had undergone in the past seventy years, was delighted to see the new Slovak border-crossing and folklore festivals, because they meant that she could now have closer contact with the land of her youth.

The sister-city ties serve in general to create new political and economic ties for Żywiec with other cities abroad. In this way, the town does not have to rely on the national level of political-economic planning to attempt to better its position in the emerging postsocialist order. These new relationships primarily benefit the neocapitalist class, because they reinforce their authority in the community as knowledgeable participants in the global economy. In the next section, I discuss the interaction between the community strategies of capitalism and models of authority the two elite classes propose, as well as the reactions from the nonelite populace of Żywiec.

Patronage Ideals

The contrasting community strategies in the postcommunist era in Żywiec are influenced by the differences between the two models of capitalism in Żywiec I have outlined—large-scale, international capitalism, represented by the Żywiec Brewery and other privatized enterprises, and small-scale, community-based capitalism, represented by local businesses such as bakeries, butcher shops, flour mills, and so forth. The global capital model is based on integrating into the global political-economic system, with the goal of benefiting from foreign investment. The small-scale model is based on traditionalism, which stands for closing the community to outsiders who are not controllable. However, there are some complicating cases on which I elaborate here that will show how these various community strategies, proposed by elites, affect other members of the community and how these nonelites are reacting to the proposed strategies. As I discuss ideological and financial conflicts between the town council and the brewery, I also examine Żywiecers' perceptions of the Żywiec Brewery, which represents the interests of global capitalism, and the Żywiec Metal Factory, a community-based industry with international ties. These cases illuminate the ramifications of the penetration of global capital on the community, as well as some strategies the neocapitalists are attempting to use to discipline multinationals into patterns of investment that will benefit both themselves and, ideally, the community, too. They show how traditional identity can be used to mediate globalizing influences, even by those who seek to undermine its power through folklorization.

In *Modernity at Large* (1996), Arjun Appadurai notes that "[t]he megarhetoric of developmental modernization . . . in many countries is still with us. But it is often punctuated, interrogated, and domesticated by the micronarratives . . . which allow modernity to be rewritten more as a vernacular globalization and less as a concession to large-scale national and international policies" (10). In this section, I chronicle the ways in which two of these micronarratives, those of the neocapitalists and the prewar elite, construct the idea of local strategies within globalization, and how these micronarratives obscure underlying processes of class and force alternative possibilities (such as the metal factory case) into the logic of their narratives. In the end, however, both micronarratives minimize the importance of the nation-state to the community, even as they disagree about the character of the community's relation to international capital and other global structures.

The Brewery versus the Metal Factory

The Żywiec Brewery and the Żywiec Metal Factory offered many similar services during the socialist period. Both enterprises had cultural
clubs, health clinics, childcare facilities, and athletic clubs. They arranged services such as group vacations. The brewery also ran a pre-
school for children of employees. In short, both enterprises, which
employed a large proportion of the population, continued to fulfill
those services that people had come to associate with the patronage
ideals of the Habsburg period. Even though these enterprises were
officially managed through the socialist state, they carried through on
services that benefited employees as individuals. These services also
benefited Żywiec as a community, because they maintained the feeling
that there were large, community-based patrons to whom the town
could turn in times of need.

Both the metal factory and the brewery have been privatized in
the postsocialist period, and both have involved foreign investors in
their affairs. Ironically, most townspeople believe that the metal factory *has not* been privatized, simply because it has continued to provide many benefits to employees and has not laid off as many
employees as the brewery has.[6] Why is there such a difference in the
outcomes of these privatizations, and what sorts of effects does this
difference have on the models of capitalism that Żywiecers are willing
to accept? The answers to these questions lie in the composition of
management at the two factories and the ways in which the factories
are integrated into the community.

At the metal factory, I interviewed the general director, his
secretary, the director of the cultural club, and the metal factory
band leader about the effects of foreign investment on their factory.
I also knew and interviewed a number of people in Żywiec who
worked as laborers at the metal factory. The general director, Pan
Marek, was an older man who had clearly managed the factory
before privatization, although he did not speak about the socialist
period. Instead, he focused on the changes from socialism to
postsocialism and the kinds of efforts he had made at the factory.
He emphasized that he ran a tight ship and that after the fall of
socialism, to increase efficiency, he had fired many people who were
alcoholics.[7] Pan Marek described his hard work and the many hours
he spent driving to Germany to convince customers of the metal
factory to invest in it to ensure its continued existence after
privatization. Because these investors are also suppliers or distributors, and they do not have a controlling interest in the factory, he
felt able to control their desires for greater profit. As a result, Pan

Marek believed that the metal factory would be able to continue to play the role of patron in the community, because the factory did not have to "streamline" by cutting down on benefits.

Pan Jan, the director of the cultural club (*Śrubka*, which means "little screw"), played the public role of the patron for the metal factory. In many ways, he acted as the intermediary between the neocapitalists and the prewar elite by allowing them to plan activities jointly. The cultural club sponsored many activities on its own in Żywiec, such as yoga and aerobics classes, art exhibits, speakers, and concerts. Pan Jan was also involved in planning the festivals and other cultural activities. He worked with the (neocapitalist) town council's arts and culture committee and attended meetings of the (prewar elite's) FZR and ZCC. While allowing his employer, the metal factory, to gain currency in the community, he still espoused traditionalism and was very conscious of being a proper Góral. During our interview, he castigated me because he believed that my research would focus only on the good things about privatization, instead of talking also about the deleterious effects on the "little people" and on the community as a whole. Try as I might, I could not convince him that my project was not to promote the intrusion of Americanization in Żywiec.

Pan Jan echoed Pan Marek in his determination to continue the services that were so beneficial to metal factory workers. Pan Marek's secretary was likewise full of nothing but praise for the general director in both his attainment of foreign investment and his commitment to "community values." The metal factory workers whom I knew (those who had not been fired for alcoholism or inefficiency) also insisted that the metal factory was entirely commendable as a place to work and good for the community.

In contrast to the metal factory, the brewery seemed like a breeding ground for dissent. Whereas the metal factory managers were all Żywiecers, the brewery management included outsiders both at the local management level and on the board of directors. There have been several general directors of the Brewery since the 1991 privatization, all from outside Żywiec. Thus, at the Żywiec Brewery, there was not stability in management, nor was the management rooted in the community at all. Workers at the brewery resented the outsider managers, were angry about the employment layoffs, and particularly resented the new marketing department and "marketing guys," whom they saw as the puppets of Heineken's will in Żywiec. Members of the brewery management, who claimed that they were spurred on by investors' desires for greater profits, had eliminated most of the fringe benefits for working in the brewery by 1995.

The brewery was also attempting to pull away from the expectations of the community that they would donate money for projects such as the smaller folk festivals. Instead, they focused on the large international portion of the Week of Beskid Culture and sponsored their own projects, such as rock concerts, at which they could sell a lot of beer. As I have mentioned, on the occasion of the pope's visit, the town council had requested a special donation to beautify the town. The brewery agreed to give money, with the stipulation that the town council must be more willing to negotiate with the brewery on the issue of their desire to trademark the Żywiec name.

This contentious issue was a result of the fact that a new mineral water factory in a nearby village was marketing their mineral water under the name "Żywiec Zdrój." Thus, the Żywiec Zdrój factory could take advantage of the national recognition of the Żywiec Brewery name. This was additionally complicated by the fact that the Żywiec Brewery had recently begun producing and marketing their own brand of flavored mineral waters, under the Żywiec label. As a result, these competing brands of Żywiec and Żywiec Zdrój mineral waters were placed on store shelves next to one another, and consumers did not know the difference.

The Żywiec Brewery felt that the Żywiec Zdrój usage was unfair, because the brewery had been using the "Żywiec" name for national distribution for decades. Thus, they proposed that the town of Żywiec should give them sole rights to use the name for nationally marketed products. The town council was perturbed at the massive layoffs and other effects of privatization that they seemed unable to control, and unhappy that the brewery was unwilling to donate to town causes anymore. As a result, they came up with a counterproposal: they proposed a town tax on the name "Żywiec" as it was used for any nationally marketed product, then claimed that the brewery would be in a better financial position to pay the tax than Żywiec Zdrój, because it was a much larger and more profitable enterprise. Therefore, the brewery would effectively have sole usage of the "Żywiec" name. This compromise was not at all what the brewery management had expected—thus, their attempt to soften the town council with a donation for the pope's visit. The town council was using the only tools at its disposal to bring the influence of international capital to heel and use it for their benefit and presumably the benefit of the community. This dispute had still not been settled in 1997, which benefited only the neocapitalists, because they were able to continue using this issue to control the brewery's donations to the community.

In contrast with these conflict-ridden contemporary accounts of working in the brewery that were relayed to me by managers, workers, and outsiders, elderly members of the prewar elite tended to have very positive memories of working at the brewery. In interviews, I heard idealized versions of prewar brewery employment that focused on the patronage of the archduke and the gracious working conditions they were afforded as the local elite. These prewar brewery employees emphasized that the brewery was embedded in the community in many ways, including providing housing, sponsoring community events, and even arranging for the distribution of coal and potatoes during the winter. The new brewery hardly seemed the same entity, leaving a vacancy of authority and patronage in the community.

The two enterprises, the metal factory and the brewery, interact differently with events such as the folk festivals. The brewery sponsors the large Góral and International Folk Festival, but because townspeople believe that the brewery is motivated only by profit from the beer it sells and the international exposure, they feel that the brewery is sponsoring the festivals for the wrong reasons. The metal factory, on the other hand, does not advertise much at the town festivals, but Żywiecers know that it is involved in planning most festivals because the *Śrubka* director is also on the town council's arts and culture committee and the ZCC committee that plans the festivals. He frequently takes on the role of master of ceremonies at these events, and his presence is strongly felt as a community cultural leader. In stark contrast, the brewery is absent from community festivities except when it is selling beer and/or advertising.

Both the metal factory and the brewery are examples of neocapitalism in Żywiec, because they are both large enterprises that have been privatized and have investment from abroad. Ironically, however, the metal factory is widely perceived as being an example of community-based capitalism and a staunch moral leader in the community. Both the benefits employees receive from the workplace and the emphasis on traditionalism associated with the metal factory's cultural club *Śrubka* seem to lead people to define the metal factory as nonprivatized, rather than perceiving these conditions as an alternative form of privatization. In this sense, then, the prewar elite benefit from this widespread misconception, and the metal factory is able to play both sides of the ideological fence in Żywiec.

Neocapitalists versus International Investors

The position of the neocapitalists is thus shaky as they attempt to showcase their business acumen and community authority. Traditionalism is perceived as the sphere of the prewar elite and community-based capitalism, even where it is actually being practiced as part of international investment, as with the metal factory. The neocapitalists' success at bringing in international capital to the brewery and other businesses is perceived as destructive to the community, because these businesses no longer donate money to town events or keep up with benefits to their employees.

In response, the neocapitalists have tried a number of strategies to buttress their authority as mediators of international ties, as well as discipline the capital coming into the community. This economic positioning takes several different turns: trying to get more foreign investment, trying to control the investment through economic threats and promises to the international companies, and focusing on sister-city agreements. The town council's position on the trademarked use of the name "Żywiec" is one example of their attempts to control the brewery enough to pry more money out of it. The more money the neocapitalists can obtain from outside businesses, the more their position of power is bolstered.

Another example of the neocapitalists' attempts at control over the Żywiec Brewery is their threats to turn over sponsorship of major community events to another brewery. Part of the rhetoric they use in this instance is the community-oriented ideology of Góral traditionalism. For more than a hundred years, the Żywiec Brewery has used Góral images and the "Żywiec" name in its advertising and marketing strategies, from the dancing Góral couple on the label to hiring costumed Góral bands to play in grocery stores during promotions. The brewery is thus strongly identified with Żywiec Góral identity, both by Żywiec residents and by outsiders. The town council has begun to use this identification with Żywiec and Górals against the brewery by threatening to give sponsorship of major events such as the huge Góral and International Folk Festival to another brewery in Poland, one of the main competitors to Żywiec Beer. This would clearly affect the Żywiec Brewery, because the rival brewery would gain publicity by sponsoring such a major event right in the same town with which the Żywiec Brewery is associated. The rival brewery would also gain sole rights to sell beer at the festival it sponsored, which would mean that the Żywiec Brewery would lose money by its absence as a vendor. This plan of the town council cleverly combines both ideological and financial reasons for Żywiec Brewery sponsorship of town events, in ways that clearly have an impact on the brewery.

In the fall of 1995, the town council actually made good on its threat to give sponsorship of a Żywiec festival to another brewery. It gave the sponsorship of the Days of Old Music, a minor festival with fewer overt Góral events, to a rival Polish brewery. Thus, this brewery was able to have its logo on all of the publicity materials for this festival and sell its own beer in Żywiec at the event. The rival brewery generally thumbed its nose at the Żywiec Brewery by invading its territory, both in the form of the town of Żywiec and the Góral region and identity as a whole. It remains to be seen whether this will substantially affect the Żywiec Brewery's financial interactions with the town. In 1996, however, the Żywiec Brewery still retained sponsorship of the major Góral and International Folk Festival. Because the Days of Old Music is a minor festival that draws fewer tourists, sells less beer, and has much less national and international publicity, the threat of not sponsoring that festival may not have been enough to motivate the Żywiec Brewery to increase its contributions to the town. Regardless, the actions of the town council can be seen as a strong and nuanced attempt to discipline the brewery for its actions in cutting off the town financially.

Who Benefits from Traditionalism?

What is the meaning of the rhetoric of Góral community values in the town council threats to the brewery? I believe that it serves in part to couch the neocapitalists' actions in an acceptable frame, and, thus, it helps to make their cause more palatable to the general Żywiec population. However, because the meaning of Góral identity as resistance to the control of outside forces is deeply hegemonic within Żywiec, the use of arguments based on traditionalism may also help neocapitalists to convince themselves that their strategy is appropriate. The use of traditionalism is an example of contradictory consciousness in which the neocapitalists use the rhetoric of ethnic revitalization and community-based development while working to make the ethnicity a nostalgic part of the community's past and subverting community development to the needs of global capital.

In contrast, the prewar elite have proposed a different strategy of community adaptation, and their use of traditionalism differs from that of the neocapitalists. In what regard do these two strategies differentially affect portions of the Żywiec population? Is community autonomy an effective mechanism for dealing with the transition to postsocialism, and if so, for whom? I take up these remaining questions here.

This chapter shows the two different models of capitalism proposed by the neocapitalists and the prewar elite as strategies for community survival. I examine the ways in which these classes interact with the community and how their proposed strategies are received by workers and townspeople. The two classes interact differently with the two ideologies at the community level, those of traditionalism and modernity. Góral identity and ideas of modernity are two different resources that are manipulated by these elite classes to bolster their authority both with local and international businesses and the nonelite in Żywiec.

Over the past several centuries, Żywiecers have never escaped from the sense of being occupied by outside forces and having to negotiate with them. The idea of democracy is not essential to their identity and is not particularly motivating to them at this time, when it is associated with poverty and political disenfranchisement. Thus, Żywiecers can appropriate useful aspects of the project of postsocialism without encompassing the whole package of global capitalism, democracy, and modernity.

The interaction between visions of traditionalism and modernity can be seen, for example, in promotional materials produced by the mayor and town council to promote tourism and business investment in Żywiec. Two videotapes had been produced, one simply introducing viewers to the town and region, and the other chronicling Pope John Paul II's visit to Żywiec (*Żywiec* 1994, *Na swojej ziemi* 1995). The first video mixes images of productive modern technology, a competent labor force, the beautiful regional landscape, and recreational activities, with images of people wearing traditional Żywiec Góral garb performing dances, playing music, and producing crafts. The second focuses on the papal visit, but it also shows off the town to its best advantage. A number of promotional pamphlets have been produced with similar messages of both development and traditionalism, such as the town budgetary statistics juxtaposed with pictures of arts and crafts and pictures of assembly lines paired with those of Góral dancing troupes.

These materials have several different purposes, two of which are to introduce potential investors and sister cities to the town and provide souvenirs for tourists. Perhaps most surprising, however, is that the primary consumers of these materials are Żywiec residents themselves. Whenever a slick new publication comes out, even if it has the same themes and images as previous publications, Żywiecers purchase it in droves. This discourse of combined development and traditionalism produced by the town council is similar to their use of the folk festivals: the promotional materials privilege their authority as people who understand capitalism and are capable of bringing in and controlling money from abroad. In purchasing the promotional materials, nonelite Żywiecers are literally buying the neocapitalist version of what the community strategy should be for the postsocialist era.

Certainly the emphasis on traditionalism strengthens the community identity, but how is this beneficial for both elites and nonelites? It is clear that for the neocapitalists, it is a tool to use against transnational capital, which cements their authority by showing that they can get donations from and cement ties with other communities. For the prewar elite, it provides a mechanism to bolster their position as traditional cultural authorities in the community. The nonelite do play a role, however, in accepting or rejecting these class positions and proposed strategies of community action, and some proportion of them stand to benefit from the uses to which traditionalism is put in this community.

I contend that emphasizing the Góral identity has, in the past—and particularly in the socialist era—been an effective mechanism for dealing with provincial isolation and poverty, for the nonelite in Żywiec as well as for the elites. Góral dancing and musical groups from Żywiec and several villages in the Żywiec area applied for grants from the Polish socialist government and have had the opportunity to go abroad to perform. One woman from Porabka, a neighboring town, showed me newspaper clippings going back forty years of the dance troupe she founded. They had been abroad many times during the socialist era, and they gained more than just the joy of travel. Groups who were able to go abroad during socialism benefited from being able to purchase Western goods, which they could then resell in Poland, and from making contacts abroad that could be useful for gaining sponsors for travel permits that would allow them to go abroad again to work. Thus, the groups served as a way to get out of Żywiec, to travel and to make contacts on the other side of the Iron Curtain, for the nonelite as well as the elites.

Women who participated in these groups had another benefit from traveling abroad. I was told by several people that their daughters, sisters, cousins, and friends had married foreign men whom they had met while performing in Góral dance and musical troupes. These women had a rare opportunity to get out of socialist Poland permanently, and to be in a position to aid their families who remained by sending them remittances. Access to Western money, particularly dollars and deutsche marks, could go far in socialist Poland toward obtaining tightly controlled goods. In many ways, then, emphasizing their ethnic difference gave Żywiecers tools to hold off the consequences of socialism that would otherwise affect their community.

In the postsocialist era, however, much of this national funding for the arts has been cut, and groups must apply to town budgets or directly to town businesses to sponsor them for trips out of the country. How, then, might emphasizing community difference benefit the nonelite in Żywiec? Unemployment and poverty are on the rise, and the opportunity to travel abroad is even more beneficial in the postsocialist era. Góral identity still gives dance and musical troupes a reason to exist and an excuse to travel abroad. In the case of the metal factory, which continues to fund cultural groups through *Śrubka*, its employees are still able to obtain travel benefits similar to those under socialism. The brewery, on the other hand, has cut these benefits and thus is seen as being against the community.

The new sister-city relationships fostered by the town council also benefit individual Żywiecers. These relationships, in which the town does an end run around the national polity by setting up direct relations with other nations, afford some Żywiecers the opportunity to travel to these particular cities with the assurance that they will be hosted there. Góral troupes and artisans can travel to festivals, and people who are associated with particular businesses with partners in the other sister cities can travel for several months to the sister city to learn and consult. For example, the hospitals in Żywiec and in Rhien have been exchanging doctors and administrators.

Clearly, the neocapitalists have been somewhat effective at getting money out of local businesses by emphasizing the Góral ideology of the community. But the question remains, how much of this money is benefiting anyone other than the town council and mayor? Is this money actually being funneled to meet the needs of townspeople? I do not have a definitive answer to this question, but I do have a qualified one. The national budget has slashed money for towns and villages enormously, and prices have risen enormously, resulting in many local problems for the Żywiec town budget. Certainly some notice must be taken of the fact that the neocapitalist politicians have ample, nationally supplied salaries, which are the envy of their neighbors. On the other hand, the rest of the money for running the town has to come from somewhere, and some of it is indeed coming from international business that has invested in Żywiec.

The effects of encroaching global capitalism are being held somewhat at bay by the use of Góral community identity, in both the senses that the neocapitalists and the prewar elite are using it. Some proportion of the nonelite do benefit by these community strategies, because the strategies are effective in mediating the relationship between the town and national political and economic policies, and the town and global capital. The models of authority that the neocapitalists and the prewar elite have provided are still close to the patronage models of the Habsburgs. Of course, the Habsburgs fit it better than any mayor ever could, and the prewar elite do not have the massive capital that can be mobilized by international businesses. However, the classes have each provided leadership and a vision of the community's future convincing to nonelite in Żywiec, which motivates Żywiecers to support the efforts of the two classes.

PERFORMANCES OF CLASS AND ETHNICITY, AND COMMUNITY VERSUS NATION

According to Appadurai (1996),

> [G]lobalization is itself a deeply historical, uneven, and even localizing process. Globalization does not necessarily or even frequently imply homogenization or Americanization, and to the extent that different societies appropriate the materials of modernity differently, there is still ample room for the deep study of specific geographies, histories, and languages. . . . [T]he relationship between history and genealogy is impossible to engage without a strong sense of the actualities of the longue durée, which always produce specific geographies, both real and imagined. If the genealogy of cultural forms is about their circulation across regions, the history of these forms is about their ongoing domestication into local practice. (17)

In this chapter I have argued that however much class conflict is involved in ethnic revitalization in postsocialism, in this case, the reentrenchment of this ethnicity also serves to mediate the relationship between the national polity and the local community. This is an important facet of this phenomenon to consider, given that many provincial communities have few other resources that can be mobilized in their defense, and they have been particularly hard hit by the shock therapy policies of decentralization in Eastern Europe and the former Soviet Union. Many other communities in Eastern Europe are struggling with the dialectic between communism and capitalism, and many people feel trapped because capitalism has not led to the positive changes for which they had hoped. Yet the only alternative, they imagine, would lead them "back" to communism.

Żywiec is in a unique position because members of this community vividly remember a discourse of *community* development rooted in local patronage and local authority, rather than socialist ideals or global capitalism. This discourse provides them with several options for community strategies in the postsocialist era that are neither tied to Polish nationalist development nor totally at the mercy of global capitalism. Globalization, the integration of this community into political, economic, and cultural forms with world-spanning importance and implications, is mediated through a locally remembered and constantly reconstructed history of identity.

Chapter 6

◄o►

Politics, Culture,
and Modernity
in Postcultural Poland

Pope John Paul II's visit to Żywiec was a context within which Żywiecers acted out conflicting ideologies of traditionalism and modernity. The papal visit presented an opportunity for different groups of Żywiecers to express their visions of the future for the community. On that highly charged public occasion, the two elite classes, which I have called the prewar elite and the neocapitalists, struggled for symbolic control over how the town of Żywiec and Żywiec Górals were to be portrayed. The neocapitalists had a dispute with the Żywiec Brewery, through which they gained funding to spruce up the town. Buildings on the pope's route received a fresh coat of paint and were renovated, a large stage that towered over the main square was constructed, and the "smallest rondo in the world" was completed downtown. Through these tasks, the neocapitalists publicly displayed their expertise in obtaining funds in the postsocialist era to other Żywiecers and to outsiders, which enabled the many national and international news crews in town for the visit to show a new and prosperous-looking Żywiec to the watching world. In return, the Żywiec Brewery was allowed to hand out flags with its corporate colors and its stylized version of the "Żywiec" name.

These images of modernization were countered by the prewar elite. They arranged for traditional Góral mountain horn players in colorful costumes to perform a salute as the pope entered town, and they formed a choir to sing traditional Góral songs and hymns. Many members of the prewar elite also dressed for the occasion in beautiful traditional garb. These activities were designed to show that Góral identity is not part of the nostalgic past, but rather a living part of the community and a strong force—not just an economic and political identity, but one with deep cultural meaning in everyday life as well.

Claimed as a Góral by townspeople, the Holy Father in many ways embodied in one person the complex relationship Górals have with their local community, the nation, and international forces. For example, he was born and raised in the Żywiec region, and idolized by the people of Poland as a national symbol when he was inducted into the papal office. Since his elevation, he had been a critic of the expansion of a predatory capitalism and the values that come with political and economic integration into the capitalist system at the expense of other traditional and moral values. Yet he helped to bring capitalism to Poland through both political activism and diversion of funds to the Solidarity movement. Similarly, Żywiecers are peripheral to the Polish nation-state, and through outsiders' romanticization of their ethnicity, they are held up as remnants of the traditional Polish past. They, like John Paul II, have an ambivalent relationship with capitalism: first, immediately after the fall of the socialist state, they embraced it as the panacea for fifty years of communist oppression, and then they became dissatisfied when the reality did not match their expectations.

The struggles enacted through, and the issues raised by, John Paul II's visit were the same ones that colored family land feuds, community agreements with international businesses, folk festivals, and sister-city agreements in the Żywiec region. I have discussed issues of class conflict, conflicts over the integration of international capital into the community, the relevance of the Góral identity to postsocialist life, and the increasing peripheralization of Żywiec vis-à-vis the Polish nation-state. These are all factors that play out in the everyday life of Żywiec, and which were brought into sharp relief by the visit of the pope. They continue to shape other important public occasions, as well as behind-the-scenes interactions among the town council, cultural groups, and businesses such as the metal factory and the brewery.

The myriad political, economic, and cultural changes in postsocialist Eastern Europe have altered the available resources and relations of power in struggles for control over community processes.

This is consistent with the Marxian view of political economy that "the project of development, as it has been imposed on the non-Western world, has typically involved the creation of new elites and new gaps between castes and classes, which may not have arisen except for various neocolonialist projects in the new states" (Appadurai 1996, 144). The project of development in Eastern Europe, whether it is called a "transition to capitalism and democracy," or "globalization," or even "modernization," has some structural similarities with other instances of increased integration into global capitalism in that the creation of new elites, whose interests are intertwined with global capital, results in conflicts over authority and control within the local community.

In Żywiec, these struggles for community control have been expressed in part through the re-entrenchment of stereotyped, folkloric Góral ethnicity, a strategy that I term "traditionalism." This process is driven by class conflict between the prewar elite, who have both economic power as small-scale capitalists and cultural capital as authority figures within the Góral ethnicity, and an emerging neocapitalist class with ties to global capital. Both elite classes compete for the hearts and minds of the other classes in the community (the workers, the peasants, and the unemployed underclass) through appeals to particular and conflicting ideals of traditionalism and modernity. My meaning of traditionalism closely corresponds to Appadurai's formulation of "culturalism," which he states is the "conscious mobilization of cultural differences in the service of larger national or transnational politics. It is frequently associated with extraterritorial histories and memories, sometimes with refugee status and exile, and almost always with struggles for stronger recognition from existing nation-states or from various transnational bodies" (1996, 15). I agree with Appadurai's admonition that we must not reduce ethnicity to ethnonationalism (1996, 149–57), not only for the sake of recognizing the importance of a range of kinds of ethnicity, but also because the decreasing significance of the nation-state in the context of globalization provides for fewer stimuli toward nationalism.

Contrasting with the idea of traditionalism in the Żywiec community, the idea of modernity, in the sense that it is used by the neocapitalists, refers to the idea of progress, the civilized as opposed to the primitive, the urban as opposed to the rural, and the material, commercial trappings of labor-saving devices, high-tech entertainment systems, news media that span the globe, and popular culture. Certainly, to many residents of Central and Eastern Europe and the former Soviet Union, stores such as McDonald's and Benetton, and Western-made goods in general, were symbols of modernity for which they yearned under communist regimes. The way to attain these things, as they were given to understand, was through the development of capitalism and democracy, two concepts that seemed to denote basically the same system. Capitalism-democracy was seen in contrast to their own system of socialism-communism, which was based on a centralized economy and a one-party political system. The neocapitalists claim that they are the people who best understand how to operate in the global capitalist system, and thus their vision of the community's future is the best.

However, before we uncritically accept the duality of these two systems, we must ask if the desire of Żywiecers (and other people in the former Eastern Bloc) to acquire conveniences means that they were buying into the idea that they were premodern and needed to move on to modernity. Perhaps this was somewhat true in the past, as Żywiecers were ideologically rejecting the Soviet model of modernity, with which they were dissatisfied. Currently, disappointments with transition policies have resulted in more complex points of view about capitalism and democracy, which have also translated into rethinking the idea of the modern. The present local sense of modernity in Żywiec is not centered entirely around Western goods and international capital, much as the neocapitalists have attempted to privilege that definition. Rather, as an emic category, modernity is seen by many Żywiecers to represent the freedom to make their own decisions, accompanied by a moral confusion about what those decisions ought to be. The prewar elite believe that Góral values, including those privileging family and an insular community, are effective ways of dealing with the modern era.

These current class struggles, along with the use of traditionalism around ethnic identity, and the appeals to modernity, must all be placed in their historical context from the feudal and socialist periods to the present. Many of these processes operated in previous eras— Żywiec is no stranger to fluctuating national political and economic agendas. The present "crisis" follows a long history of crises in this century alone, as the community was traded, conquered, and integrated into different nation-states—from the Habsburg Empire, to the interwar Polish state, to the Nazi occupation, to the Soviet-dominated Polish People's Republic (*Polska Republika Ludowej* [PRL]), to the postsocialist, independent Poland. The integration of capitalist markets brings new political and economic resources to bear, but the processes through which community action is mobilized and the idioms through which community ideals are expressed remain fundamentally similar to those of previous periods, in that Góral identity has been a continuing focus in periods of upheaval and resistance. The present postsocialist era, however, has seen the emergence of the neocapitalist class, which is a major contender for political and cultural power in the community in a way that even the communists were not able to achieve. The rise of this new neocapitalist class in Żywiec is in part a result of a new economic niche for transnational capital. Just as important, however, are the political and ideological strategies deployed by neocapitalists, which many Żywiecers of other classes are willing to accept for a variety of reasons.

In Żywiec, the neocapitalists attempt to justify their local authority by invoking the idea of modernity: they are the people who understand the modern world, and who will act as mediators between the outside (the national level and the global political-economic system) and the local Żywiec community. In this equation, as in national and international politics, modernity is glossed as capitalism and, to a lesser extent, democracy. Ironically, these neocapitalists, who are most invested in the idea of modernity, also need to integrate Góral themes into their proposed community strategies. Re-entrenching Góral identity brings them some local legitimacy, because they are drawing on an idiom of identity that is deeply meaningful in this community, and it also lends them cultural specificity in marketing their local culture to outsiders. However, for neocapitalists, the advantages of emphasizing Góral identity are few, and the salience of the identity remains a critical point of conflict between them and the prewar elite.

Neocapitalists have also attempted to cast Góral identity as a nostalgic remnant of the past, and themselves as the best local authorities in the new, modern world. They do so to undermine the authority of the prewar elite, the owners of small-scale capitalist businesses. The economic base of this class has reemerged in the postsocialist era because their prewar property has been returned to them. This prewar elite class benefits from ethnic re-entrenchment in a traditionalist vein: their authority as community leaders flows from their position as cultural elites within the Żywiec Góral community. If the prewar elite strategy of community insularity is followed, their businesses benefit most from restricting the penetration of global capital, because they will experience less competition. This position of local authority is contested by the neocapitalists, whose new class position is based on their middleman position between international capital and the community. If they are able to promote their strategy of community integration into the global economic system, they will benefit from their continued control over local politics and thus local community resources, as well as resources that they are able to obtain from international businesses investing in Żywiec. The neocapitalists are attempting to folklorize the ethnic identity and thus remove it from contemporary life, to buttress the idea that the community is entering the modern era and must have appropriately "modern" community leaders. In this characterization of the modern, they are influenced by what Appadurai (1996) calls the ideology of the "Enlightenment project of political participation—based on the idea of an educated, postethnic, calculating individual, subsisting on the workings of the free market and participating in a genuine civil society" (142). The prewar elite are responding to this challenge by denying that Góral identity is a nostalgic leftover from presocialist days and promoting events and ideologies of vibrant ethnic identity. These ideologies cast them in the role of cultural authorities and community patrons.

The prewar elite have constructed a public sense of Góral traditionalism defined by the performance of dialect, dress, arts, music, dance, and crafts. The neocapitalists also emphasize this performance-oriented definition of Góral identity, but they attempt to further folklorize the identity to downplay the current existence of Góral identity, which does not fit their definition of "modern." Neither faction has evoked the actually existing sense of Góral community identity, which much of the population in the Żywiec area shares. I refer to the everyday expressions of Góral identity as a host of cultural practices, including language, architectural style and other aesthetics, and a savvy, resourceful, and enduring resistance to outside forces. This sense of Góral identity is tacit, undergirding family and community life in Żywiec in these times of postsocialist political, economic, and cultural upheavals just as well as it did during the earlier eras. The nonelites in Żywiec are relatively supportive of these self-folkorized efforts at ethnic entrenchment, however, because both public and private senses of Góral identity have advantages for Żywiec residents. The ideas of Góral traditionalism, identity, and modernity are resources that can be used within families and between individuals in disputes, not just for elite factional fights. The performative aspects of Góral identity promote tourism, which benefits local business but also provides opportunities for nonelites in Żywiec to travel to other countries with folk groups, to see the world and look for foreign employment opportunities at the same time.

Which class is winning the struggle? On a return trip to Żywiec in 1997, it was clear to me that the neocapitalist vision of the community's future (and thus of how modernity was constituted, and probably of the Góral identity as a thing of the past) was triumphing. The relatively large amounts of money coming to brewery managers and others through multinational investments were being funneled into large community businesses, and the smaller stores and older businesses owned by the prewar elite were closing. More children of the prewar elite were attempting to gain entrée into the international enterprises rather than revive their parents' or grandparents' businesses. People were also worried about the increasing unemployment in town—there had been more brewery layoffs and layoffs from other firms, with yet more layoffs planned for the future. Nonelite support for the neocapitalists was waning, but the neocapitalists had so much economic capital, and their programs tied in with national and international visions of development and modernity to such a great extent, that it is difficult to see how they could be dislodged. Prewar elites were seeing their economic capital eroding as a result of competition with international business, and they no longer enjoyed the high levels of social and cultural capital they had during the socialist era. During the socialist era, the prewar elite played the role of resistance to socialism, which to an extent dovetailed with international ideas of development and modernity.

In each era, would-be elites have an edge not only because they interact more with outsiders, but also because they represent to outsiders the needs of nonelites in the community. But the needs of the community are not always clear or homogenous, and nonelites perceive those needs differently as the situation changes, further changing the situation for elites. Each elite group tries to answer the needs of the community differently, but they also try to shape the perception of what the community needs. The production of meaning by the local elite is a complex process that interacts with outsiders and their various needs, but also interacts with nonelites and rival would-be elites in the same community. The prewar elite class is a formidable opponent that continues to shape the debate over community strategies in Żywiec, yet it seems likely to me that the neocapitalist strategy will eventually assume a dominating position. The prewar elites are able to mobilize the social, cultural, and symbolic capital of their traditional place in the community, as well as the economic capital that flows from their newly returned businesses. Neocapitalists, however, have access to resources that flow from transnational businesses, and these wield considerable power. The neocapitalists have demonstrated, though, in the case of the Żywiec Metal Factory and in their interactions with the Żywiec Brewery, an ability to constrain somewhat the actions of global capital in the local setting. This leads me to consider the interaction of global, national, and community processes in the next section.

Supranational, National, and Regional Processes

The configurations of power, domination, hegemony, and resistance enacted in the articulations between class, community, nation, and the global system are by no means unique to the postsocialist transition in Eastern Europe. We can see these forces playing out, for example, in debates over purifying the French language as France moves ever closer to political and economic integration with the European Union. Similarly, as the European Union becomes more important in Great Britain, the reemergence of Scottish nationalism points to issues of community identity in the face of globalization. Thus, the concept of the nation-state becomes problematized because of the influence of supranational forces.

However, socialism and postsocialism as political and economic systems highlight comparisons with other case studies that focus on capitalism as a transformative mode. The decentralization of the state in Poland involves political and economic decentralization, two processes that are frequently glossed as a singular transition to both democracy and free-market capitalism. There are numerous examples of societies that have democratized and/or fully integrated into the global capitalist system, and Żywiec has points of similarity with many of these cases, from Eastern to Southern Europe, to Asia and Latin America. Out of all of these societies, how can we select the most appropriate cases for comparison? The importance of the nation-state in the economies of Latin America and Asia, even after decentralization, means that the dynamics of local economies are strongly shaped by national policies. In the Żywiec region, in contrast, national policies have had the effect of forcing Żywiec to become more autonomous.

A second factor in selecting comparative cases is the importance of political geography. The position of Poland between World War I and World War II was that of a peripheralized country within Europe. During the socialist period, the Polish economy was redirected toward the Soviet Union. With the dissolution of the Soviet sphere, Poland is returning to its former position as a European outpost. In this sense, it is most broadly similar to the situations of other European peripheral states, such as Spain, Portugal, and Greece, which also went through transitions to democracy and global capitalism in the mid-1970s. Even in the context of transnational capital and global processes of power, history and geography remain important factors to consider in looking at the relationship between global, national, and local change.

Similar processes are occurring across Europe. The post-Franco transition in Spain from authoritarian state capitalism to free markets and social democracy is an example of a European case study comparable to Poland, in the sense that, as Maddox (1993) demonstrates, in neither case is the nation-state an important actor on the local scene. Both states are on the European periphery, and both have a history of distinct, regional ethnic identities that are used by the upper class during a new articulation of different modes of production.

Though the processes I describe were profoundly affected by socialism, in many ways neither capitalism nor socialism has been as singular in its social, political, and economic effects as has been suggested by scholars and politicians. One explanation for this is that many of the effects attributed to capitalist industrialization are in fact merely the effects of industrialization in any mode of production. Industrialization is clearly a process that has some similarities in shaping labor and other relationships, regardless of the mode of production in which is it employed. Likewise, the lack of industrialization in peripheral regions in Spain is an important point of difference with peripheral Poland. This industrial facet of Żywiec leads to the important fact that neocapitalists in Żywiec arise from acting as middlemen between international capital and local industrial enterprises. In contrast, nonindustrial Andalusia, Maddox's case study, seems to lack a cogent contesting elite class, as the former landed elite class there was able to transform its base of economic support in the new regime.

In searching for appropriate comparisons to this case, however, it has been necessary to rethink the relevance of the late twentieth century nation-state in looking at the processes of transition. This is particularly necessary in the case of Żywiec, but it is true to some extent throughout the former Eastern Bloc and perhaps across Western Europe as well. Analyses of the transition in Eastern Europe and the former Soviet Union have tended to emphasize the nation-state as the category of primary importance. The region of Żywiec, however, has interacted with a number of different nation-states over the past four hundred years, and particularly during the last century. During this time, the community as a cultural, political, and economic unit has been able, through the actions of elite classes, to negotiate and mediate its interaction with these various states. I contend that the economic structure of Żywiec is becoming less, not more, integrated with that of the Polish nation-state. As businesses, homes, and land are privatized and returned to their prewar owners, liquidated, or sold to new investors, and as state funds to communities decrease, the decentralization of economic power in Poland means that the nation-state is less and less

involved in local processes.[1] At the same time, Żywiec's ties outside
Poland are increasing as a result of investment by global capital, opening of borders for travel and business, and the efforts of neocapitalists
to encourage sister-city relationships. The nation-state, therefore, is
becoming progressively less important as an effective category in considering community economics, in Żywiec and arguably across the
board in Eastern Europe. This process is heightened by the effects of
Poland's possible integration into supranational entities such as the
European Union and NATO.

My argument concerning the decreasing relevance of the nation-
state aligns with that of Arjun Appadurai; however, I follow a somewhat
different path than he in arriving at the same conclusion.[2] Appadurai
(1996) states, in discussing the "crisis of the nation-state," that

> Nation-states, for all their important differences . . . make
> sense only as parts of a system. This system . . . appears
> poorly equipped to deal with the interlinked diasporas of
> people and images that mark the here and now. Nation-
> states, as units in a complex interactive system, are not very
> likely to be the long-term arbiters of the relationship be-
> tween globality and modernity. (19)

He identifies the expansion of mass media and mass migration as the
primary factors producing the current situation, where the local and
the global are interconnected, circumventing the importance of the
nation.[3] I am not so confident as he in making sweeping statements
about the crisis of the nation-state writ large. Because of the factors I
consider important in the production of globalization, I confine my
view of the crisis of nation-states to the European context.[4] As I have
stated throughout this book, I see the movement of transnational capital and the integration of the European nations in NATO and the
European Union as processes that fundamentally connect localities in
Europe and undermine the role of the nation-state at the expense of
global, or at least supranational, entities.[5] In Eastern Europe, I see this
condition as exacerbated by the politics of decentralization, which
actively seek to strip the nation-state of resources and decision-
making power.

The nation-state of Poland has not been the primary site of interaction for Żywiec historically, as has been seen through Żywiec's forc-
ible integration into many different nation-states. Instead, the regional
economy has been shaped by an ideology of community insularity
based on values of Góral identity. The strength of Góral community
identity as a mechanism for coping with national intrusions can be

seen in past periods as well as in the present. In this book, I have outlined the historical trajectory of foreign aggressors and other political units imposing political and economic policies on the Żywiec region, and the way Górals have deployed their ethnic identity to mediate the relationship between nation-state and community. Górals used this strategy of relying on ethnic identity to arouse community spirit and fashion economic and political niches for their community in the midst of many changes in the nation-states to which Żywiec has belonged. In the partition period prior to World War I, when Żywiec belonged to the Austro-Hungarian Empire, Góral identity provided the community with a stable identity and reinforced the community economic system of insularity, with the Habsburgs as primary community patrons. During the interwar period (World War I to World War II), when the Polish state was reconstituted from the partitions, the Polish government ironically requested that the Habsburgs maintain their presence in the Żywiec region to promote order where the government could not. The period of the Nazi occupation, when the Habsburgs were finally driven out, saw the creation of many Góral cultural groups interested in entrenching community identity in the face of German terror and destruction. The socialist period was a veritable hotbed of oppositional activities, which were driven in part by the prewar elite class and in part by sheer resistance to the socialist project—for example, the Solidarity movement, various Catholic activities, and Góral clubs, journals, and festivals. The present re-entrenchment of the Góral identity taking place in Żywiec is thus part of a local historical pattern and a reflection of a trans-European (Appadurai might argue, global) trend, and yet it has interacted with the processes put in motion by postsocialism in unique ways.

The process of ethnic re-entrenchment in Żywiec in the postsocialist era involves an interweaving of local politics and culture, which are set in the contexts of changing national powers, the political and economic power of global capitalism, and ideologies of modernity. Local processes are intricately linked to global ones; supranational processes in Europe provide further impetus to the revitalization of local ethnic identity. For example, national political and economic policies in Poland are driven by entities such as the IMF, World Bank, OECD, and other development agencies. Poland's national political elite are determined to speed Poland's entry into other supranational entities: the European Union and NATO. The shock therapy policies that politicians are currently enacting in Poland alienate peripheral areas within Poland, stripping them of industries unprofitable to the state and eliminating jobs without replacing liquidated factories. In the face of the nation-state's abandonment, peripheral communities are left to try to salvage their local economies as best they can. In the case of Żywiec, some local elites, the neocapitalists, have responded by proposing that the community should court international capital to bring foreign investment into the community. In the process, the community is developing direct ties abroad without the mediation of the Polish state. Ironically, national attempts to effect a transition to capitalism are resulting in the alienation of regions such as Żywiec from the nation-state, thus reducing the economic importance of the nation-state. Into this vacuum of power have rushed the two competing elite classes in Żywiec, both of whom have used the idiom of the community's ethnicity to bolster their positions. This ethnic identity is expressed in community disputes with businesses such as the brewery, in the community's relationships abroad with sister cities, and on public occasions such as folk festivals and the pope's visit. The importance of Góral ethnicity in the postsocialist era is thus increasing as the importance of the Polish nation-state decreases.

The Thawing of the Cold War Paradigm

[T]he explosion of ethnic conflicts in Eastern (and even in Western) Europe is blurring the line between the West and the non-West. . . . The fact that the old language of modernization has been replaced by new talk of the obstacles to civil society and sustainable democracy should not obscure the persistence of the primordialist thesis. —Arjun Appadurai, Modernity at Large

The realization that socialism and capitalism have many points of comparison prompts us to reconsider the uniqueness of the postsocialist transition in Eastern Europe. In the wake of the fall of socialist states, we are realizing anew that socialism was never totalizing in its ability to restructure historical relations of power in communities. Class and ethnicity (as well as other social relations that I do not discuss in depth here, such as race and gender) continued to have a felt reality and explanatory power during the socialist period, and today they are still being worked out as part of their historical processes of articulation and change. The postsocialist transition does not create nor operate on a tabula rasa. The Cold War paradigm that informed so much academic and political work during socialism told us that socialist states had been able to fundamentally change social relations, wiping out previous constellations of interactions, despite some anthropological attempts to question this paradigm.

The end of the Cold War has caused the Cold War paradigm to metamorphose into its teleological successor, the transition paradigm, in which the changes in the former Eastern Bloc will erase all vestiges of socialism. Changes in social relations and cultural forms, such as expressions of ethnicity and race or conflicts rooted in class and gender, are thought in this model either to spring entirely from the new political and economic changes (i.e., to be entirely new phenomena) or to be resurgences of processes that were occurring before the socialist period and were interrupted by socialism (to be a result of the "thawing" of the Cold War, for example).

Arjun Appadurai (1996) calls this last idea the "Bosnian Fallacy," noting that "what is fascinating about Eastern Europe is that some of its own right-wing ideologues have convinced the liberal Western press that nationalism *is* a politics of primordia [primordial ethnicity becoming ethnonationalism], whereas the real question is how it has been made to *appear* that way" (21). He notes that moving away from this argument involves conceding both "first, that the political systems of the wealthy northern nations may themselves be in crisis, and second, that the emergent nationalism of many parts of the world may be founded on patriotisms that are neither exclusively or fundamentally territorial" (21).

As I have noted, I do believe that the nation-states of Europe are in crisis as a result of supranational processes specific to that region. As for the second half of the Bosnian fallacy, the Żywiec case has not yet become a case of ethnonationalism, and I have no expectation that ethnic identity in this case will develop nationalist pretensions. It is an identity that has been successively integrated and cast loose from various nation-states in the Central European region, and Żywiecers expressed to me no desire to pursue such grand and official action such as seceding from the Polish nation. The seemingly apathetic action of simply avoiding the national apparatus and creating their own independent links with other regions internationally is a case of resisting the nation-state through taking the path of least resistance, the path that will provoke no retaliatory action on the part of the Polish state.

Instead of falling into either the "invention of tradition" argument or the Bosnian Fallacy, then, I have shown in this case study that relations of ethnicity and class were continuous from the presocialist to the socialist to the postsocialist eras, and that these processes, rather than being interrupted by socialism, were important in locally shaping socialism and in turn were shaped by the resources and opportunities available during socialism. Ethnic re-entrenchment among Górals in postsocialist Poland is not simply a result of the end of socialism opening up new spaces for subnational or regional identities. Neither is it primarily a "return to tradition" driven by new interactions with capitalism. Rather, it is mainly a process driven by local class conflicts, which interact with national political and economic policy changes. It is supported on the local level by nonelites because of the strong unspoken understandings of Góral identity and community values, and because Góral revitalization also leads to material benefits for some nonelites in the community.

In moving beyond the local, micro picture of Żywiec, it is necessary to ask both how local relations of power, community, and tradition flow from a particularistic historical context and how these relations in postsocialism are similar to those in areas where socialism was never a major organizing principle. This study has attempted to answer these questions. As we have seen, there are links between the case of Żywiec and the larger changes in the former Soviet Bloc, and there are also useful comparative links to be made between the case of the Eastern European periphery and peripheral areas within Western Europe. In the previous two sections, I have discussed two broad contexts within which these links are important: views of the transition of the former Soviet Bloc and the connections among global, national, and local processes.

CONCLUSION

This case study has been concerned with the meaning of Góral ethnic entrenchment in Żywiec. In the postsocialist era, as in previous eras, this entrenchment has been driven by class relations. The postsocialist era has made new resources available for class formation and class action, yet the idiom of local identity, a constantly reconstructed local history and genealogy, has circumscribed the ways in which class conflict has been expressed.

Traditionalism and modernity are two idioms through which class conflict is expressed in postsocialist Żywiec. To bolster their claim as local authorities, the prewar elite class is attempting to keep Góral traditionalism and community insularity alive in the modern era. The emerging neocapitalist class, in contrast, claims that Góral identity is a valuable part of the nostalgic past of the community and modernity for Żywiec involves integration with the global capitalist economy and leaving behind local identity. That they are the most appropriate agents for carrying out this vision of the community's future is the unsubtle subtext of this ideology.

The salience of Góral identity has been a recurring theme across many different eras of political and social change. In *Western Times and Water Wars*, John Walton (1992) states that "[s]tate and dominion are not things that sit on top of social actors, but relationships that are sustained by legitimacy, that are changed as much by cultures and movements that germinate in local settings as by structural forces. States and domains change in important part because local people challenge them on the basis of culturally fashioned claims" (339). In each of the eras discussed here—the Austro-Hungarian partitions, the interwar Polish state, the Nazi occupation, the Communist hegemony, and now the postsocialist era—the Góral identity has played a central role in mediating the relationship between the local community and the nation-state, regardless of the national identity of the political center. I suggest that in the postsocialist, globalized context, the relevance of the European nation-state has decreased as a result of supranational entities such as the European Union and NATO, the influence of global capital, and the decentralization of the Eastern European national economic and political systems. As the nation-state declines, the importance of local geographies and genealogies increases. The Góral identity is an instance of a nonnationalist identity, or what Arjun Appadurai calls a "postnational formation" (1996, 164ff.). He notes three possible implications of postnationalism: that the nation-state is becoming obsolete and other forms of identity are replacing it, that alternative forms of identity are emerging that contest the nation-state or are peaceful alternatives to the nation-state, or that the decline of the nation-state's ability to mobilize identity will promote group loyalties that are unconnected to territorial states (1996, 168–69).

Notes

Chapter 1. The Day the Pope Came to Town

1. I am borrowing the Polish words *górale* (the people to whom I refer in English as Górals), *góralski* (Góral, an adjective), and a number of other related words. The root of these words is related to the Polish *gory*, which means mountains. There are various suggested ways of translating them into English (highlanders, mountaineers, mountain men, hillbillies), but I have opted to anglicize the words so as not to use English words that have different connotations. Also, I have decided not to use the Polish words because the grammatical structure of Polish would make this difficult for the English-language reader to follow.

2. The proportion of Poles who are self-reported Catholics is between 95 and 98 percent.

3. The Virgin Mary is frequently referred to as the "Queen of Poland" in classical nationalist poetry, Catholic masses, and everyday life. This stems from the history surrounding the conversion of Poles to Catholicism under Mieszko I, the first king of Poland. He declared that Poles would convert to Catholicism by symbolically "donating" the entire country to the Catholic church in 966 AD. This also connects in national imagery to the Black Madonna of Częstochowa, a famous painting kept in a monastery in the town of Częstochowa, which is in the same county as Żywiec. This painting of unknown origin is associated with miracles, particularly with a victory of the Poles during the Swedish invasion in the 1650s. It was also a rallying point for Polish nationalist troops fighting the partitioning of Poland between Russia, Prussia, and Austria in the 1790s. The monastery is a frequent pilgrimage site in Poland, and it was the site for the World Youth Day Catholic conference in 1993. Thus, in Żywiec, displaying flags with Mary's colors is much more than a mere expression of Catholic piety, it is also an expression of nationalism and

what can be interpreted as regional pride. This is similar to the case in Mexico, where the Virgin of Guadalupe is a multitiered symbol of Catholicism, nationalism, and regional pride (see Lafaye 1976 and Brading 1991).

4. Standard Polish and the Góral dialect are generally mutually intelligible, but there are significant differences in vocabulary and grammar. I was able to understand the Góral dialect in Żywiec in part because most speakers were code switching between standard Polish and Góral, and also because of my previous training in Russian. Góral grammar, which is significantly different from Polish, tends to be similar to Russian grammatical structure. Different grammar is often a sign that two tongues have differentiated enough to be classified as different languages rather than dialects. The question of language versus dialect classification tends to be based on mutual intelligibility, but it is also a political issue. In the case of the Góral dialect, the issue has not been taken up by Górals, even those who are working for community self-determination.

5. For simplicity, I use the term "Góral" when referring to Żywiec Górals, where they would use terms that translate as "Żywiecers" or "Górals" or "Żywiec Górals." When I am referring to other Górals, I specifically state that they are other Polish Górals or Slovakian Górals, and so forth. All of the Góral groups are in the foothills and mountains of southern Poland, the northern Czech Republic, and northern Slovakia.

6. "Self-folklorized" means that the Górals themselves have adopted a standard of what is traditional, which is frozen in the late nineteenth and early twentieth centuries.

Chapter 2. A Political and Economic History of the Żywiec Region

1. Local manuscripts state that it remained in Habsburg possession until World War II. This is somewhat a misstatement of legal fact, because the Habsburgs could not own the region in any legal sense after the reconstitution of Poland in 1919. However, there are two factors that make this line fuzzy. An ongoing argument during the interwar period erupted into pitched battles over the regions of Teschen (Polish name: Cieszyn) and Orava (Polish name: Orawa) between the Polish state and the Austrian state. Also, the Habsburg family who was in residence in Żywiec kept up its presence there until World War II and owned much of the local industry, giving it de facto local socioeconomic power.

2. Although I know of no comparative studies concerning the Góral dialect and Silesian, my statement is informed by personal communication with Elizabeth Vann, a linguistic anthropologist who was working in Silesia. Our visits to one another's research sites occasioned our noticing that there

are many similar grammatical constructions and words in Góral and Silesian that are neither Polish nor German.

3. For more on resistance in Poland during this period, see Michnik 1985, Raina 1978, Kuron 1977, and Moczulski 1982.

4. I discuss the connections between the prewar elite class and Solidarity activism in Żywiec in detail in chapter 3.

5. The avoidance in this quote of any direct reference to the Church of Saint Stanisław Kostka is typical of communist-era obfuscation due to censorship. Although the references were veiled, they were nevertheless easily understood by most Poles, who were used to reading between the lines.

6. But for an exception, see Dunn (2004).

7. See Scott 1976 for a discussion of moral economy.

8. I rely heavily on manuscripts by former Żywiec mayor Andrzej Komoniecki, local historian Grazyna Rapacz, and information kept by the Żywiec Museum.

9. This is based on the manuscript on the development of industry in Żywiec by Grazyna Rapacz. Also, materials on the brewery were provided to me by a variety of local people who had worked there during the prewar period or who knew the Habsburgs at that time.

10. This factory was in Zabłocie, the Jewish village adjacent to Żywiec, and the owners were Jewish. It was thus a particular target during the German occupation and also had a somewhat different relationship to the town than other, non-Jewish factories.

11. See Walton and Seddon 1994 for a discussion of the general phenomenon.

CHAPTER 3. ELITE CLASS STRUGGLES AND AUTHORITY

1. Some small percentage of the Żywiec community belongs to the Evangelical Protestant church. The fact that virtually none of these people are from the elite classes suggests some interesting relationships between class and conversion—a subject that bears further scrutiny, given the large numbers of missionaries of various religions who have flocked to Central and Eastern Europe in the years following the fall of the Iron Curtain.

2. Cemeteries have a central place in Polish culture. The All Saints' Day holiday is preceded by several weeks of activity in which family members go to cemeteries to clean and decorate family plots in anticipation of the mass visits on 1 November. On All Saints' Day, families visit cemeteries where their own family members are buried, as well as graves of friends, to offer up prayers and place lighted candles and flowers on plots.

3. The issue of formal or informal address is extremely important in denoting relationship. In Polish, the second-person singular pronoun *ty* and second-person singular verb form are an informal mode used with close friends and many family members. The third-person singular verb forms along with the titles *Pan* (for a man) and *Pani* (for a woman) denote a more formal relationship. People with other titles, such as aunt, uncle, and, in prewar Polish, mother and father, were also addressed by those titles in the third-person singular. Further, using the title *Pan* or *Pani* along with a first name (Pani Helena) is somewhat more familiar, and using the title with the last name (Pani Wałęsa) is very formal. To complicate this, the Góral dialect uses a modified second-person plural verb form for the formal verb form. Further, many residents code switch, so they are using both standard Polish and Góral forms within the same conversation.

4. "Old lineage" refers to the prewar upper class. It does not necessarily mean that a particular family has lived in an area longer than others; rather, it is roughly analogous to saying that this is "one of the first families" of a town.

5. The Polish People's Republic is the English translation of Poland's name during the socialist period—*Polska Republika Ludowej* (PRL).

6. Hoffman uses "apparatchik" to mean a PZPR leader, someone with political influence, as opposed to merely a member of the PZPR.

7. Though community management was taken over by the PZPR and businesses and property were nationalized, there were, of course, other venues through which political and economic power could be maintained, if not monopolized, by these families. These include apparent differential access to better high schools (perhaps due to both initially better parental education and teacher bias within the system), maintenance of bilingualism within families (many upper-class families spoke both Polish and German), and such symbols of status as beautiful antique furniture.

8. The histories and roles of these organizations will be examined in chapter 5.

9. For some overviews of the Solidarity history, see Goodwyn 1991; Kubik 1994; Laba 1991; Amin 1991, Ost 1990, Staniszkis 1989 and 1991, Jasiewicz 1991, Kuczynski and Nowak 1988; Wnuk-Lipinski 1991; Bernhard 1991, 1993; Lopinski, Miskit, and Wilk 1990; Krzeminski 1983; and Kuron 1982.

10. The Catholic church has sponsored a number of measures attempting to decrease women's rights in Poland, and during 1994–95 was attempting to have Catholicism declared the national religion. The extreme-right wing of Solidarity at the time frequently published anti-Semitic comments in labor union papers.

11. Some of these businessmen were former communists who had managed to parlay their political ties into positions of economic authority in the

new regime. For more on postsocialist class mobility in Eastern and Central Europe, see Szelenyi and Szelenyi 1995.

12. It was difficult for me to discover who exactly was involved in this failed plan. There was some coverage of the issue in the 1991 *Karta Groni* under the sensationalist title "The Habsburgs Are Returning!" and in the national newspapers at the time, but these articles were not specific about the Żywiec group's involvement. I was told by a few informants that they had met with the one Habsburg heir who was interested in the project, but I believe that a larger group had been involved and people were simply reluctant to look foolish several years after the privatization had gone through. I know that the director of the Żywiec Castle Museum spoke with the heir, and I suspect that the FZR in general was involved in the process.

13. This legal technicality is the same one under which Polish Jews whose property was seized by the Nazis are not eligible to reclaim their property under provisions for return to previous owners. Poles who know that they are now in possession of houses that once belonged to Jews, however, can become violently defensive if they believe that "foreigners" are trying to come back to reclaim those houses.

14. Berdahl 1999, Maddox 1993, and Nelson 1999 are just a few recent examples.

15. See Livezeanu 1995 and Verdery 1991a for just a few examples.

CHAPTER 4. NONELITES, FAMILY NETWORKS, AND IDENTITY

1. The names of all families in this chapter have been changed to protect their privacy.

2. In Figures 1 and 2, triangles represent males and circles represent females. A slash through an individual shows that the person is deceased. A bracket facing up, connecting two individuals, represents a marriage. Double slashes through a bracket indicates a divorce. Lines descending from brackets indicate descendants.

CHAPTER 5. THE COMMUNITY, THE NATION STATE, AND GLOBALIZATION

1. It is true that in some political contexts, re-entrenchments of ethnicity can lead to ethnonationalism. In this case, I discuss how Góral traditionalism in Zywiec connects with Góral ethnicity in Slovakia to construct cultural, economic, and political ties between these peoples and regions, lending a

transnational character to the phenomenon. However, to change this into an ethnonational movement would require greater politicization of ethnicity with regard to both nation-states. This could certainly happen in the future.

2. I should note that these two classes, and the two strategies associated with them, are ideal types. Not every member of these two classes would espouse the respective strategies; however, there is an overall pattern of action that is compelling.

3. The regional differences included languages, currencies, and other leftover disparities from the partition period, which the interwar-era leaders had attempted to minimize to foster the new Polish nation-state.

4. The Beskids, in which Zywiec is located, are the foothills to the Tatras Mountains.

5. By this they mean they think that Zakopane Górals speak only in unmixed dialect, wear turn of the century–style clothing, adhere to the ideal of small-scale farming, and practice Góral arts and crafts. In fact, it is true that many Zakopane Górals do speak more heavily in dialect, are involved in Góral artisanry, and have articles of traditionalist clothing. However, compared with Żywiec, there is very little industry in Zakopane and much of their economy is dependent on the year-round tourist trade of those who come to hike the mountains, ski, and see "real Górals."

6. Another reason why people often do not think of the metal factory as a privatized firm is that in Zywiec, privatization often is glossed as having sold stock on the open market, because that is how the brewery was privatized.

7. Alcoholism had been a major problem in Poland during the socialist period, and it continues to have many effects on the Polish family, workplace, and politics. However, under socialism, inefficient workers were more tolerated, and there were numerous sayings pointing out that it did not matter whether you worked, drank, or slept, you would still get paid. After privatization began in 1991, problem drinkers who had previously had no worries about calling in sick or drinking on the job began to lose their jobs in droves.

CHAPTER 6. POLITICS, CULTURE, AND MODERNITY IN POSTSOCIALIST POLAND

1. Given the imperialist ties of the Soviet economy to its satellites, the extent to which the Polish nation-state was an important political or economic category in the socialist era is debatable as well.

2. For a contrasting view of the importance of nations and national culture in the context of globalization, see Marden 1997 and Stevenson 1997.

3. See Sassen 1996 for a similar view that focuses on cities as the nexus of locality that is linked to globalization.

4. Rees 1993 and Amin and Thrift 1994 are two examples of recent literature in which we can see a trend toward discussing the influence of globalization on the power of the nation-state in Europe.

5. For discussions of how the European Union is reconfiguring power relations between and among European states, see Leitner 1997. For several approaches to the European Union's ability to control emerging institutions and processes of decision making in Central and Eastern Europe, see Dobrinsky and Landesmann 1995.

Bibliography

◄o►

Albert, Steve. "The Power of Precedent: French Linguistic Conservatism and the Evocation of Collective Memory." Paper presented at the annual meeting of the American Anthropological Association, San Francisco, Calif., December 1996.

Amin, Ash, and Dietrich Michael, eds. *Towards a New Europe?: Structural Change in the European Economy.* Brookfield, Vt.: E. Elgar Publications, 1991.

Amin, A., and N. Thrift, eds. *Globalization, Institutions and Regional Development in Europe.* Oxford: Oxford University Press, 1994.

Anderson, Benedict. *Imagined Communities.* London: Verso Press, 1983.

Appadurai, Arjun. "Theory in Anthropology: Center and Periphery." *Comparative Studies in Society and History* 28 (1986): 356–61.

———. *Modernity at Large: Cultural Dimensions of Globalization.* Minneapolis: University of Minnesota Press, 1996.

Ash, Timothy Garton. *The Uses of Adversity: Essays on the Fate of Central Europe.* New York: Vintage Press, 1990.

Banac, Ivo. *Eastern Europe in Revolution.* Ithaca: Cornell University Press, 1992.

Banfield, Edward. *The Moral Basis of a Backward Society.* Glencoe, Ill.: Free Press, 1958.

"Bawaria i Żywiecczyzna." *Gazeta Wyborcza* (July 14. 1995): 1.

Berdahl, Daphne. *Where the World Ended: Re-Unification and Identity in the German Borderland.* Berkeley: University of California Press, 1999.

Berend, Ivan, and Georgy Ránki. *Economic Development in East-Central Europe in the 19th and 20th Centuries.* New York: Columbia University Press, 1974.

191

Bernhard, Michael. "Reinterpreting Solidarity." *Studies in Comparative Communism* 24 (1991):317ff.

———. *The Origins of Democratization in Poland: Workers, Intellectuals, and Oppositional Politics, 1976–1980.* New York: Columbia University Press, 1993.

Bobbio, Norberto. "Gramsci and the Conception of Civil Society." In *Gramsci and Marxist Theory,* edited by C. Mouffe, 21–47. Boston: Routledge and Kegan Paul, 1979.

Bobrowska, Jadwiga. "Dzieje badan folklorystychnych w regionie żywieckim." *Karta Groni* VII–VIII (1976):114–36.

Bourdieu, Pierre. *Outline of a Theory of Practice.* New York: Cambridge University Press, 1977.

———. *Distinctions: A Social Critique of the Judgement of Taste.* Cambridge, Mass.: Harvard University Press, 1984.

———. "The Forms of Capital." In *Handbook of Theory and Research for the Sociology of Education,* edited by J. G. Richardson, 241–58. New York: Greenwood Press, 1986.

Bowers, Brent. "American Entrepreneurship in Poland Is Picking Up." *Wall Street Journal* (April 18, 1991): B2(W)–B3(E), Warsaw edition.

Brading, David. *The First America: The Spanish Monarchy, Creole Patriots, and the Liberal State, 1492–1867.* New York: Cambridge University Press, 1991.

Brinton, William M., and Alan Rizler, eds. *Without Force or Lies: Voices from the Revolution of Central Europe in 1989–1990.* San Francisco: Mercury House, 1990.

Brumberg, Abraham. "Sic Transit Post-Sovietology." *The Nation* (January 29, 1996): 29–31.

Bulka, Wladyslaw. *Góralskie jodlo.* Żywiec: Gazeta Żywiecka, 1993.

Burawoy, Michael. *Manufacturing Consent: Changes in the Labor Process under Monopoly Capitalism.* Chicago: University of Chicago Press, 1979.

———. *The Politics of Production: Factory Regimes under Capitalism and Socialism.* New York: Schocken Books, 1985.

Burawoy, Michael, and K. Hendley. "Between Perestroika and Privatization— Divided Strategies to Political Crisis in a Soviet Enterprise." *Soviet Studies* 44 (1992):371–402.

Burawoy, Michael, and Pavel Krotov. "The Soviet Transition from Socialism to Capitalism: Worker Control and Economic Bargaining in the Wood Industry." *American Sociological Review* 57 (February 1992): 16–38.

Burawoy, Michael, and Janos Lukacs. *The Radiant Past: Ideology and Reality on Hungary's Road to Capitalism.* Chicago: University of Chicago Press, 1992.

Burawoy, Michael, and Theda Skocpol, eds. *Marxist Inquiries: Studies of Labor, Class and States.* Chicago: University of Chicago Press, 1982.

Byczko, Anna. "Z historii 'Groni.'" *Karta Groni* XI (1981): 7–11.

Cahalen, Deborah J. "A Place to Stand: Social Movements and Civil Society in Poland." *Polish Sociological Review* 3 (1994):199–210.

———. "The Day the Pope Came to Town: Góral Identity and Historical Consciousness in Poland." Paper presented at the annual meeting of the American Anthropological Association, San Francisco, Calif., December 1996.

Calhoun, Craig, ed. *Social Theory and the Politics of Identity.* London: Blackwell, 1994.

Cardoso, Fernando, and Enza Faletto. *Dependency and Development in Latin America.* Berkeley: University of California Press, 1979.

Chekov, Anton. *The Three Sisters,* translated by Randall Jarrell. New York: Macmillan, [1901, rev. 1902] 1969.

Chirot, Daniel, ed. *The Origins of Backwardness in Eastern Europe: Economics and Politics from the Middle Ages until the Early Twentieth Century.* Berkeley: University of California Press, 1989.

Chirot, Daniel, ed. *The Crisis of Leninism and the Decline of the Left: The Revolutions of 1989.* Seattle: University of Washington Press, 1991.

Chudnovskii, Mikhael A. *Folk Dance Company of the U.S.S.R. Igor Moiseyev, Art Director.* Moscow: Foreign Languages Publishing House, 1959.

Coleman, James. "Prologue: Constructed Social Organization." In *Social Theory for a Changing Society,* edited by Pierre Bourdieu and James Coleman, 1–14. Boulder, Colo.: Westview Press, 1993a.

———. "The Rational Reconstruction of Society." *American Sociological Review* 58 (1993b): 2.

Coulmas, Florian. "European Integration and the Idea of the National Language." In *A Language Policy for the European Community: Prospects and Quandaries,* edited by Florian Coulmas, 1–43. Berlin: Mouton de Gruyter, 1991.

Coutouvidis, John, and Jaime Reynolds. *Poland 1939–1949.* Leicester: Leicester University Press, 1986.

Cwikowska, Monika. *Żywiec na dawnej pocztowce.* Żywiec: Monika Cwikowska, 1995.

Dabrowski, J. M., M. Federowicz, and A. Levitas. "Polish State Enterprises and the Properties of Performance." *Politics and Society* 19 (December 1991):403–37.

Davies, Norman. *God's Playground: A History of Poland. Volume 2, 1975 to the Present*. New York: Columbia University Press, 1982.

DiPalma, Giuseppe. *To Craft Democracies. An Essay on Democratic Transitions*. Berkeley: University of California Press, 1990.

Dobrinsky, Rumen, and Michael Landesmann, eds. *Transforming Economies and European Integration*. Aldershot, U.K.: Edward Elgar, 1995.

Dollinger, Zygmunt. "Struktura demograficzna i rolna powiatu żywieckiego." *Gronie* (1938): 4–8.

Donnan, Hastings, and Thomas M. Wilson. *Borders: Frontiers of Identity, Nation and State*. New York: Berg, 1999.

Drakulic, Slavenka. *How We Survived Communism and Even Laughed*. New York: HarperCollins, 1993.

Dunn, Elizabeth. Privatizing Poland: Baby Food, Big Business, and the Remaking of Labor. Ithaca: Cornell University Press, 2004.

Eley, Greg, and Ronald Grigor Suny, eds. *Becoming National*. Oxford: Oxford University Press, 1996.

Evans, Peter. *Dependent Development: An Alliance of Multinational, State and Local Capital in Brazil*. Princeton: Princeton University Press, 1979.

Fallenbachl, A., and Z. Fallenbachl. "Privatization and Marketization in Poland." *Studies in Comparative Communism* 23 (fall–winter 1990): 349–54.

Frank, André Gunder. *Capitalism and Underdevelopment in Latin America: Historical Studies of Chile and Brazil*. New York: Monthly Review Press, 1969.

Fukuyama, Francis. *The End of History and the Last Man*. New York: Free Press, 1992.

Galbraith, Maria H. "A Pole Can Die for the Fatherland, but Can't Live for Her: Democratization and the Polish Heroic Ideal." Paper presented at the annual meeting of the American Anthropological Association, San Francisco, Calif., December 1996.

Garciá, Canclini, Néstor. *Hybrid Cultures: Strategies for Entering and Leaving Modernity*, translated by Christopher L. Chiappari and Sylvia L. López. Minneapolis: University of Minnesota Press, 1995.

Giurchescu, Anna. "Power and the Dance Symbol and Its Socio-Political Use." In *Proceedings. 17th Symposium of the Study Group on Ethnochoreology. Dance and Its Socio-Political Aspects: Dance and Costume*, edited by I. Loutzaki, 15–22. Nafphlion, Greece: Peloponnesian Folklore Foundation/International Council for Traditional Music, 1994.

Goodwyn, Lawrence. *Breaking the Barrier: The Rise of Solidarity in Poland*. New York: Oxford University Press, 1991.

Grabowski, Jaroslaw. "Czasem smazę hamburgery." *Gazeta Handlowa* (*Gazeta Wyborcza*) (1995): 12, Katowice.

Gramsci, Antonio. *Selections from the Prison Notebooks of Antonio Gramsci*, translated by Q. Hoare and G. Smith. New York: International Publishers, 1971.

Grant, Bruce. *In the Soviet House of Culture: A Century of Perestroikas.* Princeton: Princeton University Press, 1995.

"Habsburgowie wroca!" *Karta Groni* XV (1991): 15.

Hann, C. M. *A Village without Solidarity: Polish Peasants in Years of Crisis.* New Haven: Yale University Press, 1985.

————.*The Skeleton at the Feast: Contributions to East European Anthropology.* Canterbury: University of Kent at Canterbury, 1995.

Hauser, Ewa. "Politics of Feminism in Poland." Paper presented at the annual meeting of the American Anthropological Association, Chicago, Ill., November 1991.

Hendry, Barbara A. "Constructing Linguistic and Ethnic Boundaries in a Basque Borderland: Contestations of Identity in Rioja Alavesa, Spain." Paper presented at the annual meeting of the American Anthropological Association, San Francisco, Calif., December 1996.

Herzfeld, Michael. *Cultural Intimacy: Social Poetics and the Nation State.* London: Routledge, 1997.

Hobsbawm, Eric. "La scienza politica." *Rinascita* 50–1 (December 1977).

Hobsbawm, Eric, and Terence Ranger, eds. *Invention of Tradition.* Cambridge: Cambridge University Press, 1983.

Hoffman, Ewa. *Lost in Translation.* New York: E. P. Dutton, 1989.

Holly, Krystyna. "Nazwy terenowe Żywiecczyzny." *Karta Groni: Wydawnictwo Spoleczno-kulturalne Poswiecone Sprawom Żywiecczyzny i Beskidów* XVII (1993): 121–37.

Hosmer, Dorothy. "Pedaling through Poland: An American Girl Free-Wheels Alone from Kraków, and Its Medieval Byways, toward Ukraine's Restive Borderland." *National Geographic Magazine* LXXXV (1939): 739–75.

Irvine, Judith T., and Susan Gal. "Language Ideology and Linguistic Differentiation." Paper presented at the Seminar on Language Ideologies, School of American Research, Santa Fe, N.Mex., April 1994.

Jasicki, Bronislaw. "Badania antropologiczne na Żywiecczyznie." *Karta Groni* XI (1981): 12–20.

Jasiewicz, Krzysztof. "Polski wyborca—w diesiec lat po Sierpniu." *Krytyka* 36 (1991): 37ff.

Kaminski, Bartolomiej. *The Collapse of State Socialism: The Case of Poland.* Princeton: Princeton University Press, 1991.

Kideckel, David A. *The Solitude of Collectivism: Romanian Villagers to the Revolution and Beyond.* Ithaca, N.Y.: Cornell University Press, 1993

Kochanowicz, Jacek. "The Polish Economy and the Evolution of Dependency." In *The Origins of Backwardness in Eastern Europe: Economics and Politics from the Middle Ages until the Early Twentieth Century,* edited by Daniel Chirot. Berkeley: University of California Press, 1989.

————. "Paradoksy odgórnych modernizacji. Miedzy romantyzem rynkowym z etatystyczną utopią." *Res Publica* (1992): 1–2.

Kolodzejczyk, R. "The Petty Bourgeoisie in Poland during the Transition from Capitalism to Socialism—an Essay on Research Problems." *Bulgarian Historical Review* 2 (1989): 21–30.

Komoniecki, Andrzej. *Kroniki Żywiecki.* Żywiec: Towarzystwo Miłosników Ziemi Żywieckiej, 1992.

Kornai, Janos. *The Socialist System: The Political Economic of Communism.* Princeton: Princeton University Press, 1992.

Krzeminski, Ireneusz. *Polacy—Jesien '80.* Warsaw: PAN, 1983.

Kubik, J. "Who Done It: Workers, Intellectuals, or Someone Else? Controversy over Solidarity's Origins and Social Composition." *Theory and Society* 23 (1994): 441–66.

————. Personal Communication, 1995.

Kuczynski, Pawel, and Krzysztof Nowak. "The Solidarity Movement in Relation to Society and State: Communication as an Issue of Social Movements." *Research in Social Movements, Conflict and Change* 10 (1988): 136ff.

Kulczycki, John J. *School Strikes in Prussian Poland, 1901–1907: The Struggle over Bilingual Education.* Boulder, Colo.: East European Monographs, 1981.

Kuron, Jacek. "Reflections on a Program of Action." *The Polish Review* 22 (1977).

————. *Solidarność, The Missing Link: A New Edition of Poland's Classic Revolutionary Socialist Manifesto: Jacek Kuron and Karol Modzelewski's Open Letter to the Party.* London: Bookmarks, 1982.

Kuznets, Simon. *Economic Change, Selected Essays in Business Cycles, National Income and Economic Growth.* New York: Norton, 1953.

Kwasniewski, Jan. "Privatization—Poland." *Eastern European Economics* 30 (Fall 1991): 41–48.

Laba, Roman. *Worker Roots of Solidarity: A Political Sociology of Poland's Working Class Democratization.* Princeton: Princeton University Press, 1991.

Lafaye, Jacques. *Quetzalcóatl and Guadalupe: The Formation of Mexican National Consciousness, 1531–1813,* translated by Benjamin Keen. Chicago: University of Chicago Press, 1976.

Lefebvre, H. *La production de l'éspace.* Paris: Éditions Anthropos, 1974.

Lefkowitz, Daniel S. "Ethnic Languages of Emotion and the Struggle over Historical Consciousness in Israel: European or Arab?" Paper presented at the annual meeting of the American Anthropological Association, San Francisco, Calif., December 1996.

Leitner, Helga. "Reconfiguring the Spatiality of Power: The Construction of a Supranational Migration Framework for the European Union." *Political Geography* 16 (1997):123–43.

Lipski, Jan Jozef. *KOR: A History of the Workers' Defense Committee in Poland, 1976–1981.* Berkeley: University of California Press, 1985.

Lipton, D., and J. Sachs. "Privatization in Eastern Europe: The Case of Poland." *Brookings Papers on Economic Activity* 2 (1990):293–341.

Livezeanu, Irina. *Cultural Politics in Greater Romania: Regionalism, Nation Building, and Ethnic Struggle, 1918–1930.* Ithaca, N.Y.: Cornell University Press, 1995.

Llobera, Josep R. *The God of Modernity: The Development of Nationalism in Western Europe.* Providence, R.I.: Berg, 1994.

Lopinski, Maciej, Marcin Miskit, and Mariusz Wilk. *Konspira: Solidarity Underground,* translated by Jane Cave. Berkeley: University of California Press, 1990.

Loranc, Boleslaw, and Tadeusz Pajda. "Dwadzieścia lat działalności Warszawskiego Oddziału TMZŻ (Towarzystwo Miłośników Ziemi Żywieckiej)." *Karta Groni* XVII (1993):282–83.

Lukaszuk, Miroslaw. "150 wesel bez wódki." *Gazeta Wyborcza* (July 25, 1995): 5. Bielsko-Biała.

Luporini, Cesare. "Marx e Gramsci: le categorie strategiche." *Rinascita* 50–1(December 1977).

Maddox, Richard. *El Castillo: The Politics of Tradition in an Andalusian Town.* Chicago: University of Illinois Press, 1993.

Maners, Lynn D. "The Hegemony (and Anti-Hegemony) of Symbols: Public Performance, Ethnic Identity and Nationality in Bosnia and Herzegovina." Paper presented at the annual meeting of the American Anthropological Association, San Francisco, Calif., December 1996.

Marden, Peter. "Geographies of Dissent: Globalization, Identity and the Nation." *Political Geography* 16 (1997): 37–64.

Marx, Karl. *Das capital, Volume Three*. In *The Marx-Engels Reader*, edited by R.
C. Tucker, 439–42. New York: W. W. Norton, [1867, 1885, 1894] 1978.

―――. *The Eighteenth Brumaire of Louis Bonaparte*. In *The Marx-Engels Reader*,
edited by R. C. Tucker, 594–617. New York: W. W. Norton, [1852] 1978.

Matustík, Martin Joseph. *Postnational Identity: Critical Theory and Existential
Philosophy in Habermas, Kierkegaard, and Havel*. New York: Guilford Press,
1993.

Meres, Magdalena. "Naukowe badania etnograficzne nad kultura ludowa górali
żywieckich i ich płon." *Karta Groni* XVII (1993): 281.

Michnik, Adam. "A New Evolutionism." In *Letters from Prison and Other Essays*, vol. 22. Berkeley: University of California Press, 1985.

Moczulski, Leszek. *Revolution without Revolution*. Menlo Park, Calif.: Center
for the Study of Opposition in Poland, 1982.

Monticone, Ronald C. *The Catholic Church in Communist Poland 1945–1985*.
Boulder, Colo.: East European Monographs, 1986.

Motyl, Alexander J. *Sovietology, Rationality, Nationality*. New York: Columbia
University Press, 1990.

Mouffe, Chantal. "Introduction: Gramsci Today." In *Gramsci and Marxist Theory*,
edited by Chantal Mouffe, 1–18. Boston: Routledge and Kegan Paul,
1979.

Na swojej ziemi: wizyta Ojca Świętego Jana Pawla II w Żywcu. Video, 30 min.
Żywiecki Urząd Miasta, Żywiec, 1995.

Nagengast, Carole. *Reluctant Socialists, Rural Entrepreneurs: Class, Culture and
the Polish State*. San Francisco: Westview Press, 1991.

Nelson, Diane M. *A Finger in the Wound: Body Politics in Quincentennial Gua-
temala*. Berkeley: University of California Press, 1999.

O'Donnell, Guillermo, and Phillipe C. Schmitter. *Transitions from Authoritarian
Rule: Tentative Conclusions about Uncertain Democracies*. Baltimore: Johns
Hopkins University Press, 1986.

O'Donnell, Guillermo, Philippe C. Schmitter, and Laurence Whitehead, eds.
Transitions from Authoritarian Rule: Comparative Perspectives. Baltimore:
Johns Hopkins University Press, 1991.

O'Dowd, Liam, and Thomas M. Wilson. *Borders, Nations and States: Frontiers of
Sovereignty in the New Europe*. Brookfield, Vt.: Avebury, 1996.

Okey, Robin. *Eastern Europe 1740–1985: Feudalism to Communism*. Minneapolis:
University of Minnesota Press, 1986.

Organizacja Rady i Urzędu Miasta. *Żywiec*. Żywiec: Urząd Miasta, 1994.

Ost, David. *Solidarity and the Politics of Anti-Politics: Opposition and Reform in Poland since 1968*. Philadelphia: Temple University Press, 1990.

Ozturkman, Arzu. "Folk Dance and Nationalism in Turkey." In *Proceedings. 17th Symposium of the Study Group on Ethnochoreology. Dance and Its Socio-Political Aspects: Dance and Costume*, edited by I. Loutzaki, 83–86. Nafphlion, Greece: Peloponnesian Folklore Foundation/International Council for Traditional Music, 1994.

Persky, Stan, and Henry Flam, eds. *The Solidarity Sourcebook*. Vancouver, B.C.: New Star Books, 1982.

Phelan, Peggy. *Unmarked, the Politics of Performance*. New York: Routledge, 1993.

Pine, Frances. "Naming the House and Naming the Land: Kinship and Social Groups in the Polish Highlands." *Journal of the Royal Anthropological Institute* 2 (1996):443–59.

Projekty Dokumentów VI Wzd NSZZ Solidarność Regionu Podbeskidzie. *Report*. Bielsko-Biała: NSZZ Solidarity, 1995.

Przeworski, Adam. *Democracy and the Market: Political and Economic Reforms in Eastern Europe and Latin America*. Cambridge: Cambridge University Press, 1991.

Raczka, Zofia. "Sprawozdanie z działalności Oddziału Żywieckiego TMZŻ (Towarzystwo Miłosników Ziemi Żywieckiej) w latach 1991–1992." *Karta Groni* XVII (1993):290–91.

Raina, Peter. *Political Opposition in Poland 1954–1977*. London: Poets and Painters Press, 1978.

Ramet, Pedro. *Religion and Nationalism in Soviet and East European Politics*. Durham, N.C.: Duke University Press Policy Studies, 1984.

Ramet, Sabrina. *Cross and Commissar: The Politics of Religion in Eastern Europe and the USSR*. Bloomington: University of Indiana Press, 1987.

———. *Social Currents in Eastern Europe: The Sources and Meaning of the Great Transformation*. Durham, N.C.: Duke University Press, 1991.

Rapacz, Grazyna. "Rozwój przemysłu w mieście Żywcu." Żywiec, 1986. Photocopy.

Rau, Zdzislaw, ed. *The Reemergence of Civil Society in Eastern Europe and the Soviet Union*. Boulder, Colo.: Westview Press, 1991.

Rees, G. Wyn, ed. *International Politics in Europe*. London: Routledge, 1993.

Reinfuss, Roman. "Polnocno-zachodnia granica górali żywieckich." *Karta Groni* XIV (1989): 129–33.

Rocznik Statystyczny Wojewodztwa Bielskiego. Bielsko-Biała: Wojewódzki Urząd Statystyczny w Bielsku-Białej, 1989, 1992, 1993.

Roos, Hans. *A History of Modern Poland from the Foundation of the State in the First World War to the Present Day*, translated by J. R. Foster. New York: Knopf, 1966.

Roseberry, William. "Political Economy." *Annual Review of Anthropology* 17 (1986):161–85.

Rosenberg, Dorothy. "Shock Therapy: GDR Women in Transition from a Socialist Welfare State to a Social Market Economy." *Signs* 17 (1991): 129–51.

Rostow, Walt Whitman. *The Dynamics of Soviet Socialism*. London: Secker and Warburg, 1952.

———. *The Stages of Economic Growth, a Non-Communist Manifesto*. Cambridge: Cambridge University Press, 1960.

———. *The Economics of Take-Off into Sustained Growth. Proceedings of the International Economics Association, 1965*. New York: St. Martin's Press, 1965.

"Rozmowa z Ojcem Joachimem Badenim." *Gazeta Żywiecka* (December 1993): 6.

Rudra, A. "From Collective Capitalism to Private Capitalism: The Soviet Transition." *Economic and Political Weekly* 25 (1990):1137ff.

Sachs, Jeffrey D. "Accelerating Privatization in Eastern Europe—the Case of Poland." *World Bank Economic Review* (spring 1991): 15–30.

Sachs, Jeffrey D., and David Lipton. "Poland's Economic Reform." *Foreign Affairs* 69 (1990): 47–66.

Sampson, Steve, and David Kideckel. "Anthropologists Going into the Cold." In *Anthropology of War and Peace*, edited by Paul Turner and David Pitt, 160–73. Hadley, Mass.: Bergin and Garvey, 1988.

Sassen, Saskia. "Whose City Is It? Globalization and the Formation of New Claims." *Public Culture* 8 (1996):205–23

Schöpflin, George. *Politics in Eastern Europe, 1945–1992*. Cambridge, Mass.: Blackwell, 1993.

Schumpeter, Joseph A. *Capitalism, Socialism and Democracy*. New York: Harper and Bros., 1947.

Scott, James C. *The Moral Economy of the Peasant: Rebellion and Subsistence in Southeast Asia*. New Haven: Yale University Press, 1976.

———. *Weapons of the Weak: Everyday Forms of Peasant Resistance*. New Haven: Yale University Press, 1985.

Senin, M. V. *Socialist Integration*. Moscow: Progress Publishers, 1973.

Shay, Anthony. "Limitations of Iranian Iconographic Sources for the Development of Historical Evidence of Iranian Dancing." In *Proceedings of the*

Annual Conference of the Society of Dance History (U.S.) Scholars, 173–86. Riverside, Calif.: Society of Dance History Scholars, 1966.

———. "Parallel Traditions: State Folk Dance Ensembles and Folk Dance in 'The Field.'" *Dance Research Journal* 31/1 (spring 1999): 29–54.

Simons, Jr., Thomas W. *Eastern Europe in the Postwar World*. New York: St. Martin's Press, 1993.

Sliz, Tadeusz. "Działkowe wspomnienia Żywczaków w Krakowie." *Karta Groni* XVII (1993):284–86.

"Spotkanie z burmistrzem." *Gazeta Żywiecka* (April 1993) 4.

Staniszkis, Jadwiga. *Poland's Self-Limiting Revolution*. Princeton: Princeton University Press, 1984.

———. *Ontologia socjalizmu*. Warsaw: In Plus, 1989.

———. "Dylematy lat osiemdziesiątych w Polsce." In *Spoleczenstwo Polskie u progu przemian*, edited by Janusz Mucha. Wrocław: Zakład Narodowy imienia Ossolińskich-Wydawnictwo, 1991.

Starski, Stanislaw. *Class Struggle in Classless Poland*. Boston: South End Press, 1982.

Stephen, Lynn. *Zapotec Women*. Austin: University of Texas Press, 1991.

Stevenson, Nick. "Globalization, National Cultures and Cultural Citizenship." *The Sociological Quarterly* 38 (1997): 41–66.

Subtelny, Orest. *Domination of Eastern Europe: Native Nobilities and Foreign Absolutism, 1500–1715*. Montreal: McGill-Queen's University Press, 1986.

Szajkowski, Bogdan. *Next to God . . . Poland: Politics and Religion in Contemporary Poland*. London: Frances Pinter Publishers, 1983.

Szelenyi, Ivan. *Urban Inequalities under State Socialism*. New York: Oxford University Press, 1983.

———. *Socialist Entrepreneurs: Embourgeoisement in Rural Hungary*. Madison: University of Wisconsin Press, 1988.

Szelenyi, Ivan, and Sonja Szelenyi. "Circulation or Reproduction of Elites during the Postcommunist Transformation of Eastern Europe: Introduction." *Theory and Society* 24 (1995):615–38.

Szuber, Izabela. "Pracowac za zasiłek. Sluzba zdrowia. W Żywcu prace znalazlo 8 pielęgniarek." *Gazeta Wyborcza* (July 19, 1995): 2.

"XXXII Tydzien Kultury Beskidzkiej Góralskie spiewanie." *Gazeta Żywiecka* (August 1995): 9–10.

Thomas, William I., and Florian Znaniecki. *The Polish Peasant in Europe and America, 1918–1920*, 5 vols. Boston: Gorham Press, 1927.

Thompson, E. P. *The Making of the English Working Class*. New York: Vintage Books, 1963.

———. *Customs in Common: Studies in Traditional Popular Culture*. New York: The New Press, 1993.

Tłustochowicz, Grzegorz. "Opinii mieszkanców Żywca o najważniejszych sprawach miasta." Magisterium, Uniwersytet Adama Mickiewicza, 1994.

Tonnies, Ferdinand. *Community and Society*, translated by Charles Loomis. East Lansing: Michigan State University Press, [1887] 1957.

Trebacz, Tadeusz, ed. *Kalendarz Żywiecki 1994*. Żywiec: Gazeta Żywiecka, 1993.

Verdery, Katherine. *National Ideology under Socialism: Identity and Cultural Politics in Ceausescu's Romania*. Berkeley: University of California Press, 1991a.

———."Theorizing Socialism: A Prologue to the 'Transition.'" *American Ethnologist* 18 (1991b):419–39.

———. *What Was Socialism, and What Comes Next?* Princeton: Princeton University Press, 1996.

"W trysk kapitalu." *Gazeta Żywiecka* (August 1993) 2.

Wallerstein, Immanuel. *The Modern World System: Capitalist Agriculture and the Origins of the European World-Economy in the Sixteenth Century*, 2 vols. New York: Academic Press, 1974.

———.*The Capitalist World Economy: Essays*. Cambridge: Cambridge University Press, 1979.

Walton, John. *Western Times and Water Wars: State, Culture and Rebellion in California*. Berkeley: University of California Press, 1992.

Walton, John, and David Seddon. *Free Markets and Food Riots: The Politics of Global Adjustment*. Cambridge, Mass.: Blackwell Publishers, 1994.

Weber, Max. *On Charisma and Institution Building*. Chicago: University of London Press, 1968.

Wedel, Janine. *The Private Poland*. New York: Facts on File Publications, 1986.

Wicker, Hans-Rudolph. *Rethinking Nationalism and Ethnicity: The Struggle for Meaning and Order in Europe*. New York: Berg, 1997.

Wiktor, Jan. "Górale od Żywca—osadnicy pomorscy w oczach Jana Wiktora." *Gronie* (1938): 8–14.

Wnuk-Lipinski, Edmund. "Deprywacje spoleczne a konflikty interesów i wartości." In *Polacy '90: Konflikty i zmiana*, edited by W. Adamski. Warsaw: IFIS PAN, 1991.

Wolf, Eric R. *Europe and the People without History*. Berkeley: University of California Press, 1982.

Wolff, Larry. *The Vatican and Poland in the Age of the Partitions: Diplomatic and Cultural Encounters at the Warsaw Nunciature.* Boulder, Colo.: East European Monographs, 1988.

Worsley, Peter. *The Three Worlds: Culture and World Development.* London: Weidenfeld and Nicolson, 1984.

Zagroszka, Danuta. "Polskie tempo." *Gazeta Wyborcza* (November 9, 1994): 14.

Zemtsovsky, Izaly, and Alma Kunanbaeva. "Communism and Folklore." In *Folklore and Traditional Music in the Former Soviet Union and Eastern Europe,* edited by J. Porter, 3–23. Los Angeles: Department of Ethnomusicology, University of California, 1997.

Żywiec: miasto, które sięga szczytów. Video, 60 min. Żywiecki Urząd Miasta, Warsaw, 1994.

"Żywieckie Zakłady Futrzarskie idą pod młotek." *Gazeta Żywiecka* (May 1993): 12.

Index

◄o►